Willy Russell
Plays: 1

Breezeblock Park, Our Day Out,
Stags and Hens, Educating Rita

Willy Russell has written some of the most popular and frequently staged plays of the last twenty years. This volume contains his key plays from the seventies, which culminated in *Educating Rita*, SWET Best Comedy of 1980, produced worldwide and made into a highly successful film. The collection is introduced by the author.

Breezeblock Park is set on a northern council estate and takes a look at the suffocating effect of possessions and possessiveness: 'Trenchantly observed . . . hilarious, upsetting and somewhat seditious.' *Variety*

Our Day Out unleashes a school coach trip, which is not only an exuberant celebration of the joys and agonies of growing up but also points up the children's day-to-day lives and future prospects. 'The skill and zest of the show derive from its success in following the adult argument through while preserving all the fun of a story for and mainly played by children . . . a Dickensian fairytale . . . I have rarely seen a show that combined such warmth and such bleakness.' *The Times*

Stags and Hens 'takes place in the Gents and Ladies loos of a tacky Liverpool club, where Dave and Linda have decided, unbeknownst to each other to hold their stag and hen parties . . . a bleakly funny and perceptive study of working-class misogyny, puritanism and waste.' *Guardian*

Educating Rita: 'One way of describing *Educating Rita* would be to say that it was about the meaning of education . . . Another would be to say that it was about the meaning of life. A third, that it is a cross between *Pygmalion* and *Lucky Jim*. A fourth, that it is simply a marvellous play, painfully funny and passionately serious; a hilarious social documentary; a fairy-tale with a quizzical, half-happy ending.' *Sunday Times*

Willy Russell was born in Whiston near Liverpool and left school at fifteen. After a succession of jobs he decided to take 'O' and 'A' levels and become a teacher. His stage plays include *Blind Scouse* (Edinburgh Festival, 1972), *John Paul George Ringo . . . and Bert* (Everyman Theatre, Liverpool; Lyric Theatre, London; winner of the *Evening Standard*'s and the London Theatre Critics' award for Best Musical, 1974), *Breezeblock Park* (Everyman; Mermaid, London, 1975), *Our Day Out* (BBC 'Play for Today', 1976; adapted for the stage, Everyman; Young Vic, London, 1983), *One for the Road* (Contact Theatre, Manchester, 1976; on tour, 1978; revised for Lyric Theatre, London, 1987), *Stags & Hens* (Liverpool Playhouse, 1978; adapted as screenplay, *Dancing Thru' the Dark*, 1990) and *Educating Rita* (RSC Warehouse; Piccadilly Theatre, 1980; RSC tour, 1982; winner of the Society of West End Theatres' award for Best Comedy in 1980; made into a film in 1983), the musical *Blood Brothers* (Liverpool Playhouse; Lyric Theatre, London, 1983; Albery Theatre, London, 1988; Broadway, 1993), and *Shirley Valentine* (Everyman, Liverpool, 1986; Vaudeville Theatre, London, 1988; screenplay, 1989). In 1983 the Open University awarded him an Honorary MA in recognition of his work as a playwright.

WILLY RUSSELL

Plays: 1

Breezeblock Park
Our Day Out
Stags and Hens
Educating Rita

with an introduction by the author

Methuen Drama

METHUEN CONTEMPORARY DRAMATISTS

10 9 8 7 6

First published in Great Britain 1996
by Methuen Drama
This edition, with a new cover, published in 2002 by
Methuen Publishing Limited,
215 Vauxhall Bridge Road, London SW1V 1EJ

Reprinted 1996, 1997

Breezeblock Park was first published in 1978 by Samuel French. Copyright ©
1978 by Willy Russell
Our Day Out was first published in 1984 by Methuen; revised 1992. Copyright
© 1984, 1991 by Willy Russell
Our Day Out songs and music copyright © 1984 by Bob Eaton, Chris Mellor
and Willy Russell
Stage and Hens and *Educating Rita* were first published in a collection with
Blood Brothers in 1986 by Methuen
Stags and Hens copyright © 1985 by Willy Russell
Educating Rita copyright © 1985 by Willy Russell

Methuen Publishing Limited Reg. No. 3543167

Copyright in this collection © 1996 by Willy Russell
Copyright in the Introduction © 1996 by Willy Russell
The authors have asserted their moral rights

ISBN 0–413–70220–0

A CIP catalogue record this book
is available from the British Library

Typeset by Wilmaset Ltd, Birkenhead, Wirral
Printed and bound in Great Britain by Cox & Wyman Ltd, Reading, Berkshire

Caution

Contents

Willy Russell
A Chronology

1947 Born in Whiston, near Liverpool.
1962 Left school to become a ladies' hairdresser.
1969 Returned to education as a mature student.
1972 *Blind Scouse* premièred at the Edinburgh Festival.
      Tam Lin (for children) produced in Liverpool.
1973 *When the Reds*, an adaptation of Alan Plater's play *The Tigers Are Coming – OK?*, produced in Liverpool.
      King of the Castle shown on BBC1.
1974 *John Paul George Ringo . . . and Bert* premièred at the Everyman Theatre, Liverpool, transferred to the Lyric Theatre, London; wins the *Evening Standard*'s and London Theatre Critics' Award for Best Musical.
      Break-In shown on BBC1.
1975 *Breezeblock Park* premièred at the Everyman Theatre, Liverpool, transferred to the Mermaid Theatre, London (1977) and then to the Whitehall Theatre.
      Death of a Young Young Man shown on BBC2.
1976 *One for the Road* premièred (as *Painted Veg and Parkinson*) at the Contact Theatre, Manchester.
1977 *Our Day Out* shown on BBC1.
1978 *The Daughters of Albion* shown on ITV.
      Stags and Hens, originally a student piece for Manchester Polytechnic, opens at the Everyman Theatre, Liverpool.
      Politics and Terror shown on television.
1979 *Lies* shown on BBC1.
1980 *Educating Rita* commissioned by the Royal Shakespeare Company; wins London's SWET Award for Best Comedy.
      The Boy with the Transistor Radio commissioned and shown by ITV.

1983   Film of *Educating Rita*, directed by Lewis Gilbert,
       starring Michael Caine and Julie Walters; screenplay
       by Willy Russell nominated for an Academy Award.
       Blood Brothers (for which Willy Russell also wrote the
       music) premièred in Liverpool and transferred to
       Lyric Theatre, London.
       Our Day Out (revised for the stage) produced at the
       Everyman Theatre, Liverpool, and subsequently the
       Young Vic Theatre, London.
       Awarded an Honorary MA by the Open University.
       One Summer shown on Channel 4.
1984   *Stags and Hens* produced at the Young Vic, London.
1986   *Shirley Valentine* first produced at the Everyman
       Theatre, Liverpool.
1987   *One for the Road* produced at the Lyric Theatre,
       London.
1988   New West End production of *Blood Brothers*.
       Shirley Valentine produced at the Vaudeville Theatre,
       London.
1989   *Shirley Valentine* nominated for the Tony Award and
       Drama Desk Award for Best Play and wins the
       Olivier Award for Best Comedy of the Year.
1990   Screenplay of *Dancing Thru' the Dark*, based on *Stags
       and Hens*.
       Screenplay of *Shirley Valentine*; film directed by Lewis
       Gilbert, starring Pauline Collins.
       Awarded a D.Litt. by Liverpool University.
1993   *Terraces* (1973) revived by Scene Drama and shown
       on BBC1.
       Blood Brothers opens on Broadway.

Introduction

There was more, much more than idle curiosity in the voice of the taxi driver; there was an intensity to his question, his phrasing of the words grave and urgent and almost whispered as he asked me, 'How . . . do you . . . write . . . a play?'

He'd stopped the cab. We still had another couple of miles to go before we got to the station. But we were stopped. And he was turned around, looking at me through the grill, his face wondering and intent, eyes wide and unblinking as he awaited the answer upon which, it seemed, his very life depended.

Why hadn't I lied? When we'd exhausted our views on weather and government (both of which we agreed were growing more appalling by the minute), when we'd grown tired of laughing at the daftness of princes and princesses, grown bored with bemoaning the increasing craziness of Christmas, when after lapsing into silence for a minute or two, he'd glanced at me in the rearview mirror and asked, 'So what is it that you do for a living?', why hadn't I lied and told him I was a teacher or a hairdresser or warehouseman? Having, in the past, done all these jobs I could convincingly have kept up some sort of conversation if curiosity and politeness had required it. But I hadn't lied. I'd confessed.

'I write,' I whispered, 'write plays,' I reluctantly mumbled, turning and gazing out of the window, hoping that perhaps he hadn't quite heard me, wondering to myself about those times when I'd feverishly dreamed of the day when I could proudly, triumphantly, declare that what I was was a writer! Those were the days in which I bought and constantly wore a corduroy jacket because I'd once seen someone I thought was Roger McGough wearing something similar, days in which I'd cultivated what I considered to be the appropriately raffish and consumptive look of the struggling but determined writer, days when I sat about significantly in the Phil or the Mask or the Green Moose, days in which, when asked what I did for a living, I longed to be able to say the word *playwright* . . . Or *poet*, or *novelist*. Any kind of *writer*, it didn't matter which. But the problem was that despite my consumptive and tortured demeanour, despite the serious air and the corduroy jacket, I hadn't actually done any writing up to that point. And reluctant to lie I would, when idly asked my occupation, reveal the mundane truth contained in the word *hairdresser* or (later) *warehouseman* and, recognising the idle inquisitor's bored nod or half smile, turn my attention back to the frayed cuffs of my corduroy jacket, dreaming again of the day when I lived not by the triple-carbon dispatch note or the blow dryer but by the pen, dreaming of the day when a similarly idle inquisitor would be transformed, attention seized, eyes suddenly bright and attentive, eager and intrigued by the revelation that I was a *writer*!

And now here he was, the idly inquisitive taxi driver, asking me again, telling me to speak up, 'What was that, mate? What is it you do?'

And me, still staring through the cab window, mute, remembering the smell of corduroy and a time in which I'd hungered for the opportunity to declare with pride and justification that I was a *writer*.

But I had learned. Somewhere between fantasy and reality I had learned. Somewhere between the days of the corduroy jacket and this taxi ride to the station I had acquired caution, reluctance, the ability to lie! During a previous taxi journey in Liverpool many years earlier the driver had asked me what job I did. Upon hearing the word *playwright*, the driver hit the brakes, turned around and, apologising for having propelled me off my seat and onto the floor, told me I was an effing genius. He reached through to the back of the cab, insisting that I shake his hand. I did. And as we resumed our journey he began his eulogy on the absolute brilliance and the stunning originality of *Boys from the Blackstuff*. By the time we'd reached Allerton roundabout, he'd reviewed every episode of that series, selecting particularly favourite moments and repeating snatches of dialogue, retelling particular scenes, his litany of glowing praise and enthusiasm spawning momentary paroxysms of delight, causing him to lift up his hands and bang them deliriously on the steering wheel. I told myself that it was concern for my safety which made me ask him to stop and drop me off. But, in fact, he'd just segued from *The Blackstuff* to *Monocled Mutineer*, a series he held in even greater regard. We were only in Ullet Road, still a good two miles from Hope Street, but I couldn't stand it any longer. As I scrambled out of the cab and stood there fumbling for a fiver he told me again what an effing genius I was. 'All your work,' he told me as I held out the fiver, 'all your work, I love it.'

And then, as if recalling some forgotten blemish on an otherwise perfect canvas, his face clouded and he said, 'Apart from that one you did, what was it called, *Educating Rita*!'

Blowing out a long breath and shaking his head in disgust, he said, 'But I suppose even geniuses have their off days, don't they?'

I thrust the fiver towards him.

'No way,' he said, pushing back the money. 'This one's on me. Just give us your autograph and that'll be payment enough.'

I took hold of the pen and the pad. And wrote the words, *Best wishes, Alan Bleasdale*, before turning and scurrying off along Ullet Road, an unworthy writer in the night.

And now this taxi driver, this one who has stopped the cab and wants me to tell him how to write a play. And if I want to catch the train (which I do) then I'm going to have to find a way of telling him quickly. I am reminded of the words of the novelist Stan Barstow who, when asked what it took to write a novel, replied, 'Twelve biros and a bloody lot of paper!'

But from the look in his eyes I can see that for my taxi driver, this answer will not do. My current inquisitor is not to be deflected by borrowed Yorkshire pith and wit. My driver isn't looking for an answer; he is patiently waiting for *the* answer. He knows that I write plays. He quotes some titles and, for once, they are plays which I and not any of the Alans have written. I know the keenness of the longing in his eyes. I

know that he has already driven one fare too many, driven
from Lime Street to Hunts Cross, from Kirkby to Fazakerly,
there and back and back again, a thousand times or more,
seeing nothing of the route, seeing only his latest idea, the
latest novel or poem or play or grand opera which he writes
on a pad on the kitchen table after the driving is done.

'You write yourself?' I ask. And he nods as I know he will.
And I know that I am going to miss the train. I know that I
owe him an attempt at the truth in the way that, years ago
when accosted in libraries or pubs or bistros by a consump-
tive-looking string of a thing in an ill-fitting corduroy jacket,
writers such as Jim Allan, Peter Buckman, Adrian Henri and
others who already 'knew how to do it' found the time and
the patience to try and pass on something of the truth.

And so I tell Stephen the reluctant taxi driver that *How do
you write a play?* is a question that has no satisfactory answer. I
tell him that the writing of each and every play is an indivi-
dual process of discovering how to write that particular play.
I explain that the *how* of writing any play (or novel or poem
or film or whatever) is an inexact process of pursuing exact-
ness; that the search for the precise word or line, the precise
scene, character, moment, plot and theme is, of necessity, an
imprecise process, a mad gathering together of instinct and
intellect, foreknowledge and discovery, technique and trust,
hunch and feeling and learning, the whole thing driven by a
mix of the author's passion and ego, fear and vanity, arro-
gance and hopelessness and endless oscillation between
belief and despair in his ability to orchestrate successfully
the particular truth that he or she has been moved to tell.

Stephen ponders this for a moment and then, modifying
his question, he says, 'All right but what about when a play
is finished? Surely you can look back on it then and explain
how it was written.' He lists a number of the plays I've written and I consider his question. And the answer is, no. We
talk about the plays he has mentioned. I think back to *Breezeblock Park* and I can explain how one of my reasons for writing that play was a desire to show off. That after writing *John
Paul George Ringo . . . and Bert* (a play written very much in the
wonderful Everyman house style created by Alan Dossor and

John McGrath) I wanted to demonstrate that I also knew
how to handle different, more traditional forms of drama,
that as well as writing in the 'epic' Everyman style, I could
also turn my hand to the 'well-made play', bringing to it (as
I then believed) a somewhat radical and revolutionary slant
by putting a working-class rather than a middle-class family
at the centre of a comedy of manners. Writing *Breezeblock
Park* was, in part, me declaring, 'I understand form; I have
something to say. I have content but I also appreciate and
understand the importance of form in theatre.' Not exactly
the most noble reason for writing a play. But, as I'd said, no
play was ever written without ego and vanity being in the
mix. And, of course, showing off was not the sole reason
behind *Breezeblock Park*. Had I merely wanted to show off in
terms of form (to reflect perhaps the fact that as well as
having a Liverpool accent and an 'ear for dialogue' I'd also
spent three of the most fulfilling years of my life studying
drama), then I would not have had a play to write. Within
that form I wanted to tell my story of the family. I wanted
to revel in (and have an audience revel in) the glorious sad
madness of that particular family and the glorious mad sad-
ness that seems to manifest itself one way or another, at one
time or another, in all families.

But even as I explain this to Stephen I realise that I'm already in danger of misleading him, of persuading him that I
knew what I wanted to do, knew how to do it, sat down and
did it. What I've just told him, although true, is the edited,
whittled, honed down truth that comes only with the benefit
of hindsight. And lest I leave him with a false (if convenient)
impression, I hastily catalogue the false starts, the fumbling
down cul de sacs, the creation of redundant character, the
over-emphasising of theme, the moments in which the
action was right but the tone was wrong, the scenes which I
knew to be crucial but which I never seemed to be able to get
right, the wrong moves, the slack moments, the false notes,
all this and much much more a necessary part of the making
of the play and all of it to be addressed again and again, written and rewritten up to the day of delivery, through rehear-
sals and even beyond.

We'd opened the play at the Liverpool Everyman. I'd been approached by members of the Workers Revolutionary Party and warned that to 'present the proletariat in such an unflattering and demeaning light was to undermine the class struggle'. I'd been grabbed by the shirt-front in the green room and told by a fellow writer that I'd written a play which should never have been allowed to appear on an English stage. Upstairs in the auditorium an audience comprising many of those whose sensibilities were of such concern to the WRP and the outraged writer were howling in joyous recognition as Betty wielded her new 'cocktail' mixer, as Vera was yet again denied her port and lemon, as Uncle Ted exposed the crucial flaw in the writing of *Waiting for Godot*. Deciding that the opinion of the audience mattered more than that of my self-appointed advisors, I straightened my shirt-front, left the WRP plotting the revolution and took myself upstairs to watch the rest of the play, especially the final scene. It worked – the scene in which Sandra winds up in the kitchen, making sandwiches with the rest of the women – it worked, there was no doubt of that. But I'd had this growing feeling, this nagging suspicion that whilst, as written, the scene worked, it didn't work in the way I'd imagined it working. On paper the scene had seemed right. But on stage . . . I couldn't quite pin it down . . . but there was something about this scene that . . . I couldn't quite . . . something . . . something about this scene. It worked, taken as a scene it worked; the staging was perfect, the acting was faultless. But . . . something . . . something about this scene. I watched it again. It worked. The audience was applauding, solid, appreciative applause. And yet . . .

On my way down to the bar I was stopped by a man demanding to know if I was the author of the play. Expecting another grabbing by the shirt-front and/or hector/lecture on class consciousness I braced myself and confessed. The big guy's hand shot out but instead of grabbing me by the shirt he was grabbing my hand and shaking it and telling me (not inviting but telling me) that he and I were going for a drink and a chat. Between ordering the drinks and enthusing generously about the play, I learned that Dave Hill was an actor

who'd come in to see the show because his partner, Jane
Wood, was playing Reeny. Continuing to pour his almost ex-
travagant praise into my ears, Dave led the way across to one
of the bistro's scrubbed pine tables. As we sat down he
grabbed me by the arm, fixed me with his stare and said,
'But, you've got the ending wrong!'

Despite his earlier praise I was suddenly cautious, suspi-
cious, instinctively defensive, resentful even of the virtual
stranger who felt he had the right to assail me with such
bald, blunt criticism. I toyed with the notion of telling him
where to stick his drink and his criticism. And yet regardless
of the sudden bruising to the ego, hadn't I been up in the
auditorium, looking at that ending and wondering about it?
Somewhere beyond the pricked ego, instinct told me that his
intention was not to wound and that if I could overcome my
defensiveness I might just learn something. Still cautious,
still cool, I picked up my drink and asked him, 'What do
you mean?'

He made two marvellous observations. Beginning with the
final scene he told me, 'As it stands it's a good scene. But it's
the wrong scene to end the play.'

I told him that I'd begun to suspect as much myself but
hadn't been able to work out why this was.

'Because,' he told me, 'it's the mother's play, not the
daughter's. Or, at least, it's as much the mother's play as
the daughter's.'

It was a wonderful note; the simple but crucial observa-
tion so often lacking in much of what passes for dramatic
criticism.

Any residue of defensiveness now dispelled, I began enthusing, agreeing, acknowledging my own blindness and, at
once, outlining how I would rewrite the scene to take account of the fact that Betty's journey had, indeed, been left
unresolved.

And that's when I first heard the term *obligation scene*, when
the wise Mr Hill made me realise that if a scene is proble-
matic then the seeds of that problem are almost always
located at some earlier point in the play.

'What do you mean, "obligation scene"?' I asked. And I
learned about explosions, about the gloves having to come
off, learned how, if you've set two forces against each other,
two opposing ideas, two different philosophies, two differing
sets of needs, two cultures, then you have to set up the expec-
tation, the *need* (in storytelling terms) for these two to clash
openly. And I hadn't done it. Throughout the play the
values and concerns and the needs of both Betty and Sandra
are constantly in opposition. But I'd not written the scene in
which their simmering resentments erupt into direct confrontation, a confrontation which, throughout, the play pro-
mised but failed to deliver. In part there was good reason or,
at least, an explanation for this; one of the play's themes was
the families' refusal to confront, how feelings and passions
and needs were sublimated or stifled or perverted into concern for purely material matters. One of the threads of the
play was Sandra's attempt to break through this, taunting
and goading and trying to force some reaction from her
mother. In what I'd no doubt considered to be my thematic
cleverness I'd been consistently unswerving in this, refusing
throughout to allow Betty to react openly to the taunts of her
daughter, having her instead sidestep open confrontation,
sometimes nimbly, sometimes crudely, but always, always
refusing the bait. But, sitting there in the bistro, with Dave
Hill's help and encouragement, I realised that whilst a play
demands a certain consistency in the way that its themes are
handled, one cannot allow that constancy to stifle character,
that, indeed, one's theme may be better served by removing
the author's gag from the character's mouth and letting him
or her, speak, yell, spit and scream and shriek from the
depths of an unpredictable soul.

I was back to rewriting.

Stephen, the taxi driver, was frowning at me. 'What?' he
said. 'Even after the play had opened?'

I nodded. Folding his arms and turning back to stare out of
the windscreen, Stephen shook his head. Catching my eye in
the rearview mirror he asked, 'Is it like that with all the plays
you've written?'

'To a lesser or greater degree, yeah,' I answered. 'I told you, each play is a process of discovering how to write that particular play.'

He blew out a sigh, started the engine and switched the meter back on. 'So you can't tell me then?' he said.

'What?' I asked.

'How to write a play,' he said, pulling into the traffic and turning into Smithdown Road.

'Well,' I said, 'perhaps you could get yourself twelve biros and a lot of paper and . . .'

Willy Russell

Breezeblock Park

Breezeblock Park was first presented in 1975 at the Everyman Theatre, Liverpool; subsequently on 12 September 1977 at the Mermaid Theatre, London; and on 3 November at the Whitehall Theatre, London by Colin Brough for the Lupton Theatre Company, with the following cast:

Betty	Prunella Scales
Syd	Bernard Gallagher
Sandra, *their daughter*	Emma Jean Richards
Vera	Julie Walters
Tommy, *Betty's brother*	Peter Postlethwaite
Reeny, *Betty's sister*	Eileen Kennally
Ted	Norman Rossington
John, *their son*	David Neilson
Tim	Anthony O'Donnell

Directed by Alan Dossor
Designed by Adrian Vaux

Act One

Syd and Betty's house on a council housing estate. Christmas Eve.

To one side is the front room, and adjoining it the kitchen. Through the door of the front room can be seen a small hall and the beginning of the stairs. A door leads from the front room into the kitchen, and another door from the kitchen to the back of the house. Although we are in a council house, we are not in the land of cloth caps and sawdust on the floor. The room is not too vulgar: it contains a fitted carpet, the famous Japanese Lady *print, a Coalglow electric fire, a radiogram, a sideboard, a glass-fronted cabinet, a three-piece suite and a colour television. This television is on throughout the entire act – though generally without sound. There is also a Christmas tree – a silver false one.*

When the curtain rises, **Betty** *is making adjustments to the Christmas tree. The door to the hall and stairs is open.* **Sandra** *is sitting at the kitchen table reading a book. After a moment* **Betty** *goes to the hall and shouts up the stairs.*

Betty   Syd! Syd, are you ready yet?

We hear a grunt from upstairs.

They'll all be here, y'know. They'll all be here if you don't get a move on.

Syd (*off*)   All right, all right, what harm will it do if I'm not quite ready? Bloody hell, Betty, it's only the family we're expectin' – not the Queen Mother.

Betty (*moving to the first step on the stairs*)   The Queen Mother I wouldn't mind. But our Reeny is a different matter. I am *not* having you only half ready when she arrives.

Syd (*off, wearily*)   All right. All right.

Betty (*turning to go back to the front room but stopping and taking a couple of steps up the stairs*)   Yes, yes it's all right for you because you don't mind giving her the chance to put one over on me. (*She turns to come down, but suddenly remembers something and turns back. Quietly, threatening*.) And listen, don't you go blabbing about the price of my new suite. (*Pause.*) Did you hear me Syd?

Syd (*off*)   How can I tell her how much the suite cost when I don't know meself?

Betty (*impatiently*)   Of course you know how much it was. You signed for it in the shop.

Syd (*off*)   Yes, I signed for it. But when I signed it cost two hundred and twenty quid. When Mrs Devlin was here the other night it'd gone up eighty quid; when y' showed it to Barbara Mac it was a three hundred and fifty quid job. No wonder the bloody country is sufferin' from inflation.

Betty   You make me sick! How the hell could it only have cost two hundred and twenty?

Syd   Well that's what it said on the form.

Betty (*getting more rattled*)   Yes, yes, well go on, go on . . .

Syd   Well, that's it – two hundred an' twenty quid . . .

Betty   How did I come to marry someone so stupid? Two hundred and twenty pounds, Sydney, with HP on top of that. With VAT on top of that. Delivery charges on top of that. The special shampoo for cleaning it. Two hundred and twenty pounds my foot. That suite has cost me every penny of three hundred pounds.

There is a grunt from upstairs.

Did you hear me? Three hundred pounds – not a penny less, and don't you go forgetting it. You try and make me look cheap in front of our Reeny an' I'll swing for you. (*She comes back into the room and mumbles to herself as she makes adjustments to the Christmas tree. Referring to* **Sandra**.) An' she won't lift a finger to help. She never does, that one. Not lately. Thinks she's a law unto herself she does. Well I'm gettin' a bit sick of it. (*She stands back and looks at tree, then shouts through to the kitchen*.) Sandra, Sandra, come an' have a look.

Sandra (*not looking up from her book*)   What?

Betty   Just come an' have a look.

Sandra   What? I'm reading.

Betty   Sandra! It's Christmas Eve, you don't want to be reading at Christmas. Come on, come an' have a look.

Sandra *reluctantly puts down her book and comes through to the front room.*

Sandra   What?

Betty (*looking at the tree, smiling, fawning, proud*)   Look, love. Look at it. (*Pause.*) You've always loved the tree, haven't you? Eh? Isn't it really lovely this year?

Sandra   I don't know why you waste your money, Mother.

Betty (*flaring slightly*)   Now don't start. Just don't start that stuff again, Sandra, I've had enough lately. It's Christmas now let's have no more of that stuff.

Sandra   What stuff?

Betty   You know very well what stuff; all this – criticizing stuff. I'm just getting really fed up with it.

Sandra   Just look at it. You could at least have got a real tree.

Betty   Don't be stupid! Who buys real trees these days? Real trees are old fashioned. And anyway – they smell.

Sandra   Yeh. Real trees are supposed to . . .

Betty   I am not arguing with you, Sandra. I want the house to be nice. Not smellin' like the inside of some forest.

Sandra *sighs and walks towards the kitchen.*

Betty (*reaching into the cabinet*)   All right, clever, if you want a smell – here! (*She produces an aerosol and liberally sprays the tree.*)

Sandra   What's that?

Betty   *That* is the smell of real trees. (*Holding up the can.*) Pine essence, lovely. (*She sniffs.*)

Sandra *resumes her passage to the kitchen.*

Sandra I've told y', Mother – stuff like that is just a con trick.

Betty (*following her through to the kitchen*) An' I've told *you* I don't want to hear any more of that stuff. It's bad enough havin' to put up with your criticizin' the whole year round but I'm certainly not havin' any of that at Christmas.

Sandra '*tuts' and goes to pick up her book.* **Betty** *beats her to it, though.*

Betty (*reading out the title*) *The Long March of Capitalism* – now what sort of a book's that supposed to be?

Sandra (*taking the book*) A murder story, Mother!

Betty (*busying herself in the kitchen*) Well, I've warned you about all this readin'. The way you're goin' on you'll be damagin' your eyes.

Sandra *goes through to the front room door.*

Betty Where are you goin' now?

Sandra Upstairs.

Sandra *exits.*

Betty Upstairs, upstairs. You live your life upstairs lately. (*She goes as if to follow* **Sandra**, *then decides against it and instead smiles at the tree. The smile fades into thought.*)

Syd *enters behind her, wearing only trousers and vest and drying himself with a towel. He starts to sniff.*

Betty (*looking at the tree*) She used to love Christmas. (*She arranges cards on the sideboard.*)

Syd (stiff sniffing, approaching the tree) That tree stinks. Is me shirt ironed?

Betty Have I ever kept washing downstairs? Have you ever come home to find clothes airing in this room?

Syd What?

Betty   Your shirt is where your shirts are always kept – in the airing cupboard. Now would you mind going and getting one on. I told you, you're not walkin' round half-dressed when there are people coming.

Syd (*lighting a cigarette*)   It's the family that's comin' – no one's gonna complain. How many times have we been round to Tommy's house an' seen him in his vest?

Betty   People expect that in Tommy's house. They don't expect it here. The head of *this* household is not an alcoholic!

Syd   Tommy's not an alcoholic. He just likes a few pints.

Betty   Syd. Have you had a training in medicine?

Syd   No – but anyone can see that . . .

Betty   I'm not talking about anyone. Was I or was I not a nurse?

Syd   Yes, but . . .

Betty   But nothing. Tommy has a severe drink problem.

Syd   Betty!

Betty   Do you know what he's bought Vera for Christmas?

Syd   No.

Betty   Well, I do. Six bottles of whisky.

Syd   Vera doesn't drink whisky.

Betty   Exactly. And anyway, you know you had to give up the car because of your health, I don't know what you think you're doing walking round in just your vest when it's the middle of winter. Course, if you'd listened to me about the central heating, you'd be all right.

Syd   Ah . . .

Betty   Take no notice of me. Ignore me if you want to. But I've warned you – to a man in your condition, a chill could be the final stroke. But that doesn't matter to you does it? Self. Self. Self!

Syd   Well – it's only meself I'm harming.

Betty   You've no consideration, have you. It'll be all right for you if you slip away in your sleep one night. But who'll be the one who has to wake up in bed – with a corpse beside her?

Betty *to the kitchen. From outside we hear carol singing.*

Syd (*laughing good naturedly*)   'Ey – Betty – listen!

Tommy *and* **Vera** (*off; singing together*)
'Christmas is comin' the goose is gettin' fat,
Please put a fiver in the old man's hat.
If y' haven't got a fiver a quid will do.
If y' haven't got a quid, y' window's comin' through.'

Syd   Here – give us a couple of bob an' I'll go an' give it them.

Betty   You'll do nothing of the sort.

Syd   Why?

Betty   Why? Because it'll be those little swines from down the street – that's why.

Syd   Betty love . . . it's Christmas.

Betty   Syd love, those kids were carol singing on July the first.

Syd (*sighing*)   Joy and peace to all mankind.

Betty   And what's that supposed to mean?

Syd (*going to get his shirt*)   Nothing – nothing.

Syd *exits upstairs.*

Betty (*going after him to the bottom of the stairs*)   Don't you start throwing Christmas up in my face. Don't you dare tell me about Christmas, I understand the meaning of Christmas. But those swines from down the road aren't getting one penny out of this house.

Syd (*off*)   All right, Betty. But don't blame me if they put a brick through the front window.

Betty   They wouldn't.

Syd (*off*) Wouldn't they? They were in court last week for stealing a police car.

Betty (*firmly*) They wouldn't touch this house. (*Hopefully.*) They wouldn't.

From outside we hear the strains of 'Why Are We Waiting'.

Where's my bloody purse? (*Frantically rushing round and finding her purse under a cushion.*) It's not right this isn't. It's nothing less than extortion. (*Getting to the front door.*) They should be locked up! (*Opening door.*) Oh – it's you two. (*Greetings. She shouts back upstairs.*) It's all right, Syd, it's not real carol singers – only Tommy and Vera. You really fooled me for a minute. I thought it was the little children from down the street. I was just going to invite them in for a warm.

Tom *and* **Vera** *come into the room with* **Betty.**

Tommy (*fairly well oiled, carrying Christmas parcels*) I'll bet y' thought y' were gonna have t' fork out a few bob, eh Betty? I'll bet that nearly ruined y' Christmas, eh? (*He laughs.*) Eh?

Betty (*not amused*) And what's that supposed to mean?

Vera (helping **Tommy** *out of his coat. His condition and the parcels in his hand make this an awkward operation*) Take no notice of him Betty. They finished work at half-twelve today. He's been drinkin' ever since.

Tommy (*out of his coat, throwing his arms around* **Betty**) Happy Christmas Big Sister. (*He shouts, hugs her, stands back and smiles.*)

Betty It's still Christmas Eve, Tommy . . .

Tommy It's not, is it?

Betty Christmas begins tomorrow. (*She takes* **Tommy**'s *coat.*)

Tommy Well – anyway, it's good to see y'.

Betty I'm surprised you can. (*She puts* **Tommy**'s *coat in the hall.*)

Tommy Where's Syd?

Betty   He's just getting changed.

Tommy (*rubbing his hands*)   Ah well – what about a little drink while we're waitin'.

Vera   Tommy! Oh Betty, it looks lovely in here, doesn't it, Tommy? Something's changed, hasn't it? What is it?

Betty *stands by the settee, smiling modestly.* **Vera** *suddenly shrieks with delight.*

Vera   Oooooooh – Betty! You've got your new suite. Oh it's really beautiful, Betty. (*She sits down to test, goes into raptures.*) Oooooooh the comfort – the luxury – I could just fall asleep.

Tommy   We can but hope.

Vera   It's just like sitting on – well, like sitting on – on – clouds. That's it. It's just like sinking into a cloud.

Betty (*showing* **Vera** *a brochure*)   That's because of the special air pockets, Vee. I mean, we were going to get a cheaper one but as soon as we saw this one incorporated the special Winterbred Honeycombe Air Pockets – well, we couldn't resist it. If you want real comfort I think it's worth paying that bit extra.

Vera   Oh it is just like a cloud, Betty. Sit down, Tommy, try it.

Tommy   I'm frightened it might start rainin'. (*He prods the suite.*) What did it cost y'?

Vera   Tommy!

Tommy   I'm only askin' Betty how much it cost.

Betty   I'll give you a guess. Go on, Tommy, one guess. What do you think?

Tommy   Beer usually, but whatever you've . . .

Vera   *Think*, not drink. Betty's askin' y' about the suite.

Tommy   Oh! (*Prodding and inspecting.*) Well, erm – let's see . . . (*He makes an exaggerated fuss of this, tutting and shaking his head.*) I don't know – I mean, with goods of this nature it depends on the supplier. I mean, if it was from a shop down town – well! (*Shaking his head.*) But there again, if it was off the back of a lorry . . .

Vera (*quietly, threateningly*)   I'm warnin' you, Tommy . . .

Tommy   I reckon it must have knocked you back a few bob, Betty. I'm glad it didn't come out of my wallet. At a guess Betty, I mean, I'm probably wrong, but at a guess I'd say that suite, that suite, Betty, must have cost you every penny of fifty quid.

Vera (*getting in quick*)   Take no notice of him, Betty, he's stupid. He doesn't know anythin' about furniture anyway.

Tommy *goes to the door and shouts up the stairs.*

Tommy   Syd – come on, Syd, we're all waitin' for y' – come on, I wanna give y' y' pressy.

Syd *enters down the stairs, greets* **Tommy** *and comes into the room.*

Syd   Christmas presents tonight?

Tommy   Ah bugger it. There's no point waitin'. Here Syd, that's yours. (*He hands him a parcel.*)

Syd   Thanks a lot, Tommy. That's very good of y'. (*He starts to unwrap.*)

Tommy   Now for Betty – a special pressy. (*Handing her a parcel.*) Very careful, Betty, it's come all the way from London that has. I got that specially for you when I was down there for the Motor Show. Never saw any motors like, but we all had a good laugh . . .

Vera   God knows what he's bought for y', Betty. I let him buy the presents this year. I couldn't get off work at all. I hope they're all right. He wouldn't even let me see them. Even wrapped them up himself.

Syd *has unwrapped his present. It is a Krooklock.* **Tommy** *beams with satisfaction.*

Syd (*dubiously*)   Well – er, yeh. Thanks, Tom – it's er, very thoughtful.

Vera   What is it?

Syd   It's a, a Krooklock. For a car, Vera.

Vera (*to* **Tommy**)   You gormless get! You're a stupid so-an'-so. Don't you ever listen to what I say?

Tommy   Not if I can help it.

Vera   I told you a fortnight ago that Syd had to get rid of the car. I told you about his health.

Tommy   Packin' up the car?

Betty (*postponing the unwrapping to join in*)   Tommy, Tommy, now you're not tellin' me that you'd expect your brother-in-law to drive a car in the state he's in.

Tommy   He looks the picture of health.

Betty   To an untrained eye he might do, Tommy. But when you're stricken, Tommy, looks can be very deceiving.

Tommy   What is it that's wrong, Syd?

Syd (*sighing and sitting down*)   I wish I knew, Tom.

Tommy   Well, what's the doctor said?

Betty   Doctor? The doctor? And what would the doctor know about it? The stupid doctor told him it was indigestion.

Syd   That's what he said, Tom.

Betty   But when that man came back from the surgery.I took one look at him, one look, didn't I, Syd?

Syd (*going pale*)   You did, Bett.

Betty   And straightaway I said – there and then, indigestion my foot; that man is a walking heart condition. Look, go on Tommy, look at him. He's in agony, agony aren't you Syd?

Syd, *now quite reduced, nods with difficulty.* **Tommy** *shakes his head.*

Tommy   I never realized, Syd.

Betty   A layman wouldn't, Tommy, but to someone trained in diagnosing illness it's as plain as the nose on your face.

Tommy   Do you think it's wise though, Betty, making judgements over a doctor's head.

Vera   But Betty was a nurse, Tommy.

Tommy   I know but even so . . .

Vera   You were an SR . . .

Betty   An SRN? No, much higher, Vera. I was an auxiliary.

Tommy   An auxiliary?

Betty   Now if you're going to start questioning my handling of this case, Tommy . . .

Tommy   But Betty, the doctor . . .

Betty (*waving him aside*)   Don't talk to me about doctors, because I've seen enough of them behind the scenes, Tommy.

Vera   Ah, he does look ill doesn't he?

Betty   That's all right Vera. I know what to give him. (*She goes into the kitchen and gets a glass of whisky.*)

Tommy (*kneeling down and talking quietly to* **Syd**)   Sorry about the old Krooklock, Syd. See, I didn't know you'd had to get rid of the car. Mind you, it'll still come in handy won't it. (*Holding the Krooklock.*) If y' need a bit of peace y' can clamp it round Betty's mouth.

Betty *returns with the glass of whisky. She gives it to* **Syd**.

Betty   Come on, Syd. Sip this.

Tommy   So that's the way to get a drink in this house.

Betty   Syd will get you a drink in a minute, Tommy . . .

Vera   Forget him an' his drink, Betty. Come on open your present. I'm dyin' to see it. If his last effort's anythin' to go by he's probably got you a bottle of after-shave.

Betty (*resuming the unwrapping of her present*)   My God, you've wrapped it up enough, Tommy.

Tommy   I told y' Betty, it's a special present that.

Betty *finally pulls off the paper to reveal a battery-operated phallic vibrator. She looks at it, not in shock but bewilderment. She does not know what it is.* **Vera** *is silently telling* **Tommy** *off.*

Tommy (*laughing*)   Great eh, Betty – I knew you'd like it. Great eh? (*He laughs.*)

Betty   It's very nice, Tommy. Erm, what exactly is it?

Tommy   'What is it?' You're a case, Betty. She's a case our Betty, isn't she? (*He laughs, nudges* **Vera**.) It's an electric organ, Betty.

Betty   No, seriously, what is it?

Tommy   It's a thingy, isn't it?

Betty   What?

Tommy (*spelling it out*)   A vibrator?

Betty (*with a little laugh*)   Oh – of course. And what is it you use it for?

Tommy (*realizing that she really does not know*)   What?

Betty   What do you use it for?

Tommy   What d' y' use it for?

Betty   Yes.

Tommy (*uncomfortably*)   Well, er, y' know, y' use it for – well, y' know like erm . . . Well, here (*He grabs it off her, grabs* **Syd***'s glass of whisky, inserts the vibrator into the whisky and switches on.*) Y' use it for mixin' drinks. It's a portable automatic drink mixer, a shake on a stick. Latest things these are, you know. Even our Reeny hasn't got one of these.

Betty (*visibly brightening*)   I'll bet she hasn't. Let's have a look, Tommy. (*She tries it.*) Ooooh. Now that's what I call a present, Tommy. You should do the Christmas shopping every year. Now where shall we put it? What about here?

(*She puts it on the television set among the candles; stands back and admires it.*) Now, Syd. Come on, are you feeling better?

Syd A bit – yeh.

Betty Good, because you know you've not taken those presents round to your people yet.

Syd It'll do tomorrow.

Betty Oh no. You can take them tonight. A walk will do you good after having an attack.

Syd I've told you. Tomorrow.

Betty And I've told you. Tomorrow will not do.

Syd '*tuts*'.

Betty Look, if you don't take those presents round to your relations they'll end up calling here and I'm afraid I don't want them, Syd. (*To* **Vera**.) I'm not having his side parked here over Christmas. Short stuff all the time it is with them. One night of his relatives and there's no short stuff left in the house. But it won't happen this year, I'm telling you. I'm not playing the mug's game this year. I don't want them here. And if they do turn up I just won't give it them. They can drink beer, beer or nothing at all.

Tommy *picks up the Krooklock, smiles and winks at* **Syd**.

Betty No, come on. You can take their things tonight. You'll only be ten minutes.

Tommy Tell y' what, Syd, if y' fancy walkin' over I'll come with y'. We could – er . . . (*He mimes drinking a pint, trying to hide it from* **Betty**.)

Betty *sees* **Tommy**'*s action.*

Syd (*getting up*) Well if y' fancy a walk, Tom . . .

Betty You stay where you are! You can take those presents tomorrow.

Syd But you just said . . .

Betty   Yes. And now I'm saying you can take them tomorrow. Now come on Syd. I'm sure everyone must be thirsty. Get us a drink will you? Port and lemon for you, Vera.

Vera *nods.*

Betty   What about Tommy?

Tommy   Have you got any beer, Betty?

Betty   Yes, Tommy, we've got plenty of beer.

Tommy   Well save it for Syd's relatives, I'll have a large whisky. Come on, Syd, I'll help you carry them. (*He goes through to the kitchen.*)

Syd (*following*)   Come on, y' can give us a hand with this crate in the shed, Tom.

Tommy *and* **Syd** *exit through the back door.*

Vera   Where's Sandra, Bett?

Betty   Going out. That's all I ever know these days, Vera. Where are you going? Out. That's all you get from her.

Vera   She must have a feller then, eh, Betty?

Betty   I've told her; Sandra, I said, if you've got a boyfriend why don't you bring him home. She didn't say a word. (*Pause.*) There must be someone, though. There must be someone who she's getting all these new ideas from.

Vera (*fascinated*)   What new ideas, Betty?

Betty   I couldn't begin to tell y', Vera. Like the other night I said to her, 'What do you think of the tree this year, Sandra?' Do you know what she said?

Vera   What, Betty?

Betty   'I don't know why you waste your money on trash.'

Vera (*shocked*)   Go on! That's not like Sandra at all, is it? She always loved Christmas.

Betty   'Christmas,' she says, 'Christmas comes from Capitalism.'

Vera   Go on. I thought it came from Jerusalem.

Sandra *enters, and on seeing* **Vera** *is slightly taken aback. She hesitates for a moment before moving down.*

Sandra   Oh, er, hello Aunty Vee.

Vera   Hia, Sand. It definitely started in Jerusalem, Sandra. It says so in the carols.

Betty   I'm just tellin' your Aunty Vee some of the things you've been comin' out with lately. Well, I hope it's just a passin' phase – that's all I can say. (*Pause.*) Go on – tell your Aunty Vera some of the things you've been sayin'.

Sandra (*with a sigh*)   What about?

Betty   A licence to rob people of their hard earned money – that's what she said Christmas was, Vera.

Vera   But people have got to have their bit of pleasure, Sandra. You can't begrudge people a bit of pleasure once a year. Can y', Betty.

Betty   I know Vera – that's what I tried to tell her. But she never listens these days. Do you. Said I didn't know what the word pleasure meant, Vera.

Vera   Oh but you do, Betty. You're always laughin' and jokin', aren't y'?

Betty   Not lately, Vera. I've been driven up the wall lately, haven't I, Sandra? She's even, you know, Vera, she's even been going on about packing in the office an' going back to school.

Vera   But y' can't go back to school when y' nineteen, Sandra. They won't let y' in.

Sandra   Not a school. A college. Like a student.

Vera   Oh God, Betty, don't let her do that. I've seen students, Sandra. I have y' know. There's a pile of them live in one of them big houses by us. It's more like a mental home y' know, for lunatics. The language that comes out of that house. 'Ey, Betty, an' y' know that peepin' Tom – well they reckon he's a student, y' know. He's up an' down the back of Parkhill Road every night y' know, an' all's he wears is a pair of gold-rimmed glasses an' a big scarf round his neck.

Betty   At this time of year.

Vera (*nodding*)   Yeah – I know. Tommy said all we need is a bit more frost and his thingy might drop off with the cold. (*She shrieks with laughter.*)

Betty (*disturbed, in the knowledge that* **Sandra** *is present*)   His thingy – Vera?

Vera   Yeah – y'know, his ding-a-ling . . . (*She laughs again.*)

Betty (*tortured*)   Vera . . . Vera! (*She draws attention to* **Sandra**'s *presence.*)

Vera (*her hand going to her mouth in apology*)   Oh.

Sandra   It's all right, Mother. I do know about the existence of the penis.

Betty *and* **Vera** (*in instant recoil; loudly*)   Sandra!

Betty   Don't be so filthy. I think this discussion's got quite out of hand.

Sandra   Mother, the . . .

Betty   *Sandra* . . . I don't want to know. I've got make-up to put on. I hope that when I come back down I won't hear any more of that sort of talk.

Betty *makes her escape, going upstairs.*

Sandra   There's nothing wrong with that you know, Aunty Vera. The word penis.

Vera (*shuddering*)   Ooh – Sandra – don't say it. I hate that word. It goes right through me. I'm surprised at you, Sandra – comin' out with words like that.

Sandra   Well, it's only a normal word.

Vera   Not very nice though.

Pause.

Sandra   Where's Uncle Tommy.

Vera   He's in the kitchen with y' dad. He's gettin' us some drinks.

Sandra   Oh. (*Pause.*) Are you stoppin' long, Aunty Vee?

Vera   Oh, I don't know, love. Why?

Sandra   Well. I've er – I didn't know anyone would be here tonight. I've, er – well I've got someone comin' round.

Vera   Oh. (*Pause.*) A feller.

Sandra   We've got to talk to me mum and dad.

Pause.

Vera (*thinking she has guessed it*)   Oh – have you got an announcement to make?

Sandra (*realizing that* **Vera** *thinks it is an engagement*)   Yeah – sort of. You won't say anything, will you?

Vera   I won't say a word, Sand. Oh Sandra, you are a dark horse aren't you? Eh? What's he like, Sand?

Sandra   He's . . . (*Going to sit with her.*) Well – he's different, Aunty Vee.

Vera (*kindly*)   They all are at first, love.

Sandra   No, but he is. I mean – really different. I mean he's not like, you know, the fellers round here.

Vera   Where did y' meet him. Out dancin'? At the disco, was it?

Sandra   It was at a dance, yeah. At his college. He's a student.

Vera   Sandra! He doesn't wear gold-rimmed glasses does he?

Sandra   Oh, stop messing about. Aunty Vee, I'm serious. It's a different world he comes from. I mean all – this. (*The room.*) He wouldn't live like this. (*Pointing to the picture on the wall.*) He wouldn't have anything like that up, you know.

Vera   Why, Sand?

Sandra   Because, Aunty Vee – it's not unique.

Vera (*as though that explains it*)   Oh.

Sandra   I told me mother – when she was buyin' it at the market. I said don't get that picture – everyone's got one of those. There's thousands of those around.

Vera   Yeh – well that shows it's a good paintin'. I mean look at that *Bubbles*. That's a good picture an' there's millions of them around. (*Pause.*) Me an' our Tommy were thinkin' of gettin' a picture for our chimney breast. But we couldn't agree. I wanted a nice little picture –

Betty *enters*.

Vera   – but our Tommy always wanted a big one.

Betty   I thought I told you to change the subject, Vera.

Vera   What! But I was . . .

Betty   Yes, I know, Vera – now let's have no more of it.

Sandra *goes to the front door*.

Betty   Where are you going, Sandra?

Sandra   I'm just going out.

Betty   Sandra! We have got visitors.

Sandra   I won't be long.

Betty   I don't think that's the point.

Sandra   I'll be back soon.

Sandra *exits*.

Betty (*shouting through the door*)   I don't know where you learnt your manners, young lady, but you certainly weren't taught that sort of behaviour from anyone in this house.

The front door slams.

Betty   Honest to God, Vera, I don't know what's got into her over this past couple of months. She could learn a thing or two from our Reeny's lad, she could. I can't say much for

Reeny, but she's brought their John up a treat. He's always helpin' out in the house you know, Vee. He'd do anything for his mother. Not like our Sandra. She wouldn't lift a finger – not lately anyway. Do you know, if there was a speck of dust on the arm of that settee and Sandra was sitting there, she wouldn't even lean across and brush it off. Now that's not right, is it, Vera?

Vera It's not, Betty.

Betty I mean that's no way to treat a three hundred and fifty pound suite. (*She 'tuts'*.) Oh Vera, it just slipped out. You'll think I'm an awful bragger, won't you.

Vera Is that what it cost you, Betty?

Betty Well you know I don't buy rubbish, Vera.

Vera Ooh, it's just like sitting on a cloud.

Betty Of course you won't mention that to our Reeny, will you?

Vera I wouldn't dream . . .

Betty With her having got a suite not so long ago. I'd hate to embarrass her. You know, she'd be a bit upset if she thought mine was a lot dearer than hers.

Vera Would she really be upset, Betty?

Betty Upset? I mean I don't like to talk about people but do you know, when she saw that new shower I've had fitted in the bathroom, she was green.

Vera I was askin' our Tommy about gettin' a shower fitted, y' know. D' y' know what he said? (*She laughs.*) He said he'd make a bargain with me. (*She laughs.*)

Betty (*all ears*) What was that, Vera?

Vera (*laughing*) Oh Betty – I'm ashamed. I daren't tell y'.

Betty Go on love. You can tell me. You know I wouldn't breathe a word.

Vera Well – (*Laughing*.) – Tommy said that he'd get me a shower fitted if I agreed to give up wearin' tights an' start wearin' a suspender belt an' stockin's.

Betty Why?

Vera Well he just thinks stockin's are sexy.

Betty (*poker-faced*) Well, that is one thing I would not have thought about our Tommy. I didn't know he was a pervert.

Vera Oh – he's not, Betty.

Betty It doesn't sound like it, either. What did you say to this request?

Vera I agreed.

Betty You didn't.

Vera Yeh. Why?

Betty Vera, Vera! Do you realize what you are saying? That swine has turned you into a prostitute, Vera.

Vera Oh Betty! All I've said is that I'll wear stockin's.

Betty Yes. But where will it end? Don't you see my point, Vera? All right, you wear kinky stockings so that he'll get you a shower; what happens when you want a fridge? A washing machine? Vera, you could end up on the streets for a colour television.

Vera (*worried*) Oh. 'Ey, I never thought of it like that.

Betty Well I'm telling you love, you wait till you can afford a shower y'self.

Vera I think I will now, Betty.

Betty Have you seen my shower? Come and have a look. I mean I don't suppose you'll be able to afford one like this but it'll give you an idea Vera. So, he's a bit that way is he, our Tommy?

They start to go to the stairs.

Vera I think he's harmless really Bett!

Betty   Well you just stamp it out now before it takes a grip of him. Don't get me wrong, I'm not saying that a couple shouldn't enjoy it. But there's moderation. I have to restrain my feller you know.

Vera   Syd?

Betty   Oooooh – he's like a ram. Unsatiable.

Vera   Go 'way!

Betty *and* **Vera** *exit upstairs.*

The lights dim slightly in the living-room and come up in the kitchen.

Tommy *and* **Syd** *enter with a crate of various drinks.*

Tommy   I mean, no messin', Syd, I've seen strippers in the clubs up here but they're not worth a carrot compared to these London tarts.

Syd (*agog*)   Go on!

Tommy   Oooooh, what! The first club me an' the lads got into, there was this little one . . .

Syd   Stripper?

Tommy   Well, I say little but you should have seen the equipment this one had.

Syd   Go 'way!

Tommy   What this little one couldn't do with her knockers wasn't worth knowin'.

Syd   What er sort of things?

Tommy   An artiste she was, Syd. Y' talk about jugglers – I'm tellin' y' – me an' the lads didn't *walk* out of that club – we pole-vaulted!

Syd *looks at him open mouthed.*

Tommy   I thought you were lookin' for lemonade.

Syd (*breaking the trance*)   O yeh. (*He starts to look in cupboards.*)

Tommy *takes some mince pies from the oven.*

Tommy But y' know what the latest thing down there is, Syd? The massage parlours.

Syd Massage.

Tommy A wonderful experience y' know. Marvellous girls. An' very clean . . .

Syd An' er what do they – er – do, Tom?

Tommy The works, the full works. I brought – (*He produces a book.*) – a book back on it. Y' know, so Vera can learn how to do it. I'll pass this one on to y' when I've finished with it. Get Betty to do it for y'.

Syd Yes, there's a chance of that an' all. She's not very – you know, Betty – she's a bit . . . (*Checking that no one can hear him.*) I mean, between you an' me, Tommy – I'm thinkin' of lookin' round elsewhere for – y' know.

Tommy (*laughing*) Now now . . .

Tommy *gets glasses from the draining board and pours out two whiskies.*

Syd No, serious. I've thought about it Tommy an' I reckon a bit of that could make a new man out of me. It could really do me good. Y' know, make me young again. It sounds daft doesn't it?

Tommy No.

Syd I remember when I was young, y'know. I was a different man, I was. The things I used to notice – y' know – like, simple things – just, well, y' know, flowers like – an' birds singin' – an' the grass. Sounds stupid doesn't it? But the grass – Christ, it used to be so bloody green. (*Shaking his head.*) I don't know! (*Starting to look in cupboards again.*) I wouldn't mind if there was something different to look forward to – but every year's the bloody same. It's like the television, like them serials that never change from week to week, apart from gettin' worse. An' Christmas. Christ, Christmas must be the worse time of all.

Tommy An' – er – so y' lookin' round for a bit of snatch, are y'?

Syd (*again checking that no one can hear*) There's – er – there's a woman serves in the canteen at our place . . .

Tommy An' have y' managed to. . . ?

Syd No, no – it's not reached that stage yet. It's more of the chattin' up stage at the moment.

Tommy How long's this been goin' on?

Syd Well, a good few months now, but I don't think it's wise to rush these things. It's coming along quite nice at the moment; y' know, we have a laugh an' that, an' I always give her a bit of a wink when I go past. I just hope no one at our place starts to suspect what's goin' on.

Tommy Well, y' not bein' what y' could call madly indiscreet, are y', Syd?

Syd No – I know that but, see, about a month ago – she started givin' me extra chips. (*Pause.*) I mean, all the other fellers have got half a dozen chips on their plates an' I come along the queue with me plate overflowin'. I've been gettin' some strange looks already.

Tommy I'll bet you have, Syd.

Syd D' y' think anyone will cotton on?

Tommy Well, what if they do? If you wanna go an' get a bit of spare that's your business. Everyone else can sod off.

Syd Yeh. Yeh. They can, can't they? (*He sighs.*) I think that sometimes y' know. Why don't I just go an' do it. Enjoy meself. She'd have me an' all, y' know, Tom. This one in the canteen. I've thought about soddin' off with her, y' know. Jackin' this lot in an' just goin' off somewhere with her.

Tommy Now, now, Syd – come on, lad. There's no need for talk like that. Get a bit on the side, like, but don't start talkin' about, y' know, jeopardizin' the family.

Syd   Well that's how I feel sometimes, Tommy, I'm tellin' y'.

Tommy   Well, I'd watch out for thoughts like that, Syd. No use goin' over the top, lad.

Syd   Agh – I suppose y'right. It's just Christmas I suppose. It gets y' like that doesn't it? (*He resumes his search for lemonade.*)

Tommy   It's not Christmas Syd – it's this bloody country. It's no friggin' use to man nor beast. I'm gettin' out, Syd, whilst the goin's good. Australia for me this year.

Syd   I thought it was New Zealand y' were goin' to.

Tommy   New Zealand, Australia, Canada – it doesn't matter which one but this year we're goin'. I couldn't stay here much longer meself. There's no life left in this country. At least not for the likes of us. It's all right if y've got money – or, status like. But y've got to be realistic haven't y'? There's nothin' left here for us. We're just like loads of Indians herded together an' stuck in a reservation. I mean – we've got no land have we? There's nothin' y' can call y' own. Nothin' that y' can make a go of?

Syd   I suppose y' right, Tommy.

Tommy   I know I am. I'm gettin' out, settin' me course for a new country. Give me a couple of years in a young country an' I'll be a new man: cuttin' the cane, tendin' the sheep, bringin' in the wood for the fire. I'll be a new feller then; an' the ciggies y' know, an' the ale, I'll knock them right on the head.

Syd   'Ey, Tommy, will your Vera drink somethin' else with her port? I can't find this lemonade anywhere. Will she have somethin' else in it?

Tommy   She'll have to if y' can't find it.

Syd   Will she . . .

Tommy   Or there again, we could – erm . . .

Syd   What?

Tommy   Well we could nip out an' get a bottle couldn't we?

Syd   There's nowhere open.

Tommy   What about the pub? (*He winks.*)

Syd   Oh Christ, Tommy – I don't know.

Tommy   Well you need the lemonade don't y'?

Syd   I suppose . . .

Tommy   Come on – we'll be there an' back in ten minutes . . . (*He goes to the back door and opens it.*)

Syd   We won't stay for a pint though, Tom.

Tommy   Course we won't.

Syd (*going to the door*)   Are y' sure now?

Tommy   Scout's Honour, Syd, Scout's Honour.

Syd *and* **Tommy** *go out through the back door.*

The lights cross-fade slightly to the living-room.

Betty *and* **Vera** *come downstairs.*

Betty (*entering the room with* **Vera** *following*)   Syd! Sydney! (*Shocked.*) Sydney! (*It dawns on her.*) I knew it – I knew I shouldn't have left Syd with that fella of yours.

Vera   What's up, Betty?

Betty   What's up? I'll tell you what's up, Vera – They've gone off to the pub, haven't they? Well, just wait till they get through that door, they'll . . .

The doorbell chimes.

Oh, no! That's all we need. Our Reeny here an' he's out at the pub. It's your feller I blame for this, you know. This is just the thing to delight our Reeny, isn't it?

The doorbell chimes again, loud and long.

Listen to her. Listen to that. She's always been jealous of my chimes and she won't be content till she breaks them.

Betty *goes to the front door, and returns, all smiles, with* **Reeny**, **Ted** *and* **John**.

Betty   Hello, Reeny love, how are you? Come on in, Ted, John.

Ted (*taking off his coat*)   I'm just wonderin' if my car's gonna be safe out there, Betty.

Betty   Oh, it'll be all right. Come on, John, let's have your coat. Aren't you takin' yours off, Reen?

Reeny   I'd rather leave it on for a bit, Betty. I'm a bit cold.

Betty   Well we can put another bar on the electric fire you know, Reen.

Ted *goes straight to the window, puts his head under the curtains and looks out.*

Reeny   Oh don't think I'm complainin', Betty. I'm not, it's just, y' know, with getting used to the central heating now . . .

Betty, *hanging up coats, is visibly shaken. She recovers and finishes hanging the coats.*

Betty   Oh – the central heating at work you mean . . .

Reeny   And at home. You did know we were having central heating put in didn't you?

Betty   No . . .

Reeny   Maybe I forgot to mention it.

Betty *is not pleased.*

Ted   Are you sure that car of mine's gonna be safe out there, Betty? I mean, it's not so bad down at end of the estate, but I'm not so sure about up here.

Betty   Well if you like, Ted, I'll go an' stand guard on it for the rest of the night. Would y' like a few blankets off the bed to stop it getting wet?

Ted (*with an unsure laugh, really more of a cracked face*)   You do have to be careful these days, though. A car owner is a vulnerable man. I hope it's all right out there.

Betty   Come on, Reen. Sit down.

John *sits near the television and watches it.*

Reeny   I'll just get warmed through first, Bett.

Betty   Well, suit yourself. (*Aside to* **Vera**.) *She* — has got central heatin'. (*To everyone.*) Now — who's having a drink?

Vera   Yeh — I'd love that port an' lemon, Betty.

Reeny   Where's Syd, Betty?

Vera   He's gone down the —

Betty   — road to take those little children home. Carol singers, y'know. Syd was upset wasn't he, Vee? Seein' small children out on their own at this time of night. He said he wouldn't be able to rest unless he saw them safely home —

Ted *starts coming away from the window.*

Betty   I mean, you never know what's out there, lurking in the night.

Hearing this, **Ted** *returns to the window.*

Betty   Our Tommy's gone with him. I wouldn't let Syd go out on his own. I don't think it's wise for a man in his condition.

Reeny   Is he still bad, Betty?

Betty   Dyin' on his feet, isn't he, Vee?

Vera   Oh he did look ill, Reeny.

Betty (*looking at* **Reeny**)   You don't look as though you've been keepin' too well yourself, Reen.

Reeny   I've had a terrible chest the past few weeks, he'll tell y'.

John   You haven't been well at all, have y', Mum?

Betty   Why don't you take the weight off your legs, Reeny?

Reeny   No. I'm all right here for the minute, Betty.

Betty   Standing isn't good for you. And you're just at the age when they start to appear.

Ted   I wonder if that vehicle would be safer round the back?

Reeny   When what appear?

Betty   Varicose veins.

Reeny (*huffily*)   I've never suffered with varicose veins. Even when I was havin' him I didn't get them. Did I Ted?

Ted   A car owner, these days – is a potential victim.

Betty (*passing cigarettes around from the sideboard*)   Oh – that's right. I'm getting mixed up. It was me who had the varicose veins when I was carrying Sandra, wasn't it?

Reeny (*vindicated*)   I told you. I've never had varicose veins.

Betty (*going over to give* **Ted** *a cigarette*)   That's right – I had the varicose veins and you had the piles. Remember, Reen?

Ted   Christmas is the worse time of all. Drunks – can't get a bus or a taxi – they don't think twice about robbin' a car to get home. An' the next thing y' know it's up against a wall somewhere. (*He lights the cigarette.*)

Betty   Are you comfortable enough there, John?

John   Yes, thanks, Aunty Betty.

Betty   Are you sure?

John   Yes, thanks.

Reeny   Oh – Betty! Trust me! I didn't notice.

Betty *smiles at the suite*.

Betty   That's quite all right, Reeny. Tasteful furniture should never be noticed straightaway. It blends in.

Reeny   Oh I know, but I should have noticed you've had your suite recovered.

Vera No, Reeny – it's a new one.

Reeny Is it? Oh it's lovely, Betty.

Betty Just wait till you sit on it.

Vera It's just like a cloud y' know, Reen.

John (*testing his seat*) I think you've hit the nail on the head there Aunty Vee. It is just like a cloud.

Reeny, *gingerly, sits on the settee.*

Betty Now isn't that comfortable, Reeny? Have you ever known comfort like that?

Reeny (*quietly*) It's certainly nice, Betty.

John It is just like sitting on a cloud isn't it, Mum?

Reeny *slowly burns him into his seat.*

Reeny You'll be all right if it stays this way, Bett.

Betty What do you mean love?

Reeny Well, you know I got a new three-piece a couple of months back.

Betty Yes.

Reeny What's it like Ted?

Ted (*coming from the window*) It's certainly a mystery.

Vera What is?

Reeny Every mornin' when we get up – there's another seam gone. Split right open.

Betty Go 'way.

Reeny I'm not telling a word of a lie. Seams just gaping open. We've had to tape it all up.

Betty Well, haven't you had them in to look at it? They should take it back.

Ted They won't though, Betty. They said the seams had been ripped apart. Split open on purpose.

Vera They didn't?

Reeny   They did.

John *gets up and goes to window, looks out at the car.*

Reeny   I said to him, didn't I, Ted? I said, are you trying to tell me that I'd damage my own suite? I've never heard stupidity like it. I mean who's going to pay nearly five hundred pounds for a suite and then rip it all to pieces?

Vera   Is that what you paid for your suite, Reeny?

Reeny   I did, Vera.

Betty   Well maybe that'll teach you, Reeny. It never does any good gettin' things on the cheap. Now – who'd like a drink?

Vera   I'd love a port an' lemon, Betty.

Ted   I could shift a nice drop of rum if y've got . . .

Reeny   I hope you've not forgotten that you're driving me home.

Ted (*sitting*)   Oh – I'm all right if I have a couple of drinks early on, Reen. We've only just got here. We're not going' yet are we?

Reeny (*putting her hand to her chest*)   No – but if my chest gets any worse . . .

Betty   Is it very bad, Reeny?

Reeny   It's this tightness I get. Y' know, this tightness across here.

Betty (*interested*)   And have you got a tickle in your throat as well?

Reeny (*surprised at* **Betty**'s *knowledge*)   I have, Betty.

Betty (*nodding*)   And a dry cough?

Reeny   Yes – that's right. God knows what's causin' it . . .

Betty (*shaking her head*)   You don't need God to tell you what's causing that. It's as plain as the nose on your face, what's causing that.

Reeny (*a little worried*) What?

Betty It's the bloody central heating! Did you know they've found it causes a multitude of illnesses. Haven't they, Vera? There's even a theory goin' round that it can cause — (*Looking round to check that no intruder is listening.*) — C.A.N.C.E.R. (*She spells it out instead of saying the word.*)

Vera (*puzzled and fascinated*) What was that, Betty?

Betty *mouths the word for her.*

Vera Go 'way!

Betty Of the B.R.E.A.S.T. Believe me, Reeny, y' don't know what it can cause. (*Smiling.*) What did you say you were havin' to drink love?

Reeny What have you got in?

Betty You name it and it's yours.

Reeny I'll have a Tia Maria then, Betty.

Betty Ah. We just finished the last bottle yesterday, Reen. I'll tell you what you'd like — why don't you have a drop of whisky and hot water and sugar. Good for that chest of yours. Right. And some beer for John, eh John?

John Please Aunty Bett!

Betty *goes into the kitchen to get the drinks.*

Reeny And don't you go drinking it all at once.

John I won't, Mum.

Vera I thought you'd be off out, John, with it bein' Christmas. They like to get out at Christmas, the young ones, don't they?

Reeny He doesn't want to be goin' out. Do y' John?

John There's nowhere to go, Aunty Vee.

Vera Oooh — I was always off down town when I was your age. You couldn't keep me away; dancin' and larkin' about.

Ted You could do then, Vera. Not now though.

John   It's not safe in town these days, Aunty Vee. You know, with the gangs an' that. There's no point goin' to town.

Reeny   He's better off stayin' in with us, Vera.

Vera   But when y' young, y' don't wanna be sittin' in with y' mum an' dad, do y'?

Ted   But what's the point of goin' out, Vera? I mean, what is there that's worth seekin' in the world? Our John's got a good family. We get on well together, don't we John? He doesn't need to go runnin' all over the place to get enjoyment.

Reeny (*quietly*)   Not like some I could name.

Vera   Who's that, Reen?

Reeny   Well, I mean, I see Sandra's not in again.

Vera   Oh. I know.

Reeny   If it was a daughter of mine, I'd put my foot down. She could be off anywhere; with fellers, runnin' round in cars . . .

Vera   In cars, yeh . . .

Ted   Now you're talkin' about cars, Vera. I know there are more expensive models on the road. Fuel injection jobs an' automatic gearboxes an' all that stuff. There's more up-to-date models on the road. But I'd defy any of them to give a better overall performance than that car of mine.

Vera   It's certainly a lovely model, Ted.

Ted   It's looked after, Vera. Our John'll tell y', how often do we clean that car, John?

John   Four times a week we clean the car.

Ted   An' that's in summer.

John   In winter we clean it five times a week.

Vera   As much as that, Ted?

Reeny   Sometimes more than that isn't it, Ted?

John   You probably don't know this, Aunty Vera, but the car has been likened to the human body!

Vera   Go 'way!

Ted   See, Vera – man made the motor car in his own image! There isn't one part of a man's body, Vera, that isn't present in the motor car.

Vera   I bet I could think of one couldn't you, Reeny? (*She shrieks with laughter but her attempt to lighten the topic of conversation is ill-timed and fruitless.*)

Reeny *looks at* **Ted**.

John   Did you know that me dad had worked it out, Aunty Vera? At home we've got this chart that he made showing all the links between man and the car. Haven't we, Dad?

Ted   See – I'm a great believer in thinking, Vera.

Reeny   Sometimes he just sits for hours, and thinks.

Vera   Do y', Ted?

Ted   Thinking, Vera, thinking is one of the last great pleasures left to man.

Vera   Oh – I'd find it borin'. Just thinkin'.

Ted   But you wouldn't, Vera. You wouldn't become bored, because the mind, the human mind is a vast warehouse of ideas!

Vera   I suppose so. If y' a feller, like.

Betty *enters with drinks*. **Ted** *stands*.

Betty   Now, everybody. I don't want you to touch your drinks yet. Not till I say. (*She hands the drinks round 'There we are, there's yours etc. . . .'*)

There is no drink for **Vera**.

Vera   Er – mine was a – er – port an' lemon, Betty.

Betty   Ah – now I can't find the lemonade, Vera. Would you have somethin' else in your port?

Vera   Anythin', Betty.

Betty   Right. Just hold on a minute and I'll get it for you. Now. (*She grabs the vibrator from its place and holds it up.*) Who's going to be first? Reeny? (*She takes* **Reeny**'s *drink and plunges the vibrator in. Smiling.*) I'll say one thing for that feller of yours, Vera – when he buys a present, he knows what to get to please a lady!

Reeny   Oh – did Tommy get you that?

Ted   I'm just wonderin' what it reminds me of.

Reeny   Ted! (*With a slight laugh.*) Don't be filthy.

Ted   Who's being filthy? That's just your dirty mind.

Reeny (*offended*)   Dirty mind! I beg your pardon. Don't you insult me in public or we'll go home now.

Betty (*finishing the mixing and putting the 'mixer' back*)   Now now, Reen. Ted's only havin' a laugh. Let's not have any arguments. Let's have your coat an' you can settle down with your drink.

Reeny (*still not shedding her coat*)   I haven't come out to be insulted.

Betty   Never mind, Reeny. Take no notice. Every marriage has its little difficulties.

They are all silent watching the television.

The back door opens, and **Sandra** *enters the kitchen. She ushers* **Tim** *in. He is anxious and ill-at-ease. Their dialogue is whispered.*

Tim (*nervously*)   Sandra, I thought you said just your parents would be here.

Sandra   Well I didn't know did I?

Tim   All right – but come on – we'll have to leave it now.

Sandra (*emphatically*)   No! They've got to be told tonight.

Tim   But tomorrow . . .

Sandra   Tomorrow I want to be out.

Tim Look – I've told you – we can't live in my flat. It's hardly big enough for me. What will the other lads say if I move you in?

Sandra They'll just have to put up with it until we find somewhere else.

Tim Well, why can't you live at home until we find somewhere?

Sandra You've never lived here. You don't know what it's like. (*Pause.*) Come on, Tim, you said you'd tell them tonight.

Tim I know but – but not with all your relations here.

Sandra Well – we'll wait till they've gone.

Tim Sandra – I'd rather leave it till . . .

Sandra (*slightly rattled*) What are you frightened of? All you've got to do is tell them. (*Appealing.*) You said, Tim. You said you would.

Her appeal works. Resigned, he sighs.

Sandra It'll be all right. You can cope with them. Just be firm and strong. (*She enters the front room, leaving* **Tim** *just out of sight in the kitchen. With a half nervous smile.*) Hia. Aunty Reen, Aunty Vee, Uncle Ted. (*She nods to* **John**.)

Betty (*after a pause*) Well, are you coming in or not?

Sandra (*looking over her shoulder*) I've – well I've got someone with me.

Betty Pardon?

Sandra I've got someone with me.

Betty Where?

Sandra In the kitchen.

Everyone cranes to see who is in the kitchen.

Betty Who is it?

Sandra   We want a word with you and me dad. I didn't know everyone was coming.

Betty   Well what difference does that make. This is your family. Now come on. You don't leave people standing in the kitchen, Sandra. (*To the others.*) I don't know what she's thinking of, come on, come on.

Sandra *opens the door so that* **Tim** *can enter, smiling all round.*

Tim (*nodding*)   Hello.

Sandra   This is me mum. This is Tim.

Tim *stretches out his hand to* **Betty**.

Tim   Pleased to meet you.

Betty   Oh – well, come in Tim, and sit down. (*She sits him on the settee.*) You won't know Sandra's relations, will you? (*She introduces him all round.*) Now, what would you like to drink, Tim?

Tim   Beer?

Betty   Well, come on, Sandra. Get Tim a beer.

Sandra   Where is it?

Betty   It's in the ice box, where it's always kept, Sandra.

Sandra   You mean the fridge? (*She goes out to the kitchen.*)

Ted *gets up to look out of the window.* **Tim** *watches him.*

Betty   Ted's just checking that his car's still there.

Tim   Oh.

Reeny   You've got to be very careful these days, haven't you?

Tim   Pardon?

Betty   Are you comfortable there, Tim?

Tim   Yes. Yes, thanks.

During the following, **Sandra** *gets out a bottle of beer for* **Tim**, *pours it into a glass, prepares a drink for herself, then sits at the kitchen table.*

Betty I suppose Sandra's told you all about our new suite hasn't she?

Vera *passes* **Tim** *the brochure.*

Tim Erm . . .

Betty What's your second name, Tim?

Tim McBain. Tim McBain.

Betty McBain! (*Pause.*) There's, er, there's no – Irish blood in your family though, Tim?

Tim Well – I don't. . . .

Betty No – I thought . . .

Ted (*laughing*) Hey, John, John – come over here an' look at this. . . .

John *gets up and goes to the window.*

Vera I see you've got one of those college scarves . . .

Tim (*putting a pair of glasses on*) Yes, well, I'm a student!

Betty (*thrilled*) Oh, he's a student.

Vera *moves down the settee.*

Ted Look at that pile of junk across the road. Hey, Betty, how long's that feller opposite you been runnin' that heap?

Betty (*to* **Tim**) Ted knows all about cars, you know, everything. Do you have a car, Tim?

Tim Yes, it's just across the road.

Ted *and* **John** *close the curtain and return to their seats.*

Betty Whereabouts are you from, Tim?

Tim Well, I'm at college up here, but my home's in Stafford.

Betty (*almost overcome*) Oh – what a beautiful part of the world that is, Tim.

Tim Yes, it's all right.

Betty All those hops! I think the people from Stafford are very civilized, don't you, Tim?

Tim Well, erm – I just don't know really.

Reeny Oh they are, you know. Your people are much more civilized.

Tim Are they?

Ted Are they? Well, I'm surprised at you. You a college lad and you didn't know that. Do you know what Northerners are called, historically speaking?

Tim Erm . . .

Ted Tell him, John.

John Barbarians!

Ted Bar—barians. Now! Do you know what the word barbarian means? (*Fully expecting him not to.*)

Tim To be barbaric.

Ted (*after a pause*) You've got it. He's right. He's right!

Betty Our Ted could have gone to a college, you know, Tim.

Tim Oh. Yes.

Reeny He's always watching the documentaries, y'know. He loves them. Don't you, Ted?

Ted Oh – I watch them all. See, with the documentaries – the whole – of human life – is there! We can learn from things like that, y' see. Now last night – she – (*Indicating* **Reeny**.) – wouldn't watch it – but I did, didn't I, John?

John You watched that documentary, didn't y', Dad?

Ted Last night I was transported, transported from my armchair to the heart, the heart of South America! Did you see it? Did you see it yourself?

Tim Er – no, I . . .

Ted Well I did, see. An' believe me – it was a bloody crime.

Betty   Ted! Mind your language please!

Ted   But it was, Betty – it was a crime. It told all this programme did. You saw them, the little black fellers, little, but hard as nails. Solid. Livin' for thousands of years, never changin' an' perfectly happy. They, didn't have much, agreed. But they could range – free – an' wide over all the rivers an' lands doin' the things they'd always done, the things they knew an' understood. See, see, they could cope! An' live! because, because – everythin' was in order! See – see what I mean?

Tim   Mm.

Ted (*throwing up his hands*)   But what happened?

Vera   What happened, Ted?

Ted   I'll tell y', Vera. Two of them sailed up the river, didn't they.

Vera (*as though that explains all*)   Oh.

Ted   Only a couple of them – but that was it. They were finished. Swapped a few skins for a tee shirt an' a bag of beads. Next thing y' know, the whole tribe's paddlin' hell for leather up the river for tee shirts. Never got back to their own lands. All pushed together in corrugated iron sheds now. Killin' each other for a packet of American ciggies. They just sit around all day now, in their tee shirts, not understandin' what's going on.

Pause.

Vera   Me an' Tommy always used to watch *Love Thy Neighbour*. It's great!

Ted   No – y' can't beat a good documentary. An' the one programme I never miss. (*To* **Tim**.) Do y' know what that is?

Tim *shakes his head.*

Ted   Tell him, John.

John   *University Challenge.*

Ted (*to* **Tim**) I admire him, you know. Have you met him?

Tim   Who?

Ted   Bamber! Bamber Gascoigne. He's a clever lad, y' know. The questions he dreams up!

Tim (*half laughing*)   But – but, you don't think *he* makes up the questions? *He* doesn't think them up.

Pause.

Betty   Oh, I think you could be wrong there, Timothy. If y' don't mind me saying.

Tim   No. The questions come from the . . .

Betty   'Ey. You haven't got a drink yet. Where's that girl got to with your drink? (*She starts to go into the kitchen.*)

Vera (*getting up*)   It's all right, Betty. I'll go through. Betty can I help meself to a port an' somethin' while I'm there?

Betty   My God, Vera – you're shifting the drink tonight aren't you?

Vera   But I haven't . . .

Betty   How many will that be? I don't begrudge it, Vee, but I don't want you gettin' like our Tommy.

Vera   But – but – I haven't . . .

Ted (*to* **Tim**)   No, son, see, Bamber Gascoigne . . .

Betty (*shouting*)   Oh John. (*Pointing to the television.*) Turn that up.

John *turns up the sound.* **Ted** *goes to the window. Everyone watches television automatically.*

Betty   Oh – I never miss the Christmas Eve carol singing.

A choir is heard singing on the television. **Vera** *gives up protesting and goes into the kitchen. The lights cross-fade slightly to favour the kitchen.* **Sandra** *still sits, in her coat, the drinks on the table by her.*

Vera   What's up, Sand?

Sandra   Nothing. I just wanted to . . .

Vera   Hey. He talks funny doesn't he? He doesn't talk like us, does he? Oh I'm not saying there's anythin' wrong, with the way he talks. He talks nice, really. Hey – you've got a good catch there, haven't y', Sand?

Pause.

Sandra   Aunty Vera. Do you like Christmas?

Vera (*as though it is a stupid question*)   Oh yeh. Everyone loves Christmas.

Sandra   I don't. I hate it!

Vera   Oh Sandra! Don't say that. That's flyin' in the face of God. You shouldn't say things like that. (*She puts the empty beer bottle away in the bin.*)

Sandra   Why?

Vera   Well you shouldn't, Sand. It's temptin' fate. An' like those things you said to your mum. You shouldn't say those sort of things.

Sandra   What things?

Vera   About Christmas comes from cannibalism.

Sandra   I didn't say cannibalism. I said Christmas is the product of Capitalism.

Vera   What's that mean?

Sandra   Well it means . . . Tim can explain it better. You don't like him, do you, Aunty Vee?

Vera   I wouldn't say that, Sand. I mean he's – er – he is . . .

Sandra   He's different, Aunty Vera. That's all. Look, see – look, his type of life is – different like, like, when I started goin' up to the college with him. You should have seen it, Aunty Vee, honest it just . . . You want to see how they live. It's . . . I went up there one afternoon, and everyone was sittin' round on the lawns, talkin' in the sun. You know, readin' and discussin' things. Honest, everyone was full of life an' interesting. You couldn't believe how people live out there, Aunty Vee. It's just – I mean – all the people he goes round with – they're just so, you know full of life. It made me feel really thick and stupid.

Vera Oh I wouldn't let yourself feel like that, Sandra. They wouldn't make me feel like that.

Sandra An' like Christmas. Like, well. *His* mum and dad – do you know how they'll spend Christmas?

Vera Oh I know they're very civilized. Aren't they? Where they come from?

Sandra They won't spend Christmas stuck in front of the telly. They'll get a big massive table out in the drawing-room.

Vera Are they old-fashioned? No one has drawin'-rooms now. (*She looks for the port.*)

Sandra They do. And a big fire in the grate. And they'll have lots of people round, interesting people, round to dinner. And it'll be a proper dinner, a special dinner, like an event and it'll take hours to get through . . .

Vera (*looking for the port*) Ooh, I'd hate to do the washin'-up in their house.

Sandra And candles on the table, and wine, and all the people will sit round the table afterwards and talk and tell stories and laugh. All the people that Tim knows are like that, Aunty Vee.

Vera (*finding the port*) They sound like snobs to me. (*She pours her drink.*)

Sandra Wouldn't you like to live like that, Aunty Vee?

Vera Oh no! Tommy wouldn't like it. He'd throw me out.

Sandra Well, I'm going to be like them.

Vera (*as if to say 'Come off it'*) Oh, Sandra!

Sandra Tim's taking me away.

Vera (*her drink completed*) Taking you away?

Pause.

Sandra (*quietly*)　Don't you know why we wanted to see me mum and dad on their own? (*Pause.*) Aunty Vee – I'm pregnant.

Vera*'s glass stops just before her mouth. She is stunned.*

Sandra　I'm going to have a baby!

Vera*'s unsipped port is dropped. She does not know which to worry about more,* **Sandra** *or the spilt drink.*

Vera　Oh God! Oh Christ, I shouldn't say 'God' at Christmas. Oh God – I shouldn't say 'Christ'. Oh Jesus – oh frig it! (*She bends down and hurriedly tries to clear up the mess.*)

Sandra *helps her.*

Vera (*in a whisper*)　An' does y' mum know?

Sandra　Not yet. Tim's going to tell her.

Vera (*alarmed*)　When? Tonight?

Sandra　It's all right, Aunty Vee. Tim knows how to deal with situations.

Betty *enters the kitchen.*

Betty　What's goin' on?

Vera　It's all right – it's just the port wine Betty. (*She holds up the empty glass as an explanation.*)

Betty　Vera! I think you *are* gettin' to be like Tommy. (*Taking her by the arm.*) Guzzling in the kitchen! Now come on, I think you've had enough drink for one night. (*Realizing that* **Sandra** *is not following them out.*) Well come on Sandra, he's waiting for his drink.

Sandra *picks up the two drinks and follows the two of them through to the front room. The lights cross-fade slightly to the living-room.* **John** *turns down TV sound.*

Ted　No, Reeny, I would go on *Mastermind* if I was ten years younger, but not now.

Betty　You'd be very good an' all, Ted. Now, Tim, come on.

Tim (*standing*)   Erm? Yes?

Betty   You can mix the drinks for you and Sandra. (*She grabs the vibrator and hands it to* **Tim**.)

Tim's *look is of sheer horror. He looks around for help. They all look at him.*

John   Haven't you ever used one of those before?

Tim   Pardon?

John (*getting up and taking it from him*)   You've got to stick it in. (*He sticks it into his glass.*) Look. See. (*He carries on mixing.*) Isn't it fantastic, Dad, the things they can do these days?

Ted *holds out his hand.* **John** *passes the vibrator to him.*

Ted   It is marvellous y' know. When y' look around an' consider some of the things that have been achieved. (*Pause.*) And do you know, what strikes me, as the most wonderful thing of all?

Pause.

Vera   The wheel, Ted?

Ted (*looking at her, but choosing to ignore it*)   The most marvellous thing, Vera, is that two hundred years ago our class of people – had nothin'. Not a thing. But look – just two hundred years later, a mere flicker in the passage of time, and we've got – well, what haven't we got?

John   We've got everything, Dad.

Ted   In this day and age, the working man – is a king. This is the nation of monarchs. Just think how far we have come in the past two hundred years. Look what we've got – cars, colour televisions, holidays abroad. They talk about the French Revolution, the Russian Revolution. Insignificant. Do you know, can you tell me, Tim, the one significant revolution that man has known?

Tim   Yes, the er . . .

Ted   No. You're miles out, lad, miles out! The only revolution that did anythin' for the ordinary man was the

Industrial Revolution. The Industrial Revolution. That's
how we gained our liberty. Nights? Who could work nights
two centuries ago? Who could get overtime in those days?
Who could have foreseen then, that the day would come
when a man could stand at his bench – and let the work –
come to him! Just think about that!

Vera It's marvellous, isn't it?

Ted (*now totally dominating the room*) They talk about the
civilization of Greece, they say it was rapid progress! It was a
snail's pace, a snail's pace compared with the progress of the
working man in the last two hundred years.

Reeny Ted's going to write a book about it, aren't y', Ted?

Ted I am.

John What is it that you're goin' to call it, Dad?

Ted (*writing titles in the air*) *From a Peasant to a King.*

Vera Ah. (*Clapping.*) I'll buy that when it comes out, Ted.

Sandra It might have been better if they'd stayed as
peasants!

Betty Who's hungry? I'll go through and get some
sandwiches ready. Come on, Sandra – you can give me a
hand in the kitchen.

Sandra Have you ever thought about that, Uncle Ted?

Betty Sandra! Your uncle's studied these things.

Sandra I've started studying them as well.

Betty Look, why don't all us girls go through to the
kitchen? Come on – we can have a natter.

Reeny I'll give you a hand if you're goin' through, Betty.

Sandra Do you think us, this family, do you think we're
well off, Uncle Ted?

Betty Now don't start, Sandra. Come on, John. You've
not played us your record yet.

Sandra Don't start what, Mother?

Betty   Don't start with your awkward questions. It's Christmas.

Sandra   Well? I was just saying to Uncle Ted . . .

Betty (*becoming more and more rattled*)   You're just too critical for your own good. You just want to find fault with everything. Now give it a rest. Your Uncle Ted's much older than you and he doesn't want to be interrogated by a slip of a girl.

Sandra   I am *not* a slip of a girl!

Ted   No, no. What y' mum's saying Sandra love – see, you've got it wrong, what she means is . . .

Sandra   – is because I'm a girl I've got nothing to say on the subject. Well, well, there are some girls who *do* think.

Betty (*appealing to the crowd*)   See, see – that's another thing she's been going on about – this, this Women's Lib thing.

Ted   Oh – bloody hell!

Vera (*laughing*)   Have y' burnt y' bra, Sand? (*She laughs.*)

Sandra   I haven't been going on about Women's Lib. (*She glares at the wall.*)

Betty (*feeling that the crowd is with her*)   You should all come round here when Sandra's in an' listen to some of her ideas. Come on, what are you goin' to tell us today, Sandra?

Sandra   It wouldn't matter what I told you. You wouldn't listen anyway. You never listen to anything. You don't want to hear anything new. You're deaf!

Betty   Now this has gone far enough. I am not being insulted in my own house!

Sandra   See – you don't, do you? You don't listen.

Betty   Come on, John. Let's have some of those records on. Let's have this. Some nice Christmas songs. (*She takes an album and goes to the radiogram.*) Do you like pop music, Tim? (*She puts the needle on.*) Right, now what about a drink for everyone?

Betty *goes into the kitchen to prepare drinks. From the radiogram comes the song 'Wombling Merry Christmas'. They all listen to it, tapping feet, nodding heads, smiling, except* **Tim** *and* **Sandra** *– who glares.* **Betty** *returns with the drinks, including a Coca-Cola with a straw for* **Vera**.

Sandra (*over the record*)   Tim's got something to tell you, Mother.

Tim *terrified, shakes his head at* **Sandra**. **Betty** *joins in the nodding and tapping, mumbling at the Wombling Song.*

Sandra   Mother, I said Tim's got something to tell you.

Betty (*still wombling*)   What's that, Tim?

Tim   Erm – it's – well – a bit – you know . . .

Sandra   Tell her.

Tim   Well . . .

Sandra   Go on – tell her . . .

Tim   Sand – the time isn't . . .

Betty   Stop pestering, Sandra. Tim's trying to listen, aren't you, Tim? Do you like pop music, Tim?

Tim   Well, you know, heavy albums.

Betty   Well, I don't know what this one weighs but it's good. (*She sings half a line to him, smiling.*) 'Wombling, Merry Christmas . . .'

Sandra   Mother – I am pregnant!

A shock hits the room. **John** *goes to the radiogram and lifts the needle.*

Betty   Pardon!

Sandra   I'm pregnant.

In the silence that follows **Tim** *does not know where to hide.* **Ted** *gets out of it by going to the curtains and checking his car.* **John** *puts the record away.* **Reeny** *and* **Vera** *look at* **Betty**, *who stares at* **Sandra**. *It is a long silence.*

The silence is broken by **Syd** *and* **Tommy**, *off, singing drunkenly,* '*You'll never walk alone*'. *They burst into the room from the hall with shouts of* '*Merry Christmas*' *and* '*All the best*', *and stand swaying together in the centre of the room: then slowly they realize that something is wrong.*

Tommy   We only – only – slipped out – Betty.

Syd   For – for a bottle of – lemonade. (*He laughs.*) We – we forgot it, though.

Tommy   'Ey.

Syd   What?

Tommy   We'll have to go back – for it . . .

Tommy *and* **Syd** *turn as if to go.*

Betty (*still glaring at* **Sandra**)   Don't you move.

Syd *and* **Tommy** *stop.*

Betty   Sandra. Would you like to repeat what you have just said? For your father's benefit?

Sandra   I'm pregnant!

Syd (*looking at everyone*)   What did she say?

Tommy (*whispering loudly in his ear*)   She said – she's pregnant.

Syd   Is it a joke?

Tommy (*looking round*)   I don't think – so.

Syd   Pregnant! How?

Betty (*still controlled, but beginning to boil*)   How? How?

Reeny   How do women usually get pregnant Syd?

Syd   But not our – our Sandra. Our Sandra – she wouldn't – she wouldn't do that! (*Pause.*) All right. OK. So our Sandra's pregnant. OK. It doesn't matter, does it?

Betty   Will you shut up?

Syd (*looking at her*)   No . . . (*Staggering.*) Why don't you shut up? You're stupid you are Betty. (*He grabs the vibrator.*) See that. See it? He's just told me in the pub. Drink mixer! Well, it's not – d' y' know what it's for? It's a sex thing Betty. Look – a sex thing – it's for . . .

Syd *goes to* **Betty** *and whispers. She is still staring at* **Sandra**. *Suddenly she snatches the vibrator.*

Betty (*to* **Syd** *and* **Tommy**) You – and you . . . You disgust me. Sandra, will you come into the kitchen, please?

Sandra I don't want to.

Betty I don't care what you want or don't want. Come into the kitchen.

Sandra No!

Betty Are you defying me?

Sandra I don't want to go into the kitchen, Mother.

Betty I want to have words with you, young lady.

Sandra Well you can talk to me here.

Betty You deliberately did this in front of my family, didn't you?

Sandra No!

Betty Will you *stop* saying no to me?

Sandra No!

Betty Stop it!

Sandra No!

Betty (*shrieking*) STOP IT, STOP IT, STOP IT! (*In her anger she raises the vibrator as though she is going to hit* **Sandra** *with it. But she flings it on the floor. She stamps wildly on it, smashing it to pieces.*)

Tommy *and* **Syd** *try to restrain her.*

Syd Come on Betty. This is no way to spend Christmas.

Ted (*from the window*) 'Ey – I don't wanna worry anyone, but there's somethin' very suspicious-lookin' on the side of my car.

Tommy (*staggering over to him*)   Ted – Ted – if I'd known it was yours, lad – I wouldn't have. I couldn't help it, Ted. God knows – I tried to keep it down, but it just rushed up from me stomach. There was no stoppin', it spewed right out – didn't it Syd?

Ted (*disgusted and horrified*)   You dirty bloody get! (*He points at him, threatening, thinks and changes his course.*) John, John, quick, get a cloth an' let's get out there. Christ knows what the acids in that lot are doin' to my paintwork . . .

Ted *and* **John** *rush out.*

Syd (*still holding on to the trembling* **Betty**)   Now come on, Betty. Just settle down. (*He laughs.*) I don't even know what the fuss is about. (*To the others.*) She was four months gone herself, when we got married!

Betty *pulls away from him and goes to the hall door.*

Betty   Get out! All of you! Get out!

Betty *runs out and upstairs.*

Syd   – Ah – take no notice. She'll be – all right . . .

Sandra (*going quickly to the door; as she passes* **Tim**)   Come on!

Sandra *exits:* **Tim** *follows, embarrassed.*

Tommy (*noticing* **Tim** *for the first time*)   Merry Christmas, pal! (*To the others.*) Ignorant pillock. Who is he, anyway?

There is a long, awkward moment as the four people left in the room look at one another. **Reeny** *gets up as if to go, but instead she finally takes off her coat, sits down and makes herself comfortable, as –*

the curtain falls.

Act Two

Reeny's house. Late afternoon, the following day.

The shape of the set is similar to Betty's house, but in reverse. The arrangement of the furniture also, with minor alterations, is the same, in reverse. In place of the sideboard there is a long wall radiator, and there is no electric fire downstage. Reeny's settee has strips of tape running along the seams. The set as a whole immediately indicates that the two women cancel each other out.

As the curtain rises, Reeny, Ted, John, Tommy and Vera are watching television. Each of them has a card and a pencil. One or two are wearing party hats from crackers – Ted being one. From the television sound it is evident that they are watching an Opportunity Knocks / New Faces *type of programme.* Tommy *is fairly bored with it, and* Reeny *is fairly preoccupied. As the programme ends, Ted rises and switches off the sound. He is enthusiastic, a bit like a scoutmaster.*

Ted   Now! Right! In part one of today's programme we have seen nine different acts. Before we start to give marks to those acts I want to remind you – (*He verbally underlines his instructions.*)   the comments we have heard from the television judges are irrelevant! Not worth a fig! It's only *our* votes, the votes of the viewers, that count! *We* are the people who will make or break the performers we have seen tonight. When you make your judgements on those acts I want you to remember – their destiny – is in your hands!

Reeny (*to* **Vera**)   She won't turn up, y' know. (*Shaking her head.*) No.

Ted   Now, it's Reeny to vote first. The first act we saw today was the juggler from Yorkshire, Mr Johnny Perry – Reeny.

Reeny (*finding her voting card*)   Oh – er . . .

John Come on, Mum.

Ted Come on, Reeny – your marks, your marks.

Reeny Who was first – that juggler? Seven for Content.

Ted (*marking it on the master sheet*) Presentation?

Reeny Eight.

Ted Star Quality.

Reeny Erm – eight again.

Ted Right. Good. Now we turn to John. Give us your marks on the juggler, Johnny Perry.

John For Content – I can only give Johnny Perry five marks.

Ted Five? Five?

John Well, there was nothing original in his act, was there?

Ted Do you know how difficult it is to learn the art of juggling? Do you?

John (*after a pause, sighing*) All right – six for Content.

Ted OK. Presentation?

John I'll give Johnny Perry seven for Presentation. He did dress very well, and I think that's important.

Ted Good, good. Now. Star Quality?

John Four for Star Quality.

Ted You can't just give him four.

John Why?

Ted We've got to give encouragement to up and comin' stars – that's why. Imagine what he's going to feel like when I send our votes in and he sees that someone somewhere thought he was only worth four votes.

John But it is Star Quality we're talkin' about, Dad, and jugglers never get to be stars. It's a speciality act.

Ted Six for Star Quality . . .

John No, four – I said . . .

Ted And now we turn to Tommy. This is Tommy's first appearance on our panel, so Tommy can we have your marks and perhaps a few comments on the juggler Johnny Perry?

Tommy Well I thought Johnny Perry *looked* very good! His taste in dress was impeccable and he managed to sustain a smile throughout the whole of his act; even when he dropped six of his seven plates, the smile was still there, reassurin' you of his confidence. It was, of course, most unfortunate, when he threw his balls too high an' got them caught in the studio lights!

Vera Tommy!

Tommy If I have any great criticism of Johnny Perry it is that he is over-ambitious. I think he should just stick to the juggling instead of trying to sing an' dance a Russian Cossack dance at the same time!

Ted All right. (*He goes around taking the cards off people. He is in a huff.*) OK. Give me the cards – I'll do the votes meself. OK . . .

Tommy What's up, Ted?

Ted If people want to make a pig's arse of everything, that's all right by me. But I'm gettin' a bit fed up of this flippant attitude . . .

Tommy Ah, come on, Ted – I wasn't bein' . . .

Ted Votin', Tommy – votin' on matters like this might not be a serious issue as far as you're concerned, but it is to the people who depend on these votes. It is to the television companies who put faith in us. If it was left up to the likes of you, Tommy, we wouldn't get the chance to share in things like this.

Tommy Ah, come on, Ted – I was only . . .

Vera   Ted's right – you were messin' round. You're always messin'.

Tommy   Ah, I'm sorry, Ted.

Ted   No – it's all right, Tommy. Don't apologize. I'll do the votes myself.

Ted goes out of the room.

Vera   See – see what you've done now!

Tommy   All right, all right! What d' y' want me to do? Jump under a passin' reindeer?

Vera   Just be quiet an' give us a bit of peace.

They all fall silent watching the silent television. There is a long, long pause which sums up the excitement and joy of Christmas.

Vera (*at length*)   I love Christmas! (*Another pause. Quietly.*) I love Christmas! (*Another pause. Quietly.*) Oh, Reeny! Peter's gone. You've got rid of the budgie!

John   We had to get rid of him, didn't we, Mum?

Vera   Oh, he's not – er – y' know?

Reeny   No. He's still livin'. We found a good home for him. Didn't we, John? We couldn't keep him though, Vee. Not when we got the new wallpaper up. If I'd thought about it I would have got somethin' different – y' know, that he could have blended in with; but as it was. . . ! Oh – he clashed terrible, didn't he, John? Didn't Peter clash with the wallpaper, John?

Tommy (*quietly*)   Y' should've given him a coat of paint, Reen.

Reeny   We did wonder about gettin' him tinted. But the vet said no, didn't he, John? We got him into the aviary, in the park.

Tommy (*quietly*)   I'm glad you never had any kids with red hair, Reeny.

Vera (*looking at him*)   What are you on about?

Tommy (*loudly, leaning over and spelling it out for her*) Well, they'd look a bit stupid flyin' round the bloody branches in the park aviary, wouldn't they?

Vera What's he on about, Reen?

Tommy Ah – forget it.

Pause. They all look at the television.

Reeny That poor, poor woman.

Vera Think she'll come round, Reeny?

Reeny Never. She won't be able to hold her head up any more. She must be dyin' with shame. (*Pause.*) Mind you, it's her own fault. If she'd kept her eye on that girl it mightn't have happened. I mean, they might look grown up when they get to that age, but they don't know anything about the world. It's like him. (*Pointing to* **John**.) He brought a girl home about six months ago, didn't you? He thought the sun shone out of her. But she didn't fool me – I could tell straightaway she was no good. A very murky girl, she was. It upset him like, didn't it, John?

John (*absently, still glued to the television*) Mmm.

Reeny But I had to explain to him. I mean it was my duty, Vera. I would never have forgiven meself if I'd kept quiet.

Vera What was wrong with her, Reen?

Reeny What was right with her Vera? She had those eyes, y' know – very close together. His life would have been a misery if he'd carried on seein' her. Wouldn't it, John?

John (*repeating what he must have been told many times*) She wasn't the right girl for me. It was just infatuation.

Reeny As I say – he was upset for a bit – but our doctor's very good. He put him on Valium straightaway. They're marvellous things for settling you down. Show Aunty Vera your tablets, John. They do him a world of good. Don't they, John?

John *takes out a box of pills.* **Reeny** *takes them to show* **Vera**, *and retains them.*

Reeny See, Vera, he's sensible, our John is. When me an' Ted saw how things were going with this girl, we said to him, didn't we, John, we said look, she'll do you no good, get rid of her, an' we'll see about gettin' you that little blue mini you've always fancied. It meant a bit of overtime but we didn't mind.

Vera So John got the mini, did he, Reen?

Reeny I've told you Vera – that lad has got sense. He was brought up to think. Weren't you, John?

John Yeh.

Tommy (*suddenly*) Hey John – I've got just the thing for you. Have y' got a Krooklock on your car?

John I haven't got the car any more, Uncle Tom.

Tommy Not another heart condition?

John There was no point me keepin' it, Uncle Tom. It was daft really, like me mum said. I mean I could always go out in their car with them. There was no point in having two cars parked outside.

Reeny See – we're a family here, Vera. We take an interest in our child. I mean, I'm not sayin' Betty's neglected that girl – but events speak for themselves. (*Pause.*) God! How that woman must be sufferin' now. She's got my sympathy today.

Vera She's got all our sympathy, Reen.

Reeny Tortured! Tortured with grief she'll be!

Tommy Ah well – at least there'll be a weddin' to go to. I haven't been to a weddin' for ages.

Vera Oh yes. Trust you to think of that.

Tommy Well there's nothin' else to think of is there? It's happened, done, finished. They'll get married an' that's that.

The doorbell rings.

Reeny (*getting up*)   Who's that? (*She looks out of the curtains. She is excited.*) It's them – it's her – our Betty. (*Going to the front door.*) Ted!

Vera (*getting up to follow*)   Go 'way!

Vera *and* **Reeny** *go out to the hall and open the front door. They return with* **Betty** *and* **Syd**.

Reeny   Oh, Betty, Betty, love. Ah poor love – come on in. We were just saying we hoped you'd make the effort. (*To* **Syd**, *quietly.*) You go through with Ted, Syd. We'll look after Betty.

Ted *comes downstairs and takes* **Syd** *into the front room.*

Betty *is ushered through the front room to the kitchen by* **Vera** *and* **Reeny** *who appear to be coping with an invalid.* **Tommy** *and* **John** *watch television. The lights cross-fade slightly to favour the kitchen.*

Reeny   Come on Betty, love, you'll be all right with us. Don't worry, we'll look after you, won't we, Vee? It's at times like this, Betty, you realize what relations are for. Come on love.

Vera *holds out a chair but* **Betty** *ignores it and stands with her back to the sink.*

Vera   We want y' to know that you've got all our sympathy, Betty.

Betty   Sympathy, Vera?

Reeny   Tortured – wasn't I sayin' Vera? Tortured! Now let's get the kettle on. (*She sets about it.*) I always think a cup of tea's a great comfort in times like this.

Vera (*looking at* **Betty**)   I must say Bet, you look as though you're taking it very well.

Reeny   Shock Vera! Delayed shock.

Vera   Oh!

Reeny   A woman at our place, she seemed all right after her dog had been knocked down by a one-man bus. Six months later she dropped dead of a heart attack. She did.

The kettle on, **Reeny** *tries to take* **Betty***'s arm and lead her to a chair.* **Betty** *gently, but firmly pulls away and remains standing. She is smiling.*

Betty   Isn't it funny − the way things turn out.

Vera *and* **Reeny** *look at each other.*

Reeny   Erm − how d' y' mean Bet?

Betty (*still smiling*)   Well, you know, with your John being older than Sandra − I mean, I always imagined, me an' Syd did, naturally − we thought, with John being older − we always thought that it would be you and Ted who'd be the first couple to be blessed with a grandchild! (*Smiling.*) It is funny isn't it, the course − of life.

Reeny *resumes making the tea. She prepares it with controlled, but shaking anger.*

Vera   Ah − yes. It will be lovely havin' a little baby in the family won't it? We'll all have to start knittin' 'ey, Reen?

Reeny *reacts.*

Vera   Where will they be livin', Betty?

Betty   Oh, with us! Like I said to Syd, Timothy is only a student y' know. He won't have a lot of money, not for the time being − they couldn't afford a place of their own, could they? Syd says he'll put a little cooker in Sandra's room − they can make it like a little flat up there. An' the baby can have the front box room.

Reeny (*shaking her head*)   Don't y' think it'll be a bit draughty for a baby, Betty? After all . . .

Betty   Not when we get the central heating in. As you know, Syd and me have been plannin' the central heating for a long time and now with the baby on the way we thought we might as well . . . You know, I sometimes think I have second sight. I mean, I didn't know about our Sandra's condition when I was in town last week, but I stopped outside Mothercare, and I distinctly remember thinkin' how nice those new carry-cots are − you know the ones with the transporter wheels. I'm going down to order one next week. They're really dinky. An' when y' think, Reen, remember those great big prams *we* had to trundle round?

Reeny I do remember. An' if you've got any sense that's what you'll be gettin' for your Sandra, a proper full-size pram. Carry-cots – they're not safe.

Betty Yes they are, Reeny. They're double tested.

Reeny Betty! I don't care if they're triple tested and blessed by the Pope himself. They're not safe! There's no support for a little baby's back.

Betty Reeny, of course there's support. The hood folds down an' that acts as the support.

Reeny You don't call that proper support – for a baby's spine do you?

Betty Look, Reeny . . .

Reeny Listen, Betty, if you don't want my advice – all right, I won't give it. But look at it this way: when our John, an' your Sandra were babies – what were they wheeled round in?

Betty Well, I just said – big prams.

Reeny Big prams – exactly. An' have they got twisted spines? Have either of them got humpety backs?

Betty No, but . . .

Reeny No. Right. There's me point! I know, Betty, I know that a full-sized pram *costs* quite a bit more but I'm the baby's great-aunt an' I don't mind puttin' the extra . . .

Betty (*exploding*) The cost! The cost? You talk about cost to a woman who's just paid out a thousand pounds for a three-piece suite? Don't talk to me about cost. (*She laughs.*) Reeny love, if my grandson needs something, he gets it, whatever the cost. I know you're his great-aunt, an' I appreciate your concern, Reeny, I'm very grateful, but after all, I am Wayne's grandmother. (*She pours out the tea.*)

Vera (*in raptures*)   Ah – Wayne! What a lovely choice, Betty.

Betty   It is a nice name isn't it, Vee?

Vera   It's funny isn't it? The way names always make y' think of things. Wayne makes me think of the Rockies. Wayne! (*She tries out the sound.*) Wayne McBain . . .

John *enters the kitchen.*

Vera   Very distinguished, Betty.

John   Mum, me Uncle Tommy said can he have a drink?

Reeny (*looking at him in disgust*)   Are you still in?

John (*puzzled*)   What?

Reeny   You're always stuck in this house, you are. Why don't y' get y'self out now an' then an' find yourself a nice girl.

John (*still puzzled*)   I'm watchin' telly. Can me Uncle Tommy have a drink?

Reeny   It's here, it's here, can't y' see I'm makin' it? (*She hands him a cup of tea.*) Here. An' when this holiday's over, you get yourself out a bit. Sittin' in the house all the time . . .

John (*looking at the tea*)   I think me Uncle Tommy meant . . .

Reeny (*waving him out*)   Now go on . . .

John *gives up and returns to the front room. The lights come up to full in the front room.* **John** *takes the tea to* **Tommy**, *who looks at it.*

Tommy   Has your mother suddenly developed a sense of humour?

John (*going back to look at the television*)   I think she's in a bad mood.

Tommy   I'm not over the moon meself.

They watch the television.

Betty   I'll be back in a minute, girls.

Vera Where y' goin', Betty?

Betty Don't worry, Vera – I will be back. (*Going into the front room.*) I'm only goin' to the loo.

Betty *exits upstairs.*

Reeny (*almost to herself, nodding*) Yes. And to have a look at my shower.

Vera Yeah. Tommy was gonna get me a shower y' know, Reen. (*Pause.*) But y' could become a prostitute for a colour telly. (*Pause.*) Tights are OK, though.

Reeny (*still half to herself*) She's not right y' know. I mean, I've seen them carry-cots in the catalogue. She's not right y' know, Vera.

Vera No.

Reeny I'll show her. Come on. I've got the catalogue upstairs. Now just come and have a look at this, Vera, and see what *you* think. With little babies you can never be safe enough in my book.

Reeny *and* **Vera** *go through the front room and upstairs.*

The lights cross-fade to the front door.

Tommy Well Syd, when's it gonna be?

Syd (*wearily*) What, Tommy?

Tommy The weddin' – the weddin'.

Syd Ah – Jesus! Don't talk to me about it. There's not goin' to be a weddin', is there?

Tommy (*sitting up*) Y' what?

Ted You mean he won't marry her?

Syd Last night – when y'd all gone home an' Betty was in bed, he come in an' told me. 'Sandra an' I,' he says, 'Sandra an' I have decided to live together without goin' through a ceremony of marriage.'

Tommy Good Christ. You're jokin'. What did our Betty say t' that?

Syd   I haven't summoned up the courage to tell her yet.
She's goin' ahead makin' weddin' plans an' all that.
(*Appealing to them.*) Well, what could I do? Would you have
told her?

Ted   So he won't marry her then, Syd?

Syd   I've told y' what he said.

Tommy   I knew last night, as soon as I saw him I said to
meself, he's a mean-lookin' get, that one. The bloody cheek
of him, though.

Ted   You know I had a long talk with him last night don't
y'? Very strange ideas he's got, y' know.

Tommy   I don't think I like this, Syd; gonna live together?
We'd all bloody well like to do it that way, wouldn't we?
Who does he think he is, Syd? In this life we'd all like to do as
we bloody wanted — but we don't, do we? We do our duty, we
marry them an' live properly. Sod this feller's game. I mean,
it's like you, isn't it Syd? All right — so you got our Betty in the
club before y' were married, it's a mistake, fair enough. It
can happen to anyone, apart from puffs, like. No one blames
a feller for that; but y' did y' duty didn't y'? Y' married her
when y' knew she was in the club.

Syd   She wasn't in the club, Tom.

Tommy   What?

Syd   Betty — she wasn't in the club before we got married.

Tommy   But you said — last night y' said . . .

Syd   I know what I said — but I'd got it all wrong, Tom.
See, Betty explained to me. She wasn't in the club before we
got married — it was just that Sandra was a premature baby.

Tommy   Er — yeh. Well, all right, Syd, that's fair enough.
OK. But anyway — it's not you we're concerned with is it. It's
this bloody cowboy we wanna sort out. It's him who should
be answerin' the questions.

Syd   He's supposed to be comin' down here with Sandra.

Tommy (*getting up, rubbing hands together*)   Oh, is he now?
Right. OK. We'll soon sort this one out won't we, lads? I
reckon he's picked the wrong bunch if he thinks he's gonna
tangle with us! You don't walk over fellers in this family an'
get away with it. I know we sometimes have little differences
amongst ourselves – (*To* **Ted**.) – but if anyone tries to give
short change round here, he finds himself facin' a team.
That's what this family is – a team! An' if one player gets
fouled – the whole team feels it.

Ted (*rising*)   Well this feller's certainly committed a foul,
Tommy.

Tommy   In my book it's more than a foul.

Ted   You're right. It's a bloody penalty, Tommy.

Tommy   A serious infringement.

Ted   Well in that case he should be booked.

Tommy   Booked? He should be bloody sent off! (*Gradually
becoming more incensed.*) Not marryin' her? We're not standin'
for this are we? We're not just gonna stand by an' see that
little girl treated like this are we? I don't know about the rest
of y', but I love that little niece of mine, an' I'm not seein' her
treated like this.

The others grunt support.

Just wait, just wait till this feller gets here; we'll have him in
here an' sort him out once an' for all.

Ted   Is there likely to be any violence, Tommy?

Tommy   It depends on him, Ted. If he starts swingin' his
fists I can't guarantee to remain a pacifist.

Syd   If he starts swingin' his fists at you I'll be right behind
y'. I know I might be a sick man, but I won't have my family
terrorized.

Tommy   Don't you worry, Syd, he won't touch you. One
false move an' I'll put him straight through that wall.

Ted   Is it any wonder y' can't go out on the streets these days. (*He puts his hand in his pocket and brings out his car keys.*) Here – John, John. Make sure that the garage is locked.

John *gets up to take the keys.*

Ted   I want to make sure that car's safe. Y' don't know what this feller might try and do.

John *exits through the hall.*

Ted   I just hope he's not carryin' a knife. I don't mind fists, but when there's a knife around there's no tellin' where it might end up.

Tommy (*thinking*)   Y' don't reckon he'll have a knife do y', Ted?

Ted   Well y' can never tell can y'? I mean don't forget, Tommy – he is a student.

Tommy (*relieved*)   Is that what this feller is? A bloody student? Jesus! 'Ey, look out Syd, y' might get stabbed to death with a Parker Fifty-one.

Syd   'Ey, I wouldn't start bloody jokin' about it, Tommy. They're not airy-fairy these days y' know. They're violent.

Ted (*leaning the coffee-table against the television to protect the screen*)   You see them at demonstrations on the telly. Syd's right Tommy; they have to get the riot squads out – swinging clubs, kickin', puttin' the boot in, punchin', clawin' . . .

Tommy   I've told y' – let him try it on with me an' he'll find he's picked the wrong feller. I don't care if he comes through that door fightin' mad an' armed to the teeth. He won't make me budge, he won't make me move a bloody inch.

Tommy *stares defiantly at the door. It suddenly starts to open.* **Ted**, *nearest to it, dives against it and holds it shut.* **Syd** *is stuck to his chair.* **Tommy** *drops behind the settee.*

Ted (*frantically, to* **Syd**)   The bottle! The bloody bottle. Pass me the bottle.

Syd *gives* **Ted** *the bottle from the radiogram.*

John *(off)*   Can I come in please, Dad?

Ted *moves from the door and lets* **John** *in. The door remains slightly open.*

John   What's me Uncle Tommy doin' on the floor?

Tommy *(getting up)*   Just dropped me matches there, John, just pickin' them up. *(He laughs.)* I would have been with y' though, Ted, if there'd been any trouble like.

John *(opening the door fully)*   Come in. He was just goin' to knock so I let him in.

Tim *enters.*

Ted *(holding up his hand)*   Now before you start . . .

Tim   Is Sandra here?

Pause.

Syd   I thought she was with you.

Ted *(putting the bottle on the table)*   Just sit down quietly, and there'll be no trouble.

Tim *(sitting)*   Thanks. She was with me but we – erm – well, we had a disagreement.

Syd *(looking at him)*   I don't know. A fine pair you're gonna make if y' arguin' already.

Tim   It wasn't really an argument. More a disagreement really.

Tommy *(bravely)*   Listen, pal – I don't know where you come from, but round here a nark's a nark!

Tim *(to* **Syd**, *ignoring* **Tommy**)   We were on our way down here. I think she will turn up eventually. *(To* **Ted**.*)* You don't mind if I wait for her?

Ted *(looking to others for support)*   Well – erm – er . . .

Tim   I won't get in the way. I'll just sit here. You carry on as normal.

Ted   Eer − , yes. Thanks.

Silence. Everyone idly looks at the television set, occasionally glancing at **Tim** *and at one another questioningly.*

Tommy (*eventually*)   Student, aren't y'?

Tim   Yes. Yes, that's right.

Tommy   Didn't fancy workin' then?

Long pause.

(*Leaning across conspiratorially.*) Got any drugs?

Tim (*putting his hand in his pocket and bringing out a packet of Number Six*)   Only these. Want one?

Tommy (*slightly alarmed*)   What are they?

Tim   Cannabis Number Six.

With grudging recognition of the gag **Tommy** *takes a cigarette.* **Tim** *lights it for him with a lighter. Pause.*

Tommy   D' y' collect the coupons?

Tim   No.

Tommy (*taking the coupon from the packet and returning the cigarettes to* **Tim**)   Ta. (*Pause.*) D' y' get up to much at that college of yours?

Tim   Such as?

Tommy   Y' know − orgies an' that?

Tim   Only on weekdays.

Tommy   What d' y' do at the weekends?

Tim   Have a rest!

Tommy *gives a short laugh, and realizes he is going to have to change his tactics.*

Tommy   So y' a student, are y'?

Ted   Give me the name of the British general who died at Corunna?

Tommy (*looking at him*)   Ted − Ted, what are y' on about?

Ted   The Peninsular War.

Tommy   D' y' reckon that's gonna solve our little problem like?

Ted (*smiling, smugly*)   He doesn't know.

Tim   Sir John Moore.

Ted *is stung. He goes to the shelves and begins leafing through a book.*

Tommy (*to* **Tim**)   Look – er, what's your name?

Tim   Tim.

Tommy   Look, Tim – I mean, well, y' know, we know y' a student – an' well, y' know, y' a Southerner an' all that; a bit different from us like, different background – but y' see, I don't know about your family. I've never met them – but this family . . .

Syd   It's a team!

Tommy   A team, see. An' with us there are ways of doin' things that are the right ways, acceptable like, sort of, in the rules. An' then there are other ways that are wrong, definitely not in the rules.

Syd   Like committing fouls.

Tommy   An', well, see – the rules are there so that the game can be played properly. The game's no good if the rules are broken. Now, all right, you've not met our team before – fair enough. You might have thought we were playing by a different set of rules – your rules. But we're not, 'cos you've come playin' on *our* ground. It's an away game for you. We're playin' by our rules. (*Pause.*) See? D' y' get me meanin'. Y' follow me, don't y'?

Tim   No, actually. Well, not exactly.

Tommy (*kindly*)   Well look – let me make it a bit easier for y'. What we're sayin' is simple: if y' don't make a respectable woman out of our little Sandra we'll kick your teeth right down your fuckin' throat. D' y' get me meanin' now, Tim?

Tim   You want me to marry Sandra?

Tommy (*to the others, indicating* **Tim** *and smiling*)   See – the taxes we pay are not wasted if they go towards producing minds like this. You've summed it up exactly, Timothy.

Tim   And what if she won't marry me?

Syd   Y' what?

Tim   I have said to Sandra that I'll marry her. But she doesn't want it like that.

Syd   What d' y' mean, she doesn't want it like that.

Tim   I've said that we'll get married but Sandra says she'd rather us just live together.

Syd (*after a pause*)   Don't be bloody stupid.

Tim   I'm not being bloody stupid. She said . . .

Tommy (*interrogating*)   *When*, did she say that?

Tim   Well – when we first learned that she was pregnant.

Tommy (*laughing at him*)   Well! Well, what d' y' expect? Hasn't anyone ever told y' lad? Y' never believe a word from the lips of a woman when she's got one in the oven. Didn't you know that? They go mental when they're havin' a kid. In the first few months they get all sorts of ideas, stupid ideas; but y' don't take any notice of them. They go like lunatics.

Tim (*puzzled*)   Why's that?

Tommy   I don't know why, I just know they do. Round the bloody twist. What was that one like next door to us, Syd? When she was in the club?

Syd (*shaking his head*)   Terrible – terrible . . .

Tommy   She was, y' know. She kept eatin' coal, this one did.

Tim *laughs.*

Tommy   I'm not jokin', mate. She did, didn't she, Syd? Coal. Coal an' chips every night, she had. The delivery wagons couldn't keep up with her. Bags of nutty slack comin' in by the hour. An' this one next door to us, kept on devourin' the stuff. Mind you — she came a right cropper in the end.

Tim   Why? Did the coal affect the baby?

Tommy   No. It affected the Corporation though; if it'd been coke she ate she would have been all right. Coal's not allowed see. She got prosecuted for eatin' coal in a smokeless zone!

Tommy *looks at* **Tim**, *who starts to laugh.* **Tommy** *joins in the laughter.*

Tommy   Good one that, eh? Eh? Like a laugh do y'? 'Ey, have y' heard the one about the three-legged beauty queen at Butlins? She . . .

Syd   I thought we were goin' to sort out my daughter's future.

Tommy   Well, you heard what the lad's said Syd. He's just told y' he offered to marry her. That's it, it's settled isn't it? Start makin' the arrangements.

Syd   How do I know he offered? I've only got his word for it, Tom.

Tim (*to* **Tommy**)   I don't think you've understood exactly how Sandra feels. She doesn't want to get married.

Tommy   Look lad, how long have you known her? Eh? Eh? Well, we've known her all her life an' I can tell you one thing here an' now — once Sandra gets used to the idea of bein' in the club she'll drag you off to that church an' y'll be married faster than y' can say boo! Look, right now Sandra thinks she's still a girl, but she'll realize soon that she's a woman, an' she'll start lookin' forward to bein' with the rest of the women in the family. Y' know why they say 'in the club', don't y'? Y' know that expression don't y'?

Tim   Yeh.

Tommy   Well that's what it means. It really does mean joinin' a club. Sandra's never been part of the women's club before, well not a full member anyway; so she probably can't

see the benefits. But she'll be able to become a part of it now –
now that you've given her the membership card. Girls are
always moanin', but once they turn into women they're
different altogether. (*Pause.*) That lot in the kitchen now;
what d' y' think they were like when they were younger?
Don't y' think they had all these soft ideas? They did! But
look at them now – they're always together – they love it.
When them three get out to the pub with us on a Saturday
night – what they like, Syd? Tell him what it's like on their
side of the table.

Syd Can't get a word in edgeways.

Tommy We can't y' know. It's a bloody secret society
they've got goin'. They have a great time. An' they get out to
the shops together, havin' a laugh an' that. An' that kitchen;
it's private territory y' know. We can't just go in. It's
reserved for the women. You see them when they've got
somethin' to talk about, straight into that kitchen, havin' the
time of their lives. Now, once Sandra realizes that she can
share all that with them she'll be in there like a shot. She's
just got to realize that she knows the password now.

Tim Erm – yes. But look – I don't think you understand.

Tommy Of course we understand! Stop worryin'. I've
told y' – she'll change her mind. When she gets here we'll let
the women have a word with her.

Tim Er, no, I don't think so. You see, when she gets here
we're going.

Tommy Goin'?

Syd Goin' where?

Tim Look – that's why, well, why we had the
disagreement! Sandra has got all her things together and
packed them in my car. She wants to go immediately.

Syd (*shocked*) Go where?

Tim Away. To my flat. We're supposed to be moving in
today. (*Pause.*) You see – she didn't want to see any of you.
She just wanted to go. She said she was afraid, but I insisted

that we had to come down here and tell you first. It did seem wrong to me – just going away without telling you all. Well, anyway, we disagreed about that and Sandra stormed off. Said I didn't understand.

Pause.

Syd No – I don't bloody understand either. (*Quietly.*) Doesn't want to see us? Wants to go? (*Pause.*) What's wrong with us, Tommy? Are we infected? Eh? Is that it? Have we got some bloody disease?

Tim (*trying*) No – look, Mr Dobson – it's just that, I think Sandra – wants a change.

Syd (*offended, loudly*) A change? What d' y' mean, a change?

Tim Well – oh, it's difficult to explain. She just wants something – different. At least, that's the impression I get.

Syd We've never stopped her doin' anythin'.

Tim No, I know you haven't, Mr Dobson, but I'm – you see, I'm just trying to explain to you how Sandra feels. *Why* she wants to go.

Syd Go on, then. Go on. Explain it to me. Go on!

Tim Well . . .

Ted, *who since his question on Corunna has been leafing through his books, suddenly slams a big one shut and comes to join the others.*

Ted Name the five Cup finalists since nineteen sixty whose surnames begin with F.

Tommy For Christ's sake Ted. Can't y' see . . .

Ted (*excitedly*) Don't tell him, don't. Don't give it away.

Tommy Look, go give the car a wash will y', Ted? (*To* **Tim**.) Now come on, what were y' sayin' to Syd?

Tim Well, Sandra . . .

Tommy (*to* **Ted**) What is the answer, anyway?

Ted I'm not tellin' him. He's a student – let him find out for himself. (*He beams at his victory.*)

Tim (*resuming*)   You see, I think the main thing with
Sandra is that, she wants – she's discovered – well, she's –
she's found new things in her life. Do you see? I mean things,
things that well – things you don't understand. (*He frowns at
the sound of what he has said.*)

Syd   We're thick are we? We're clever enough to bring her
up but now we need a university degree before we can talk to
her . . .

Tim   No, no, no – it's not like that. It's more – well,
recently Sandra has started – getting into things that you
don't – don't, I suppose, care about.

Tommy (*suspiciously*)   Like what?

Tim   She's responding to things that you don't particularly
want to respond to . . .

Syd   Yes, well you've told us that already. Now come on,
what sort of things eh? Come on, you tell us – you're
supposed to be clever – you tell us what sort of things.

Tim   Well, things like – like music and – er – conversation
and – and theatre, and . . .

Tommy (*puzzled*)   Well, we understand all that sort of
stuff. Are you sayin' we're ignorant?

Tim   No, I'm not saying anything of the sort. I'm merely
trying to explain Sandra's . . .

Tommy   Well, I'm glad y' not. We understand things like
that. Conversation? We never stop talkin' in this family.

Tim   No, no, not talking. I don't mean . . .

Tommy   Well you said conversation didn't y'? Eh? I
mean, all right, you've got a posh name for it, but we call it,
talkin' an' it's the same thing. An' theatres an' that . . .

Tim   Yes I know that. It's just . . . (*Silence.*)

Ted   Is that all she's worried about? Goin' to theatres? She
wants to have a talk to me – I'd tell her about theatres.

Tommy (*to* **Tim**)   Ted's an educated man y' know. Y' might think we're thick, but there's a lot of brains in this family.

Tim   I'm not saying . . .

Ted   Don't talk to me about theatres. I went to one once. 'Ey, John, what was the name of that play, that play I took you an' y' mother to see when it was rainin' in town? Remember?

John (*still absorbed in the television*)   Waitin' for somethin' wasn't it?

Ted   *Waitin' For Godot*. That was it. I'll tell y' about theatres. We went in to see this thing, it was about these two tramps waitin' for this mate of theirs. Well, I'm not kiddin' you? All this audience were sittin' there waitin' for him as well. I could see straightaway what was gonna happen though. I'd been in there about five minutes an' I knew. I opened me programme didn't I, John? An' I looked down the list, y' know where it gives the names of the characters like? An' straightaway I knew, didn't I? His name's not there in the programme y' see, this Godot's. Well, it's common sense, if his name's not in the programme he's never gonna show up. Y' could wait a hundred years an' he'd still never walk on to the bloody stage. But all the rest of these stupid buggers in the place – they didn't have the sense to look in the programme an' work it out for themselves. I slipped out to this café next door an' read the paper. I laughed meself silly at the rest of them next door. When our John come out with his mum, I said to him, didn't I, John? I said to him – don't tell me – the Godot feller didn't turn up!

Pause.

Syd (to **Tim**)   See, what I can't understand, son, is why she wants to run away. I mean, we wouldn't stop her doin' stuff like that, goin' to theatres an' that. If that's what she wants to do? Why does she want to run away?

Tim   Mr Dobson, to be quite honest, I've no idea myself why she's in such a hurry to leave. I suppose you think I've encouraged her, but in fact it's just the opposite. (*Confessing to them, shaking his head*.) Between you and me I've been worried out of my mind about how we're going to live. But Sandra – well, Sandra seems to think that all she has to do is leave here and everything will be all right (*Looking at the others*.) I don't know what we're going to do.

Tommy   Well why haven't y' put y' foot down?

Tim   Oh God, I don't know. I suppose it's because I love Sandra.

Tommy (*to the others, with eyebrows raised*)   Well, that's no bloody excuse is it? I mean, I suppose I love our Vera, but if she started upsettin' me I'd soon bat her one in the mouth.

John (*still looking at the television*)   She's got to run away.

Ted *and* **Syd**   Pardon?

John   You'd all try and stop her.

Ted   Who?

John   You – the family, me Aunty Betty, me mother . . .

Ted (*a little upset*)   What are you on about at all?

John (*still looking at the television*)   I'm just tellin' y', Dad.

Ted   Just tellin' me what?

John   Just tellin' y' that y'll try and stop Sandra goin' away.

Syd   Who's said anythin' about stoppin' her goin' away, John?

John   See, you never let people do what they want; you never even let yourselves do what you want.

Ted (*outraged*)   'Ey, 'ey, 'ey. Who d' y' think you're talkin' to, clever arse? When have we ever stopped you doin' anythin' y' wanted to do?

Silence.

Well?

John   I don't know.

Ted   I don't think y' do know. I don't think you know y' arse from y' elbow.

John   I do.

Ted   Well that's about all y' do know.

John   I know about Sandra. I wish I was her. I wouldn't come back.

Ted   Wouldn't come back? Just what the hell are you on about?

John   I'd leave. I'd go. Get away on me own.

Ted   (*knowing that he has got to knock* **John** *back into place*)   Don't talk so stupid. You? Go an' live on your own. You wouldn't last a week. How the hell would you get by on your own? You know nothin' about the world; you couldn't walk down the street without me an' y' mother holdin' your hand. You, leavin' us? Don't bloody make me laugh. (*He turns away by the settee.*)

John *stands up slowly, then moves towards* **Ted** *by the settee. The others watch, embarrassed, fascinated.* **John***, standing by the settee, faces his father.*

Ted   We've looked after you, made sure y' didn't have to face up to half of it. You've never had to face a problem in your life without me an' your mother standin' each side of y'. (*He laughs.*) You wouldn't know where to start, sonny boy. Sit down, go on, sit down an' don't poke y' nose in where it's not wanted.

John *takes one of the strips of tape on the settee. Still looking at his father he rips it off in one move.*

Ted   Stop it!

John *takes another strip and rips it off.*

Ted   What are you doin'? Now stop that!

John *carries on ripping tape from the settee.*

Ted   Get off it! I'm warnin' y', get off it. (*He goes round to the front of the settee and tries to stop* **John**.)

John *holds* **Ted** *off and continues until he has ripped off the final strip. A long pause.*

John (*looking at the ragged settee*)   That's how I meant it to be . . .

Ted (*after a pause*)   *You* meant it to be? What d' y' mean – *you* meant it to be?

John   When I cut it.

Ted (*forcefully, as a statement*)   You didn't.

John   Yes, I did.

Ted (*shouting*)   Stop bein' so bloody stupid! You didn't do it. How could you do it? It was the seams, the seams that came apart. You didn't do it! (*He goes to door shouting*.) Reeny – Reeny, where's his tablets? Reeny! (*He turns back to* **John**. *Pointing*.) It's all the excitement that's brought this on. I thought Christmas might be too much for him.

Reeny *rushes in with the bottle of pills.*

Reeny   What's up, what's wrong?

Ted   He's gettin' excited, Reeny. Come here, let's have one of them. (*He rushes to the kitchen for a glass of water*.)

John   I don't want a tablet!

Reeny   Now what did the doctor say? He said you've *got* to take them.

John   I don't want a tablet.

Reeny (*holding out a tablet*)   You take that tablet John.

John   No!

Reeny   John!

John   No!

Reeny   Now don't you start your cousin's antics in this house. Take it.

John *stares silently.*

Reeny Ted. (*She takes the water.*)

Ted *gets hold of* **John**. *He struggles as* **Reeny** *makes him take the tablet.*

Reeny He's got to take them. It's no good. Nobody likes takin' tablets but the doctor said . . . There! (*She replaces the glass in the kitchen.*)

Ted All right John – all right lad. You'll feel better now.

Tommy I'd go an' check y' car an' all if I was you, Ted.

Ted (*quietly a look of horror breaking across his face*) You wouldn't. (*To* **John**.) Not to me car. You haven't? Oh Jesus Christ!

Ted *rushes out to the front door.*

John *returns to his place to watch television.* **Reeny** *comes back from the kitchen.*

Reeny (*seeing the settee*) Now who in the name of God's been pullin' at that settee? Eh?

Tommy Well y' know what it's like Reen? Y' pull a bit, absent-minded like, while y' sittin' here, an' the next thing y' know . . . (*He gestures hopelessly.*)

Reeny Trust you. John, go an' get the tape will y'? (*Pause.*) John, are you listening to me? What's wrong with you today? Go and get that tape – go on . . .

John *gets up and goes to the kitchen cupboard.*

Reeny Just look at it – the money I paid for that . . .

Tommy Ah, shoddy goods, Reeny, definitely shoddy goods . . .

Reeny I've a good mind to bring in the Trades Description people over that suite, y' know.

Tommy I don't blame y' Reen. I mean, it's not on, is it?

John *returns with a roll of tape. He begins to tape up the settee.*

Ted *enters, looking relieved. He leans against the door.*

Ted   It's all right. It's OK. (*He watches* **John** *at work for a moment quietly, then goes to him.*) No – look son. With tape, it's easier if y' rip off one piece at a time. Approximate, John, approximate how much y' need for each strip. Here, I'll rip it – you stick it.

Ted *and* **John** *begin working together.*

Reeny (*to* **Tim**)   Where's our Sandra?

Tim   She – erm . . .

Syd   She's comin', Reeny. She's on her way down here.

Reeny   Why don't you fellers nip out for a pint? They'll be opening in a couple of minutes.

Tommy (*immediately standing*)   Funny y' should mention that, Reeny.

Reeny   Well, go on, get y'selves off. As long as it's not all night.

Tommy   Why the rush to get rid of us? Have y' got a few fellers comin' in? Eh?

Reeny   Look, if Sandra's comin' she doesn't want to be facin' you lot does she? An' we'll have a lot to talk about. You don't want to be here talkin' about havin' babies, do y', Tommy?

Tommy   Reeny! You're turnin' me stomach. Y'll put me off me ale. (*To* **Tim**.) Come on. Don't y' fancy a pint? Or is it Pimms where you come from?

Tim   Yes, I fancy it, but er, I thought I'd better wait for Sandra. I mean, she . . .

Reeny   Sandra won't want to see you. She'll want to talk to us women. Go on, get off with y'.

Tim   Well, if you think . . .

Reeny   Go on – get out an' enjoy yourself with the lads.

Syd (*getting up and moving to the door*)   Yes, come on. I think y' could do with havin' a few words with us.

Tommy   Come on, Ted.

Ted (*looking at his watch*)   Well I want to be back for the second half of the programme. I don't want to miss the votin', Tommy. There's still a lot of performers to be judged.

Tommy   Oh come on, we'll be back for that.

Ted   Right. You comin', John?

John (*getting up to go with them*)   Yeh. (*On his way out.*) It's good tape that isn't it, Dad?

Ted   It's the best son. The very best. Did you know this tape, this tape can be used under water. They use it on the oil rigs up north.

John   Under water?

Ted   Yes. (*Pause.*) 'Ey, John, go on. (*Indicating* **Tim**.) Tell him. ·

John   What?

Ted   The five players whose names begin with F.

John   Flowers – Wolves. Fraser – West Brom. Foulkes – Man. United. Farnham – Sheffield Wednesday . . .

Tim (*cutting in*)   Fairbrother – Leicester City. Farnham – Sheffield Wednesday, that was the one I couldn't think of.

Tommy (*surprised*)   Oh! Y' know a bit about football, do y'?

Tim   Football? Yes, I love it.

Tommy   Great. 'Ey – fancy comin' to the Boxin' Day match tomorrow? We're all goin' like. (*Moving to the door.*) It's the one thing I'll miss – the game. It's not the same abroad.

Tim (*following*)   Are you moving abroad?

Tommy   Oh aye. New Zealand this year for me. New Zealand. Or I might try Canada like . . .

Ted, **Tommy**, **Syd**, **John** *and* **Tim** *go out through the front door.*

Reeny *stands looking at her settee.*

Betty *and* **Vera** *come downstairs.*

Vera (*on the stairs*)   But will Wayne like it at grammar school, Betty?

Betty (*on the stairs*)   It's not a question of liking it; if Wayne's got the intelligence to pass the scholarship then he'll have to go, Vera. (*Noticing that the men have gone.*) Where've they gone?

Reeny   I sent them out for a pint.

Betty   You didn't.

Reeny   *He* was here. Y' know, Tim.

Betty   Well, where's Sandra?

Reeny   She's comin' down on her own, he said.

Betty   Well, I don't know if it's on – out to the pub again . . .

Reeny   Look, it'll be a good chance for the men to get to know him.

Vera   Yeh, they soon get to know each other in the pub, fellers, don't they?

Reeny   An' we don't want them around when your Sandra gets here. I mean, we'll want to talk an' that won't we? (*Turns and looks at her settee.*) Well what do you think, Betty? I mean, re-covered it could look very nice.

Betty   It would, Reeny.

Reeny   Well then – it's up to your Sandra. If she doesn't mind havin' cast-offs she can have this suite. It'll help them get started. If she wants it I'll see about a van and get it sent round to yours.

Betty   Well, you know I never take cast-offs myself, Reeny – but seeing as it is for Sandra . . .

Reeny   Like I say, it'll do her for a while. With new covers on she'll have almost a new suite.

Betty (*quietly, sincerely, choosing not to fight*)   Thanks, Reen. Thanks.

Reeny   That's all right, Betty love.

Betty (*after a pause*)   I wish – well, y' know – I wish she had – saved herself. Not because I'm a prude. I'm not! But it does, y' know, it does make it that bit harder when they start off like this. (*Pause.*) Still, if they're as happy as me an' her father have been . . .

Vera   Ah, you've been very happy, haven't you, Betty.

Betty   I believe we have, Vera, when I look back, I have to say it's been a very happy life that I've had. I think there's only one regret I've got . . .

Vera   What's that, Bet?

Betty   I think that was the only thing I ever really yearned for, a little place of our own. I mean, I'm not saying our house isn't nice, it is, but y' never get away from the feelin' that y' livin' in – y' know – a compound. A little house I could do up on me own, without having to get the Council's permission. I still look at the houses for sale in the paper, the little bungalows, there's some lovely places goin' y' know – peaceful. (*Brightening.*) When Sandra was little, y' know, we used to go for walks up round the back of the estate, y' know where the private houses are – all different from each other – set back off the road, with names instead of numbers on them. We used to look at this one house, on a hill it was – it probably still is – I haven't been that way for years, an' I used to say to Sandra, 'That's where we'll live one day, love. That'll be us, y' know, like in the song, "The folks – who live on the hill".' I always thought that was us – the folks who live on the hill.

Vera   Ah! Yeh. (*She thinks.*) Y' know – y' know what I've always wanted to live in? Y' know – y' know those stone cottages on those islands in Scotland where only a few people live? I'd love t' live there, y' know.

Reeny Well, y'll be all right when y' get out to New Zealand, Vee.

Vera (*shocked*) Where?

Reeny New Zealand. I thought this was the year you and Tommy moved out to New Zealand.

Vera (*laughing*) Y' jokin', aren't y'?

Reeny Well, that's what he told Ted.

Vera Well that's what he *tells* everyone isn't it? But y' take no notice of him. Tommy?

Reeny Oh. I thought he was serious.

Vera No – that's just him dreamin', that is. You know what he's like. He keeps saying y' can't breathe on this estate but he'll never move off it. He'll live an' die here.

Pause.

Reeny (*to* **Betty**) Will – erm – where will they be gettin' married Betty?

Betty In church. Why?

Reeny And will Sandra be dressed in – y' know?

Betty What?

Reeny In white?

Betty Of course she will. Oh yes. Nobody bothers about things like that these days. You've got to get with it, Reeny. You're too old-fashioned, Reeny.

Reeny Whiteness does stand for purity, Betty.

Betty And how many white weddings have you seen at that church?

Reeny Plenty.

Betty Yes, and you can count on the fingers of one hand the girls who went up that aisle as virgins.

Vera   I did, Betty. I went up the aisle a virgin.

Betty   Yes, Vera. And the state your husband gets into every night, it's a wonder you haven't remained one.

Sandra *enters the kitchen and crosses into the front room, wrapped in a large coat. She is hesitant, almost nervous.*

Reeny (*after a pause*)   Oh, Sandra! Where've y' been, love? Y' look frozen.

Vera   Y' do look cold, Sand!

Sandra   It's all right. I've been walking. I'm not cold.

Reeny   Well you want to be very careful, doesn't she, Betty? Walkin'? In the first few months it can be very dangerous . . .

Sandra   Is Tim here?

Betty   Now stop worryin' about him.

Sandra   Where is he?

Reeny   It's all right. He's not run away, y' know. He's just gone down for a pint with the men.

Sandra   With the men?

Betty   With your dad and them.

Sandra   Oh. Right. (*She turns, about to go.*)

Betty   Where are y' going? Sandra . . .

Sandra   To the pub.

Vera *and* **Reeny**   To the pub?

Sandra   Yes.

Betty   Why?

Sandra   I'll have a drink. With Tim.

Reeny   Sandra, you can't go wanderin' into the pub with the men – they'll be in the bar.

Sandra   Well?

Reeny   Now look, Sandra, if you want a drink I'll get you one. What d' y' want? A nice cup of tea. Right, you sit down there and I'll get you one. Come on, you take your coat off and I'll . . .

Sandra   No, it's all right, Aunty Reeny. I'll go down to the pub.

Reeny (*taking her by the arm*)   Sandra! You'll be wasting your time, love. They only went for the one drink. They'll be on their way back. Y'd probably miss them. They'll be here in a minute. Now come on. I'll make a pot of tea. Take your coat off and sit down.

Reeny *goes to kitchen to make a pot of tea.* **Sandra** *remains standing. Long pause.*

Vera   It's not good for y', y' know, Sandra – standin'. Why don't y' sit down?

Betty   It's not only y'self y've got to think of now, y' know.

Vera   You've got little Wayne to think of now.

Sandra   Who?

Reeny *comes back from the kitchen.*

Reeny   Now that won't take a minute. Come on Sandra. It's very warm in here. You'll be stifled in a minute; let's have that coat.

Sandra   No, I'm all right. (*She sits on the very edge of an armchair.*) I want to keep it on.

Vera   I was just tellin' Sandra, Reeny, she'll have to make sure she looks after herself now, won't she?

Reeny   Oh Sandra you've got to. You've got to so that when y' time comes y'll be able to cope. You don't want to be like I was when I was havin' our John.

Vera   Oh, you had a terrible time, didn't y', Reen.

Reeny   A thirty-six-hour labour's no joke y' know. (*She relishes the following account, putting accentuated stress on the key words.*) It was agony! Sheer agony. The sweat, the

perspiration that came off me could have filled a lake.
Moppin' it up they were, moppin' it up in pools off the bed.
An' they don't care y' know, you're just like cattle when y'
get in there, common cattle. I was screamin' at them to let
me die. But they wouldn't. He was a big baby, our John was.
That was the trouble. I hope for your sake, Sandra, I hope
you don't have a big one.

Betty   She will though, look at her. Y' can see already.
Well, I can anyway. You get to know the signs when you've
worked at a hospital. Sandra won't have an easy time. It's
always a big baby when they start holdin' themselves like
that. (*She points at* **Sandra**.)

Sandra   I'll be all right. Tim will look after me.

Betty   *Tim?*

Sandra   Tim'll come in with me – help me get through it.

Betty, **Vera** *and* **Reeny** *look at one another*.

Vera   I suppose a lot of fathers go in these days, don't they?

Reeny (*shaking her head*)   No, I'm sorry – I don't care, I just
think it's unnatural meself . . .

Vera   It must be nice though, Reen – havin' him there to
hold y' hand.

Reeny   No, I'm sorry – but if y' want my opinion, it's goin'
against nature. Havin' the husband in while you're givin'
birth to a child is flyin' in the face of nature.

Vera   Oh I don't know though, Reen. The thing is . . .

Reeny   Listen, Vera. Just tell me one thing.

Vera   Yeh, go on . . .

Reeny   Why, since the beginnin' of time, have they always
built waitin'-rooms at the side of labour wards? See my
point?

Vera   Erm – yeah – I suppose.

Reeny   Exactly. Right, Vera, come on. You can give me a
hand makin' the tea.

Vera *gets up to go with her.*

Reeny   Now don't be daft Sandra, you take that coat off.

Vera *and* **Reeny** *go to the kitchen and make tea.*

Betty (*conspiratorially*)   You leave your coat on, love. I wish I'd had the sense to keep mine on. She might have had central heatin' put in, but it's obvious she can't afford to switch it on.

Sandra (*looking out of the window*)   Did Tim talk to you?

Betty   No, we were upstairs when he was here, love. He stayed with the men.

Sandra (*turning to her*)   Has me dad told you?

Betty   Told me what, love? (*Standing back and taking a good look at her.*) 'Ey, you're beginnin' to show already you are. Aren't you?

Sandra *turns away again.* **Betty** *smiles affectionately at her back.*

Betty (*quietly*)   Sandra. Sand. You do know that I'm sorry about last night don't you? It was a shock but – well, listen love – it's all right. I want you to know that whatever I said last night – I didn't mean it. It was just the shock. I'm happy, Sandra, I'm glad that there's a little baby coming into the world. No one's more thrilled than me, Sandra. (*She goes to her and puts her arm around her.*) I know we've had our rows in the past, Sandra. But – but let's forget them now, shall we? Let's put them behind us. Look – come on. We're going to be grandmother and mother soon. The little lad will be a bridge between us.

Sandra (*firming moving out of her mother's grip*)   I think you should sit down, Mum.

Betty   Sit down? Sit down? Can't y' see I'm too excited to sit down? I could dance, Sandra. It's almost as if that little baby is inside me, not you.

Sandra   Please sit down. I've got something to tell you.

Betty   And I've got something to tell you love. (*Quickly.*) Listen, I planned it all out last night. Now the upstairs of the house – it's wasted most of the time isn't it? So what I'm going to do is get your dad to turn it, Sandra, into a little flat for you and Tim. We'll have a little cooker up there an' I'll be able to baby-sit an' help you out an' that . . .

Sandra (*shaking her head*)   No, Mother. No!

Betty (*unheeding*)   Why should the kids be paying rent to some landlord? I said that to Reeny. We're not having that when they can live with us for free. I thought about it in bed last night – you know, with it being Christmas and that – I thought to meself, well, there was one baby, once, who had nowhere to rest. But this little baby of ours – he'll have a proper home. (*Pause.*) I realized last night . . . the real meaning of Christmas.

There is a long pause. **Betty** *looks at* **Sandra**, *who is looking out of the window. Very quietly* **Betty** *starts singing.*

Betty
    'Away in a manger
    No crib for a bed
    The little Lord Jesus . . .'

Sandra *turns to face* **Betty** *who continues singing, urging* **Sandra** *to join her, moving to her.*

Sandra   Mother listen to me.

Betty
    'Lay down his sweet head
    The stars in – '

Sandra (*backing away*)   Will you listen to me?

Betty (*still singing, walking towards* **Sandra** *who is backing away*) ' – the bright sky . . .'

Sandra *is backed into the corner. She is up against the Christmas tree.* **Betty** *still sings.*

Sandra (*in a scream*)   Mother! (*She flings the nearest object, the tinsel tree, across the room.*)

Betty *stops singing, shocked.* **Vera** *and* **Reeny** *rush in and stop, gaping.* **Sandra** *is firm, deliberate.*

Sandra   We are not coming to live with you an' me dad! I'm moving into Tim's flat — today! We're not even going to get married. We're going to live together.

Pause.

Right? Did you hear that? Did you hear what I said?

Betty *does not answer.* **Sandra** *goes up to her.* **Vera** *and* **Reeny** *dare not move.* **Sandra** *shouts at* **Betty**.

Sandra   Did you?

Betty (*quietly*)   Yes. I heard.

Sandra   Good — good. Because you've got to know I don't want any of that. Why should I stay, Mother?

Betty *is tight-lipped and not even looking at* **Sandra**.

Sandra   What is there to stay for? If there was some — some point, I could stay. But what do you ever do? All of you, you just sit around all day, not understanding what's going on, ripping each other to pieces. There's no meaning, is there? Look at Christmas — what does Christmas mean to you? It's just more telly, that's all isn't it? Three days of telly an' then back to work. (*Pause.*) When Tim comes for me I'm going because I don't want any of that.

Betty (*leaning forward angrily, shouting directly into her face*) Well *what* — do you want?

Sandra (*shouting back*)   I want a *good* life Mother. I want something that's got some meaning left in it. I want to sit around and talk about films and — and music. I want a house where we don't have the telly on all day, where we don't worry about the furniture. I want books on the shelves. Mother — and — oh — for God's sake, I want paintings on the wall and red wine on the table and lots of different cheeses. I want — I want—I want . . .

Betty (*venomously, deliberately scornful and vicious*)   Want — want — want! And what about what *I* wanted?

Sandra (*quickly*)   What you wanted, you got! Y' got it all, Mother – y' three-piece suites, y' fridge, y' plastic pedal bin. What you wanted – you got! (*She turns and looks out of the window.*)

Betty   You begrudge me every bit of pleasure I have ever had – don't y'? (*Pause.*) Well, let me tell you – it's more than pleasure – much more. (*To* **Vera**.) You know what she wants to do, Vera, when we're out shoppin'? She expects me to call the supermarket manager and tell him off because he's makin' a profit out of me. What do I care if he makes a profit out of me. It gives me pleasure. Let me tell you, Lady Muck – if it wasn't for the things I buy – I would have cut my throat years ago! But *she* begrudges me my few pleasures. I wouldn't mind, but I'm not askin' for very much am I? I live on an estate that's like a – a – a camp for refugees, me only entertainment's a Saturday night in a social club. I work forty-nine weeks of the year doin' a job that took me half a day to learn. An' she begrudges me the few pleasures that I get. Well, I'm tellin' you, Miss Criticize – many's the time, many's the time that a trip round the supermarket an' a new find on the shelves has stopped me goin' home an' puttin' my head in the gas oven. (*She stares at* **Sandra** *who is looking out of the window. She turns and sits on the settee.*)

Sandra   I'm going away with Tim, Mother. Today.

Betty *stands tight-lipped, staring at the wall.*

Reeny   Your mind's made up then is it Sandra?

Sandra *nods.*

Reeny   You're goin' t' live tally with him? (*Philosophically.*) Well, I suppose I should be shocked. But it's like someone was sayin' – you've got to get with it, haven't you? I suppose there's lots of young couples who live together these days. An' it's no use being old-fashioned. (*Turning to* **Betty**.) It's just your mum I feel sorry for. (*Knowing she has got her at last.*) But don't worry, Betty. We won't breathe a word about it. Just let anyone say a wrong word about you, Betty, and they'll get what's what from me. I won't have my sister

talked about no matter what sort of cross she has to bear.
We'll stand by you, Betty.

Vera, *who is full of sympathy and very near to tears, goes across and
puts her arm around* **Betty** *to comfort her.* **Betty**, *blind with anger, is
unaware of this. Her breathing is getting wilder and she is twisting her
fingers and pulling at the tape.* **Reeny** *goes across to* **Sandra**.

Reeny   I was just sayin' to your mum before you got here,
Sandra – I was saying you could have this suite of mine. I'm
getting a new one. Have you seen the new type, with the
reclining backs on them – oh, they're lovely. So look, I was
going to send this round to your mother's but – erm – well, do
y' want me to send it round to the flat? It would look nice re-
covered. It's a good suite.

Betty *suddenly leaps up, screaming the word.*

Betty   Suite? You call this a suite? (*She starts to pull the tape
off.*) Look, look – just look at it. It's rubbish. I wouldn't put it
in a dog's kennel. (*Putting wildly at the tape.*) A suite? This?
(*Pulling out handfuls of foam rubber.*) It's nothing more than a
cheap – (*Handfuls of foam.*) – stuck together – (*Foam.*) –
shoddy – (*Foam.*) – second-hand – (*Foam.*) – stinking shitty
load of SHITE! (*She has effectively reduced the settee to a wreck.*)

Vera *sits in the middle of tape and foam rubber.* **Betty** *stands
glaring, wild.*

Vera   Something's upset you hasn't it, Betty?

Reeny (*to* **Vera**, *quietly*)   It's all right, Vera. Leave it to me.
Nerves. (*Putting her arm around* **Betty**.) Come on Betty – it's all
right, come on – don't worry about the settee – I know you
didn't mean it, love. Come on now. Come on Vera. You
come with us. Let's go and make some sandwiches for the
men gettin' back. (*To* **Vera**.) Best if we keep her occupied.
Come on, Betty love.

Betty *allows herself to be led through to the kitchen by* **Reeny** *and*
Vera. **Sandra** *left alone in the lounge takes the tape and begins
mending the settee and replacing the Christmas tree.*

Ted, **Syd**, **John** *and* **Tim**, *led by* **Tommy**, *enter the front room from the hall. They still have their coats on and it is obvious they have come back with a purpose.*

Sandra, *aware of this, looks at* **Tim**, *who nervously faces her. The other men are grouped around him, a supporting tribe. They are not drunk, but have had a few rushed pints, followed by a brisk walk in cold weather. If possible we hear their breathing. They are grouped in such a way that they form a semi-circle behind* **Tim**.

Sandra   Where have you been?

Tim   To the pub.

Sandra   Come on then, we're goin'.

Pause.

Tommy (*looking at* **Sandra**)   Tell her, Tim, lad.

Tim (*looking at the others, then turning to* **Sandra**)   Now look, Sandra, I've got something to tell you. (*He looks at the others.*)

They nod – they are all with him.

Tim   Er – I've been talking to your father, to Syd. Now, Sandra, he's made us a very kind offer . . .

Sandra *goes to interrupt.*

Tim (*firmly*)   Don't interrupt, Sandra. He's made us a very gracious offer, and we, Sandra, are going to accept it!

Sandra   Come on, we're goin', you said.

Syd   Now 'ey. (*Pointing.*) Just hold your mouth for a minute and listen to the lad.

Pause.

Ted   Go on, Timothy.

Tim   Your fath . . . Syd has said that we can share his house. He's told me, Sandra, that we can have the top half of the house as our own flat.

Ted   But obviously, Sandra. Sandra y' dad can't have you livin' there in what we call – sin. So you'll have to get married.

Sandra   Get married.

Tim *jumps in quickly — trying in his own way to be authoritative.*

Tim   Yes. We've got to be realistic. You're pregnant! You're not a girl any longer. You're a woman and that means you've got responsibilities now.

Sandra (*quietly, slowly approaching him*)   You bastard.

Ted (*pointing*)   Ay. Ay. I'm not having language like that in my house. I'm sorry, but I'm not. Especially when it comes from nothin' more than a slip of a girl.

Sandra (*after a pause, looks at the men gathered round her*)   Well, if you don't like my language, then I'll get out.

Sandra *turns to go, but* **Tommy** *deliberately blocks her way.*

Sandra   Excuse me. (*She waits.*)

Tommy, *defiant, will not move.*

Sandra   I said, excuse me.

Tommy *still does not move.* **Sandra** *goes to push past him, but he forces her back.*

Tommy (*pointing, loudly and viciously*)   Now listen, you! You're not goin' anywhere. You've caused enough friggin' trouble in this family, and we're not puttin' up with any more of it.

During the above, **Vera**, **Reeny** *and* **Betty** *come through from the kitchen, drying their hands, etc. There is now a complete circle of people around* **Sandra**.

Vera   Just look at the state your mother's in over you.

Reeny   You want to grow up, Sandra Dobson. That's your trouble.

Syd   You've upset everyone, you have. You've got a bloody good lad here. He's trying to do the best by you. Now he's told you how things are. Until you can afford a place of your own, you're comin' to live with me and your mother.

Sandra's *way is blocked on all sides. She walks up to* **Tim**.

Sandra Let me past.

Tommy Don't you move, Tim.

Sandra (*to* **Tim**) You're taking me away. Now.

Tim (*shaking his head*) No, Sandra. You've got to be sensible. Where could we live? How could we exist? This is the best way.

Sandra (*desperately*) We're going.

Tommy You just shut that mouth of yours. That's your fella you're talking to.

Sandra *turns to* **John**.

Sandra Excuse me.

John *looks at* **Sandra**. *He does not know what he is going to do until* **Ted** *moves to his side: then it becomes obvious that* **John** *is not going to let* **Sandra** *through. She goes to each member of the family in turn. No one is going to let her through. Finally she comes to* **Betty**. *She looks at her mother. There is a long pause in which the two women look at each other. Slowly,* **Betty** *stands aside.*

Sandra *walks past* **Betty**, *through to the kitchen, and out.*

They all look at **Betty**: *she sits down. There is an uncomfortable silence.*

Ted Well – um – er – well, come on everyone, sit down. Come on, John, get it switched on. We're missing the second half of the programme, come on – let's get the cards dished out. (*He starts handing out the voting cards and pencils.*) You playin', Tim? Here – here's your card.

Bewildered, **Tim** *passively takes the card.* **Ted** *hands out all the cards. They all group themselves around the television.* **Ted** *gets to* **Betty**. *He has no more cards left.*

Ted Oh – erm – I'm sorry about this, Betty. It looks like I've run out of cards.

Betty *stares straight ahead.*

Ted Still. I don't suppose y' feel up to playin' right now eh? No.

Vera (*sitting on the settee next to* **Betty**)   The New Year Sales next week, eh, Betty?

Reeny   Y' goin', are y', Vee?

Vera   Ooh yeah. Never miss the January Sales. Some smashin' bargains.

Reeny   We'll all go down together if y' like, me, you and Betty. Fancy that.

Vera   Yeah.

Reeny   What about you, Betty?

Betty *turns to* **Reeny**. *She sees* **Tim** *standing there.*

Reeny   Do y' fancy that, Bet?

Betty (*to* **Tim**)   Are you still here?

Tim   Well . . .

Betty   Y' better get going hadn't y'? Y' don't know where she'll be roaming.

From the television is heard the introduction to the Opportunity Knocks/New Faces *programme. The first performer is introduced, and the following dialogue is heard over the performers' song, which is as follows – to the tune of 'And did those feet in ancient time . . .'.*

Television
'The holly is hung
The carols are sung,
The yule logs are burning on the fire . . .

Hear the church bells ring
Hear the voices sing
Christmas has come to all mankind . . .

The frost is on the window pane
The mistletoe is hanging high
Mince pies and gifts to give, how glad we live,
To share the joy of Christmas time.'

Vera   New Year eh? It hardly seems ten minutes since we were all makin' this year's resolutions. I don't suppose it'd be long before we're makin' next year's.

Ted   Well I know what my resolution's gonna be this year, Vera.

Vera   Y' gonna write that book are y', Ted?

Ted   I am that, Vera. I am.

Tommy   I know what our Syd's resolution's gonna be. Don't I, Syd?

Reeny   What is it, Syd?

Syd   I'm gonna pack up eatin' chips, Reeny.

Betty (*to* **Tim**)   Well, go on. What y' waitin' for?

Tim *nods. He starts to move, notices the card in his hand, puts it on the back of the settee, and goes to the kitchen.*

Tim *exits through the back door.*

Betty *goes to the window.*

Syd (*listening to the song*)   He's good this feller. He's good.

Ted   Good voice. (*To* **Betty**.) 'Ey, Betty – come on – y' missin' the votin'. Come on, love.

Betty *turns from the window and picks up the spare voting card from the settee. They all move up and make a space for her on the settee.* **Ted** *hands her a pencil. He smiles. The sound of the song swells, as –*

the curtain falls.

Our Day Out

with songs and music by
Bob Eaton, Chris Mellor
and Willy Russell

Our Day Out was originally written as a television play and transmitted as a BBC 'Play for Today' in 1976. It was subsequently adapted for the stage and first performed on 8 April 1983, with the following cast:

Mrs Kay	Linda Beckett
Bus Driver/Zoo Keeper/Les	Carl Chase
Colin/Headmaster	David Hobbs
Mr Briggs	Robert McIntosh
Susan/Café Owner	Christina Nagy

The Children

X Company*: Sue Abrahams, Michaela Amoo, Danny Ayers, Maria Barrett, Angela Bell, Andy Broadhead, Maxine Cole, Vernon Eustace, Brian Hanlon, Michael Kagbo, Andrea Langham, Victor McGuire, Mary Shepherd, Paul Spencer, Charlie Thelu, Jason Williams

Y Company*: Hannah Bond, Peter Bullock, Shaun Carr, Mary Farmer, Danny Jones, Anne Lundon, Ritchie Macauley, Keith Maiker, Jacqui McCarthy, Victor McGuire, Jocelyn Meall, Joanne Mogan, Joanne Oldham, Joanne Pennington, Ben Wilson, John Winstanley

    *X and Y performed on alternate nights

Directed by Bob Eaton and Kate Roland
Musical direction by Chris Mellor
Designed by Sue Mayes
Lighting designed by Kevin Fitzsimons

Our Day Out was subsequently seen at the Young Vic
Theatre, London, from 20 August 1983, with the following
cast:

Mrs Kay	Rosalind Boxall
Bus Driver/Zoo Keeper/Les	Martin Stone
Colin/Headmaster	William Gaminara
Mr Briggs	Stephen Lewis
Susan/Café Owner	Christina Nagy

The Children: Matthew Barker, Paul Billings, Gillian
Blavo, Maura Hall, Michelle Bristol, Richard Cotterill,
Brian Warrington, Tony Fuller, Jane Gibbs, Claire
Mitchell, Paul Harbert, Roy Spicer, Sally Hobbs, Tony
Jones, Darragh Murray, Darryl Niven, Marie Quetant,
Jason Robertson, Jaqueline Rodger, Elizabeth Toone

Directed by Bob Eaton
Musical direction by Stuart Barham
Designed by Sue Mayes
Lighting by Andy Phillips

Author's Note

Language and Setting
For the purpose of publication I have retained the play's
original settings of Liverpool and Wales but this is not
intended to imply that productions of the play in other parts
of the country should strive to observe the original setting or
reproduce the idiom in which it is written. If being played in,
say, Sheffield, the play would, I feel, be more relevant to both
cast and audience if adapted to a local setting and the local
accent.

Following the play's original production in Liverpool it
was staged at the Young Vic where it became a Cockney
play: the setting of the school became Hackney, the Mersey
Tunnel became the Blackwall Tunnel, Conway Castle

became Bodiam Castle, the Welsh Coast, the South Coast and so on.

I can foresee a problem where the play is set in an area which has no road tunnel or bridge and if this is the case, would suggest that you simply cut this small section of script.

Staging

Although it would be possible to present the play on a proscenium stage I think it's much better suited to a more flexible area. The play was originally presented in the round, with a set that consisted of a number of simple benches. These benches were used as the seats on the coach and then rearranged by the actors to suggest the various other settings – the café, the zoo, even the rocks on the beach.

Two platforms were built at a higher level and were used as the castle battlements, the cliff and the headmaster's study.

In both the Everyman and Young Vic productions the coach carried about fifteen to twenty passengers. Obviously this number could be increased for large-cast productions.

Music

Again, in the original productions of the play, the production budgets demanded that the musical accompaniment be kept to an absolute minimum – i.e., piano and percussion. Should you be in the happy position of knowing no such constraints and have at your disposal a band or orchestra, please feel free to arrange the music accordingly.

Willy Russell

Act One

As we hear the musical introduction for the first song, we see **Les**, *the lollipop man, enter. He is very old, almost blind and can hardly walk. A group of* **Kids**, *on their way to school, enter, shouting 'Hia Les,' 'All right there Les' and singing:*

Kids
> We're goin' out
> Just for the day
> Goin' off somewhere far away
> Out to the country
> Maybe the sea
> Me Mam says I can go . . . if it's free

During verse two the **Kids** *exit singing and* **Carol** *enters also singing.*

Carol *and* **Kids**
> The sky is blue
> The sun's gonna shine
> Better hurry up cos it's nearly nine
> This is the day that's
> Just for us
> We're goin' out . . . on a bus

Carol *is about to make her way to the school when she notices* **Les** *on the other side of the road.*

Carol   Hia Les.

Les (*trying to see*)   Who's that?

Carol (*crossing to him*)   Carol, it's Carol, Les.

Les   Hello love. 'Ey, can y' see me back across the road? (*As she takes his arm and leads him back.*) You're early today aren't y'?

Carol   Yeh. We're goin' out. On a trip.

Les　Where to?

Carol　I dunno. It's somewhere far away. I forget.

Les　Are they all goin'?

Carol　Only the kids in the Progress Class.

Les　The what?

Carol　Don't y' know what the Progress Class is? It's Mrs Kay's class. Y' go down there in the week if y' can't do readin' or sums or writin'. If you're backward like.

Les　By Christ, I'll bet she's kept busy. They're all bloody backward round here.

Carol　I know. I better be goin' now, Les. I'm gonna be late. An' there's Briggs!

We see **Briggs** *approaching as* **Les** *calls to* **Carol**.

Les　Tarar girl. Mind how you go.

Carol　(*running off*)　See y' Les.

Les　(*to* **Briggs** *who is about to cross the road*)　'Ey, you! Don't move.

Briggs　I beg your pardon.

Les　Wait. There.

Briggs　Look, I've not got the time to . . .

Les　No one crosses the road without the assistance of the lollipop man, no one.

Briggs　Look man . . .

Les　The Government hired me!

Briggs　But there's nothing coming.

Les　How do you know? How do you know a truck or a car isn't gonna come speedin' out of one of them side roads? Eh? How can you set an example to kids if you're content to walk under the wheels of a juggernaut?

Les *goes to the centre of the road and waves* **Briggs** *across*.

Les That's why the Government hires me!

Mrs Kay *and* **Kids** *enter*.

Kids (*singing*)
Mrs Kay's Progress Class
We're the ones who
Never pass
We're goin' out
Off with Mrs Kay
We're goin' out . . . today

Mrs Kay All right all right . . . Will you just let me have a
bit of peace and I'll get you *all* sorted out. Right, now look
(*She spells it out.*) all those . . . who've got permission to come
on the trip . . . but who haven't yet paid . . . I want you to
come over here.

She separates herself from the group. Every kid follows her. **Briggs**
passes and surveys the scene with obvious disapproval.

Mrs Kay (*bright*) Morning, Mr Briggs.

Briggs (*grudging*) Morning. (*He turns towards the school as a
couple of* **Kids** *emerge.*) Come on, you two. Where are you
supposed to be? Move!

The **Boys** *rush to the safety of* **Mrs Kay**'s *group and* **Briggs** *goes
off.*

Kids (*sing as a round*)
Got a packed lunch
Got money to spend
Gonna get a seat near my best friend
Just can't wait to get
Away from here
Gonna bring me Mam . . . a souvenier

As the round ends the **Kids** *are blacked out. They rearrange the
benches to form the coach, as we see* **Briggs** *enter the*
Headmaster's *study.*

Briggs When was this arranged?

Head   Don't talk to me about it. After the last trip of hers I said 'no more', absolutely no more. Look, just look. (*He indicates a file.*) Complaints from the residents of Derbyshire.

Briggs   Well how the hell's she arranged this then?

Head   When I was away at conference. George approved it in my absence. He wasn't aware of any ban on remedial department outings.

Briggs   It'll have to be cancelled.

Head   If it is she'll resign.

Briggs   Good. The school would be better off without her.

Head   There's not many of her type about y' know. By and large I reckon she does a good job. She keeps them well out of the way with their reading machines and plasticine. It's just when she gets let loose with them.

Briggs   OK. I'll have to go with her, won't I?

Blackout **Head**'s *study as we bring up* **Mrs Kay** *talking to a young teacher,* **Susan**. *Around them are lively excited* **Kids** *in random groups. Two* **Kids** *are pulling and pushing each other.*

Mrs Kay   Maurice! Come away from that road!

Maurice   I'm sorry, miss.

Mrs Kay   Come on, keep on the side where it's safe.

Two older **Kids** *(fifteen) come rushing out of school and approach the teachers.*

Reilly   'Ey, miss hang on, hang on . . . can we come with y', miss. Can we?

Digga   Go on miss, don't be tight, let's come.

Reilly   Go on, miss . . . say yeh.

Mrs Kay   Brian, you know it's a trip for the Progress Class.

Reilly   Yeh, well, we used to be in the Progress Class didn't we?

Susan   But Brian, you're not in the Progress Class any longer, are you? Now that you can read and write you're back in normal classes.

Reilly   Agh, miss, come on . . .

Mrs Kay   Brian, you know that I'd willingly take you, but it's not up to me. Who's your form teacher?

Reilly   Briggsy.

Mrs Kay   Well . . . I'll take you, if you get his permission.

Reilly (*as he and* **Digga** *run off*)   Ogh . . . you're sound, miss.

Mrs Kay   BRIAN!

He stops.

Bring a note.

Reilly   Ah miss, what for?

Mrs Kay   Because I wasn't born yesterday and if I don't ask you to bring a note you'll hide behind that wall for two minutes and then tell me Mr Briggs gave permission.

Reilly   As if we'd do something like that, miss.

Mrs Kay   I want it in writing.

Carol (*tugging at* **Mrs Kay**'s *arm as* **Reilly** *and* **Digga** *go off*)   Where we goin' eh miss?

Mrs Kay   Carol! Miss Duncan's just told you: Conway, we're going to Conway.

Carol   Is that in England miss?

Susan   It's in Wales Carol.

Carol   Will we have to get a boat?

Colin *enters, running.*

Colin   Sorry I'm late . . . Car wouldn't start.

Linda   Hia sir.

Jackie   Hia sir.

Colin Hello girls. (*Avoiding them. Or trying to*.) Erm, Mrs Kay . . .

Linda Sir, I thought for a minute you weren't comin' on the trip. I was heartbroken.

Colin Yes erm . . . er . . .

Carol Miss, how will we get there?

Mrs Kay Carol! We're going on a coach. Look. There. (*She shouts to all the* **Kids**.) You can get on now. Go on . . .

There is a wild rush of **Kids** *to the coach but suddenly the* **Driver** *is there, blocking their way.*

Driver Right. Just stop there. No one move!

Kid Miss said we could get on.

Driver Oh did she now?

Kids Yeh.

Driver Well let me tell youse lot somethin' now. Miss is not the driver of this bus. I am. An' if I say y' don't get on, y' don't get on.

As we hear the intro for 'Boss of the Bus'.

Driver (*sings*)
   This is my bus
   I'm the boss of the bus
   I've been drivin' it for fifteen years
   This is my bus
   I'm the boss of the bus
   So just pin back your ears
   I'm the number one
   I'm the driver man
   And you kids don't get on
   Till I say you can

   This is my bus
   I'm the boss of the bus
   And the lesson I want learned
   This is my bus

I'm the boss of the bus
And as far as I'm concerned
If you wanna put
One over on me
You're gonna need a damn sight more
Then a GCE

Don't want no lemonade, no sweets
Don't want no chewing gum
Cos the bleedin' stuff gets stuck to the seats
And respectable passengers' bums
This is my bus
I'm the boss of the bus
And I've seen it all before
This is my bus
I'm the boss of the bus
And I don't want no spew on the floor
I don't want no mess
Don't want no fuss
So keep your dirty hands
From off of my bus
This is my bus

Kids
He's the boss of the bus

Driver
This is my bus

Kids
He's the boss of the bus

Driver
This is my bus

Kids
He's the boss of the bus

Driver
This is my bus

Kids
  He's the boss of the bus
  There's nothing wrong with us

Driver (*heaving off a* **Kid** *who managed to get onto the bus*)
  Get off of my bus.

Mrs Kay   Is there something the matter, driver?

Driver   Are these children in your charge, madam?

Mrs Kay   Yes.

Driver   Well you haven't checked them have y'?

Mrs Kay   Checked them? Checked them for what?

Driver   Chocolate and lemonade! We don't allow it. I've seen it on other coaches, madam; fifty-two vomitin' kids, it's no joke. I'm sorry but we don't allow that.

Mrs Kay (*to* **Susan**)   Here comes Mr Happiness. All right, driver, I'll check them for you. Now listen, everyone: if anyone has brought chocolate or lemonade with them I want them to put up their hands.

A sea of innocent faces and unraised hands.

There you are, driver, all right?

Driver   No it's not all right. Y' can't just take their word for it. They have to be searched. You can't just believe kids.

Pause. She could blow up but she doesn't.

Mrs Kay   Can I have a word with you, driver, in private?

The **Driver** *comes off his coach. She manoeuvres it so that the* **Driver** *has his back to the* **Kids** *and other teachers.*

Mrs Kay   What's your name, driver?

Driver   Me name? I don't usually have to give me name.

Mrs Kay   Oh come on. What's your name?

Driver   Schofield, Ronnie Schofield.

Mrs Kay   Well, Ronnie. (*She points.*) Just take a look at those streets.

He does so and as he does she motions, behind his back, indicating that the other teachers should get the **Kids** *onto the coach.*

Mrs Kay   Ronnie, would you say they were the sort of streets that housed prosperous parents?

Driver   We usually do the better schools.

Mrs Kay   All right, you don't like these kids, I can see that. But do you really have to cause them so much pain?

Driver   What have I said? I only told them to wait.

Mrs Kay   Ronnie, the kids with me today don't know what it is to *look* at a bar of chocolate. Lemonade Ronnie? Lemonade never touches their lips. (*We should almost hear the violins.*) These are the children, Ronnie, that stand outside shop windows in the pouring rain, looking and longing, but never getting. Even at Christmas time, when your kids from the better schools are singing carols, opening presents, these kids are left, outside, left to wander the cold cruel streets.

Ronnie *is grief-stricken.*

Behind him, in the coach, the **Kids** *are stuffing themselves stupid with sweets, chocolate and lemonade.*

Mrs Kay *leaves* **Ronnie** *to it and climbs on board. As* **Ronnie** *turns to board the coach all evidence of sweets and lemonade immediately disappears.* **Ronnie** *puts his hand in his pocket, produces a few quid.*

Driver (*to the* **Kid** *on the front seat*)   Here y' are son, run to the shops an' see what sweets y' can get with that.

Susan (*leaning across*)   What did you say?

Mrs Kay   Lied like hell of course.

She gets up and faces the **Kids**.

Mrs Kay   Now listen everyone. Listen. We'll be setting off for Conway in a couple of minutes.

Cheers.

Listen. Now, we want everybody to enjoy themselves today and so I don't want any silly squabbling and I don't want anybody doing anything dangerous either to yourselves or to others. That's the only rule we're going to have today, think of yourselves, but think of others as well.

Reilly *and* **Digga** *come rushing onto the coach.*

Reilly   Miss, we're comin' miss, we're comin' with y' . . .

Mrs Kay   Where's the note, Brian?

Reilly   He didn't give us one, miss. He's comin' himself. He said to wait.

Reilly *and* **Digga** *go down the aisle to the back of the coach.*

Colin   He's coming to keep an eye on us.

Susan   To make sure we don't enjoy ourselves.

Mrs Kay   Well . . . I suppose we'll just have to deal with him the best way we can.

Mrs Kay *sits down, next to* **Carol.** **Reilly** *and* **Digga** *are at the back seat.*

Reilly (*to a* **Little Kid** *on the back seat*)   Right. You. Move.

Little Kid   Why?

Reilly   Cos we claimed the back seat, that's why.

Little Kid   You're not even in the Progress though.

Digga   'Ey, hardfaced, we used to be, so shift!

Reilly   Now move before I mince y'.

Unseen by **Reilly** *and* **Digga, Briggs** *has climbed on board. All the* **Kids** *spotting a cloud on a blue horizon.* **Briggs** *glaring. Barks suddenly.*

Briggs   Reilly, Dickson sit down!

Reilly   Sir we was only . . .

Briggs (*stacatto*)   I said sit lad, now move.

Reilly *and* **Digga** *sit on the* **Little Kid** *who is forced out. He stands, exposed in the aisle, terrified of* **Briggs**.

Briggs   Sit down. What you doing lad, what you doing?

Little Kid   Sir sir sir . . . sir I haven't got a seat. (*Almost in tears.*)

Briggs   Well find one, boy, find one!

Colin *gets out of his seat and indicates the* **Kid** *to sit there.*

Briggs (*to* **Mrs Kay**)   You've got some real bright sparks here Mrs Kay. A right bunch.

Mrs Kay   Well I think we might just manage to survive now that you've come to look after us.

Briggs   The boss thought it might be a good idea if you had an extra member of staff. Looking at this lot I'd say he was right. There's a few of them I could sling off right now. (*Barking.*) Linda Croxley, what are you doin'? Sit down girl. (*He addresses all the* **Kids**.) Right! Now listen: we wouldn't like you to think that we don't want you to enjoy yourselves today, because we do. But a lot of you won't have been on a school outing before and therefore won't know *how* to enjoy yourselves. So I'll tell you:

Throughout the last few lines of dialogue we have heard the intro for 'Instructions on Enjoyment'.

Briggs (*sings*)
　　To enjoy a trip upon a coach
　　We sit upon our seats
　　We do not wander up and down the aisles
　　We do not use obscenities
　　Or throw each other sweets
　　We talk politely, quietly nod and smile
　　There'll be no shouting on this outing, will there?
　　(*Screaming.*) WILL THERE?

Kids   No sir.

Briggs
　　No sir, no sir.
　　We look nicely through the windows
　　At the pretty scenery
　　We do not raise our voices, feet or fists
　　And I do not, are you listening girl

I do not want to see
Two fingers raised to passing motorists
To enjoy this treat
Just stay in your seat
Be quiet, be good and beháve!

As **Briggs** *finishes the song the* **Kid** *who went to get the sweets rushes on board loaded with bags.*

Kid   I've got them . . . I've got loads . . .

Briggs   Where've you been?

Kid   Sir, gettin' sweets.

Briggs   Sweets? SWEETS!

Mrs Kay (*reaching for the sweets*)   Thank you Maurice.

The **Driver** *is tapping* **Briggs** *on the shoulder.*

Driver   Can I have a word with you?

Briggs   Pardon?

Driver   In private.

He leads the way off the coach. **Briggs** *follows.* **Mrs Kay** *gives the sweets to* **Colin** *and* **Susan** *who start to dish them out.*

Kids   Ogh, great – Give us one, miss – What about me, sir?

Driver (*outside the coach, to* **Briggs**)   The thing is, about these kids, they're like little souls, lost an' wanderin' the cruel heartless streets.

The **Driver** *continues his lecture to* **Briggs** *outside the coach as we go back inside.*

Colin *is at the back seat giving out sweets to* **Reilly** *and Co.*

Reilly   How are y' gettin' on with miss, sir?

Digga   We saw y', sir, goin' into that pub with her.

Further down the aisle **Susan** *is watching and listening as she gives out sweets.*

Colin (*covering his embarrassment*)   Did you?

Reilly   Are you in love with her, sir?

Colin (*making his escape*)   All right, you've all got sweets have you?

Reilly (*jeering*)   Sir's in love, sir's in love . . .

Reilly *laughing as* **Colin** *makes his way back along the aisle.*

Susan   Watch it Brian!

Reilly (*feigned innocence*)   What, miss?

Susan   You know what.

Reilly   Agh, hey, he is in love with y' though, isn't he, miss?

Digga   I'll bet he wants to marry y', miss.

Reilly   You'd be better off with me, miss. I'm better lookin', an' I'm sexier.

Susan *gives up playing it straight. She goes up to* **Reilly** *and whispers to him.*

Susan   Brian, little boys shouldn't try and act like men. The day might come when their words are put to the test!

She walks away.

Reilly   Any day, miss, any day.

Digga   What did she say, what did she say?

Reilly   She said she fancied me!

Briggs *and the* **Driver** *come on board.* **Briggs** *goes to sit opposite* **Mrs Kay**.

Briggs   Well . . . We've got a right head-case of a driver.

The engine comes to life. The **Kids** *cheer.* **Briggs** *gives a warning look. Looks back. As he does so we see a mass of hands raised in two-fingered gestures to anyone who might be passing. Simultaneously the* **Kids** *sing:*

Kids
We're off, we're off
We're off in a motor car
Sixty coppers are after us
An' we don't know where we are

We turned around a corner
Eatin' a Christmas pie
Along came a copper
An' he hit me in the eye
I went to tell me mother
Me mother wasn't in
I went to tell me father
An' he kicked me in the bin

Which segues into the 'Travelling Song':

Our day out
Our day out
Out day out

Which fades to:

Our day . . .

The following split between all the **Kids***, each taking a different line.*

Look at the dogs
Look at the cats
A broken window in Tesco's
Look at the empty Corpy flats

Look at the streets
Look at the houses
Agh look at that feller
With the hole in the back of his trousers

Look at the pushchairs
Look at the prams
Little kids out shoppin'
With their mams

Oh there's our Tracey
There's my mate
He's missed the bloody bus
Got up too late

Look at the men
All on the dole
Look at the workers
Layin' cable down that hole

Look at the cars
Look there's a train
Look at the clouds
God, I hope it doesn't rain

Which segues back into the refrain 'Our Day Out', repeated and fading.

On the back seat the **Little Kid** *overhears a conversation between* **Digga** *and* **Reilly**.

Digga   Reilly, light up.

Reilly   Where's Briggsy?

Digga   Up the front. Y' all right, I'll keep the eye out for y'.

Little Kid   Agh 'ey, you've got ciggies. I'm gonna tell miss.

Digga   Tell her. She won't do nothin' anyway.

Little Kid   I'll tell sir.

Reilly   You do an' I'll gob y'.

Digga   Come on, open that window you.

Little Kid   Why?

Reilly   Why d' y' think? So we can get a bit of fresh air.

Little Kid   Well there is no fresh air round here. You just want to smoke. An' smokin' stunts your growth.

Reilly   I'll stunt your bleedin' growth if y' don't get it open.

Andrews *gets up and reaches obligingly for the window.*

Andrews   I'll open it for y' Reilly.

Reilly *ducks behind a seat and lights up.*

Andrews   Gis a ciggie.

Reilly   Sod off. Get y' own ciggies.

Andrews   Ah go on, I opened the window for y'.

Digga   Be told, y' not gettin' no ciggie. (*Suddenly whispered to* **Reilly**.) Briggs! (*As we see* **Briggs** *leave his seat at the front and head towards the back*.)

Reilly *quickly hands the cigarette to* **Andrews** *who, unaware of the approaching* **Briggs**, *seizes it with enthusiasm.*

Andrews   Ogh . . . thanks Reilly.

He ducks behind the seat and takes a massive drag. He comes up to find **Briggs** *gazing down at him and the ciggie.*

Briggs   Put it out.

Andrews   Sir I wasn't . . .

Briggs   Put it out lad. Now get to the front of the coach.

Andrews *gets up and makes his way to* **Briggs'** *seat as* **Briggs** *remains at the back.*

Briggs   Was it your ciggie, Reilly?

Reilly   Sir, swear on me mother I didn't . . .

Digga   Take no notice of him, sir. How can he swear on his mother, she's been dead ten years.

Reilly *about to stick one on* **Digga**.

Briggs   All right. All right! We don't want any argument. There'll be no smokin' if I stay up here will there?

Briggs *takes* **Andrews'** *seat. The rest of the coach sing: 'They've all gone quiet at the back', one verse to tune 'She'll Be Coming Round the Mountain'.*

Mrs Kay *and* **Carol** *are sat next to each other.* **Carol** *next to the window staring out of it.*

Carol   Isn't it horrible eh, miss?

Mrs Kay   Mm?

Carol   Y' know, all the thingy like; the dirt an' that. (*Pause*.) I like them nice places.

Mrs Kay   Which places?

Carol Know them places on the telly with gardens, an' trees outside an' that.

Mrs Kay You've got trees in Pilot Street, haven't you?

Carol They planted some after the riots. But the kids chopped them down an' burnt them on bonfire night. (*Pause.*) Miss . . . miss y' know when I grow up, miss, y' know if I work hard an' learn to read an' write, would you think I'd be able to live in one of them nice places?

Mrs Kay (*putting her arm around her*) Well you could try, love, couldn't you, eh?

Carol Yeh!

The **Kids** *take up the 'Our Day Out' refrain, repeating the line three times.*

On the back seat, **Reilly** *and* **Digga**, *stifled by* **Briggs's** *presence.*

Briggs (*suddenly pointing out of the window*) Now just look at that.

Digga *and* **Reilly** *glance but see nothing to look at.*

Digga What?

Briggs (*disgusted*) What? Can't you see? Look, those buildings, don't you ever observe what's around you?

Reilly It's only the docks, sir.

Briggs You don't get buildings like that any more. Just look at the work that must have gone into that.

Reilly Do you like it down here then, sir?

Briggs I'm often down here at weekends, taking photographs. Are you listening Reilly? There's a wealth of history that won't be here much longer.

Reilly My old feller used to work down here.

Briggs What did he think of it?

Reilly He hated it.

Briggs   Well you tell him to take another look and he might appreciate it.

Reilly   I'll have a job; I haven't seen him for two years.

Reilly *turning away and looking out of the window.*

A few seats further down **Linda** *suddenly kneeling up on her seat.*

Linda (*to* **Jackie**)   Ogh . . . look, there's Sharon. (*She shouts and waves.*) Sharon . . . Sha . . .

Briggs   Linda Croxley!

He gets up and moves towards her.

Only at the last moment does she turn and sit 'properly'.

Briggs   And what sort of an outfit is that supposed to be for a school visit?

Linda (*chewing and contemptuous, staring out of the window*) What?

Briggs   Don't you 'what' me, young lady. (*She merely shrugs.*) You know very well that on school trips you wear school uniform.

Linda   Well Mrs Kay never said nott'n about it.

Briggs   You're not talking to Mrs Kay now.

Linda   Yeh I know.

Briggs (*quietly but threatening*)   Now listen here young lady, I don't like your attitude. I don't like it one bit.

Linda   What have I said? I haven't said nott'n have I?

Briggs   I'm talking about your attitude.

She dismisses him with a glance and turns away.

I'm telling you now, miss. Carry on like this and when we get to Conway you'll be spending your time in the coach.

Linda   I don't care, I don't wanna see no crappy castle anyway.

Briggs   Just count yourself lucky you're not a lad. Now I'm warning you. Cause any more unpleasantness on this trip and I shall see to it that it's the last you ever go on. Is that understood? Is it?

Linda (*sighs*)   Yeh.

Briggs   It better had be.

He makes his way to the front of the coach and addresses the **Kid** *next to* **Andrews**.

Briggs   Right, you, what's your name? Wake up.

Maurice   Sir, me?

Briggs   What's your name?

Maurice   McNally, sir.

Briggs   Right McNally go and sit at the back.

Maurice   Sir, I don't like the back.

Briggs   Never mind what you like, go and sit at the back.

Maurice *does so*.

Briggs   Right, Andrews, shove up. (*Sitting by him.*) How long have you been smoking, Andrews?

Andrews   Sir, I don't . . . Sir, since I was eight.

Briggs   And how old are you now?

Andrews   Sir, thirteen, sir.

Briggs   What do your parents say?

Andrews   Sir, me mam says nothin' about it but when me dad comes home sir, sir he belts me.

Briggs   Because you smoke?

Andrews   No sir, because I won't give him one.

Pause.

Briggs   Your father works away from home does he?

Andrews   What? No sir.

Briggs   You said 'when he comes home', I thought you meant he was away a lot.

Andrews   He is. But he doesn't go to work.

Briggs   Well what does he do then?

Andrews   I don't know. Sir, he just comes round every now an' then an' has a barney with me mam. Then he goes off again. I think he tries to get money off her but she won't give him it though. She hates him. We all hate him.

Briggs   Listen, why don't you promise yourself you'll give up smoking? You must realise it's bad for your health.

Andrews   Sir, I did sir. I've got a terrible cough.

Briggs   Then why don't you pack it in?

Andrews   Sir, I can't.

Briggs   Thirteen and you can't stop smoking?

Andrews   No, sir.

Briggs   (*sighing and shaking his head*)   Well you'd better not let me catch you again.

Andrews   No, sir. I won't.

Kids various   There's the tunnel, the Mersey tunnel, we're goin' throu the tunnel . . .

All the **Kids** *cheer as the bus goes into the tunnel (probably best conveyed by blackout).*

Kids (*sing*)
>   The Mersey tunnel is three miles long
>   And the roof is made of glass
>   So that you can drive right in
>   And watch the ships go past
>   There's a plug hole every five yards
>   They open it every night
>   It lets in all the water and it
>   Washes away the sha na na na na na na na na . . .

Briggs *rising as they are, he thinks, about to sing an obscenity; sitting down again as he fails to catch them at it. The* **Kids** *repeat the verse and* **Briggs** *repeats his leap to try and catch them. Again they merely* *sing 'Sha na na na' etc. They repeat the verse once more. This time* **Briggs** *doesn't leap to his feet as the* **Kids** *sing:*

And washes away the shite!

As **Briggs** *leaps to his feet, too late, the* **Kids** *are staring from the windows at the 'pretty scenery'.* **Briggs** *stares at them.*

Girl   Sir, are we in Wales yet?

Boy   Sir, I need to go to the toilet.

Briggs   Yes, well you should have thought of that before you got on the coach, shouldn't you?

Boy   Sir, I did, sir. I've got a weak bladder.

Briggs   Then a little control will help to strengthen it.

Maurice   Sir, sir I'm wettin' meself.

Digga   Are we stoppin' for toilets sir?

Which all the **Kids** *take up in one form or another, groans, moans and cries of 'toilet', 'I wanna go the toilet.'*

Briggs   For God's sake. Just shut up, all of you shut up!

Mrs Kay   Mr B . . .

Briggs   I said shut up. (*Then realising.*) Erm, sorry sorry. Mrs Kay?

Mrs Kay   I would like to go to the toilet myself!

Briggs *staring at her.*

Milton (*hand raised*)   Sir . . . Sir . . .

Briggs (*snaps*)   Yes. Milton.

Milton   Sir, I wondered if you were aware that over six hundred people per year die from ruptured bladders.

Briggs (*seeing he's defeated, turning to the* **Driver**)   Pull in at the toilets up ahead will you? (*He turns to the* **Kids**.) Right, I want everybody back on this coach in two minutes. Those who need the toilets, off you go.

Most of the **Kids** *get off the coach and go off as if to the toilets.*

Reilly, Digga *and a small group form some yards away from the coach, obviously smoking.*

Colin (*approaching them*)   All right lads. Shouldn't be too long before we're in Wales.

Little Kid   Wales, that's in the country isn't it, sir?

Colin   A lot of it's countryside yes but . . .

Reilly   Lots of woods eh, sir?

Colin   Well, woods, yes mountains and lakes.

Reilly   An' you're gonna show miss the woods are y' sir?

Colin   Just watch it Brian, right?

Reilly   Ah, I only meant was y' gonna show her the plants an' the trees.

Colin   I know quite well what you meant. (*He turns to go.*) And if I was you I'd put that fag out before you burn your hand. If Mr Briggs catches you you'll spend the rest of the day down at the front of the coach with him and you don't want that to happen do you? Now come on, put it out.

Reilly *puts out the cigarette and* **Colin** *walks away.*

Reilly (*shouting after him*)   I'll show miss the woods for y' sir.

Throughout the above all the other **Kids** *have made their way back onto the coach.*

Mrs Kay (*returning*)   Come on, Brian, come on . . . (*She ushers them on board.*) OK Ronnie, I think that's the lot.

The bus starts.

Little Kid   Miss miss . . .

Mrs Kay   Yes.

Little Kid   Miss I wanna go the toilet.

Kids   Agh shurrup . . .

Driver   Get ready, a humpety backed bridge . . .

As they go over the bridge all passengers are bumped off their seats.

Two bored girls (*in unison*)
     It's borin'
     It's bleedin' borin'
     Another minute here an' I'll be snorin'
     Lookin' at loads of roads, miss
     When are we gonna stop?
     There's nothin' to do
     Only look at the view
     An' if you've seen one hill
     You've seen the bleedin' lot

     God! It's borin', isn't it borin'
     It's borin'
     It's bleedin' borin'

The other **Kids** *take up, quietly, the refrain of 'It's borin', it's bleedin' borin'.'*

At the front of the coach **Mrs Kay** *is having a word with* **Ronnie**.

Mrs Kay   Ronnie, I was wondering if there was somewhere we could stop for a little while, have a cup of tea and let them stretch their legs?

Driver   All right Mrs Kay, there's a café just up ahead; d' y' want me to pull in?

Mrs Kay   Thanks Ron.

The song begins as the **Kids** *dismantle the coach and re-set the seats to form the café/shop and picnic area.*

Note: if doubling is necessary the actress playing **Susan** *changes here to play the café/shop proprietress.*

Briggs (*sings*)
     All right! Let's get this straight
     We're only stopping for a quarter of an hour
     When you leave the bus you will get in line and wait
     We do not want this visit turning sour

Mrs Kay
     It's all right everybody, there will still be lots of time
     For you to stretch your legs and let off steam
     You're free to leave the bus now but please don't go

getting lost
The shop's that way, for those who want ice cream

The **Kids** *cheering as they set up the shop/café.*

Briggs
All right! Now that's enough
You're behaving like a gang of common scruffs.

Mrs Kay
By the book, Mr Briggs?

Briggs
Yes, why not by the book?
I want them looking tidy.

Mrs Kay
That's one thing they'll never look.

Briggs
Come on now get in line, I said line up, do what you're
told.

Mrs Kay
For a straight line is a wonderful thing to behold.

As the music continues as underscoring **Briggs** *addresses the* **Kids***.*

Briggs   Now the people who run these places provide a
good and valuable service to travellers like ourselves and so I
want to see this place treated with the sort of respect it
deserves. Now come on, let's have a straight line, in twos . . .

Mrs Kay *at the front of the queue which is being formed. Inevitably
there are* **Kids** *who don't conform exactly to* **Briggs'** *concept of a
straight line.*

Briggs   Come on you two, get in line. You two! Reilly, get
in line lad. I said in line . . .

Mrs Kay   Mr Briggs . . .

Briggs   I think it's under control Mrs Kay, thank you.
(*Barking at* **Kids**.) Come on! Cut out the fidgeting. Just
stand. Straight! That's more . . . RONSON. Come here lad.

Mrs Kay   Mr Briggs . . .

Briggs It's all right Mrs Kay! (*To* **Ronson**:) Now just where do you think you are lad?

Ronson (*a beat as he wonders*) Sir . . . Sir, Wales?

Briggs (*almost screaming by now*) Get in line lad.

Briggs (*sings*)
All right. That's looking fine
Chaos turned to order in a stroke

Mrs Kay
Quite amazing Mr Briggs, they're standing in a line!

Briggs
And it's important Mrs Kay, it's not a joke

Mrs Kay
Oh yes, of course it's awfully serious. I'm terribly
    impressed
Such achievements are the hallmark of the great
A quite remarkable example of a very straight, straight
    line
Congratulations Mr Briggs it's . . . well it's straight!

Briggs
I think that's good, don't you?

Mrs Kay
They do so well at standing two by two

Briggs
They do us credit, Mrs Kay

Mrs Kay
Perhaps that's true
If you stake your reputation on a stationary queue!

Briggs
Come on, it's better than a rabble, there they are as good
    as gold

Mrs Kay
Oh, a straight line is a wonderful thing to behold

Briggs (*spoken*)   With organisation Mrs Kay, with organisation it can be done.

Mrs Kay, *the other teachers and the* **Kids** *hitting the song finale as per Hollywood, splitting into two lines, hands waving and legs kicking.*

All
    A straight line is a wonderful thing to behold!

And on the last note they are back in twos, lined up.

The Shopkeeper   Right, two at a time.

The **Kids** *charge as one into the shop.*

Briggs (*apoplectic*)   Stop, I said stop . . . stop . . .

Mrs Kay *takes his arm and diverts him.*

Mrs Kay   Oh let's forget about them for a while. Come and have some coffee out of my flask. Come on.

A sea of **Kids** *in front of a sweet counter and a harrassed* **Shopkeeper**.

Shopkeeper   Fifty-four, the chocolate bars are fifty-four.

Maurice   That's robbery.

Kid   They're only thirty pence down our way.

Girl 1   Yeh, an' they're twice the size.

Kid   Ey missis, give us one of them up there.

As she turns her back the **Kids** *begin robbing sweets.*

Shopkeeper   Hey. Put that down, give that here. Where's your teachers? They should be in here with you.

Kid   What for? They couldn't afford to buy anything, the prices you charge.

Shopkeeper   There's a surcharge for school parties and if you don't like it you can get out.

Blackout and freeze as we see **Briggs** *and* **Mrs Kay** *outside,* **Briggs** *reluctant, keeping an eye on the shop.*

Mrs Kay   Isn't it nice to get away from them for a few minutes?

Briggs   To be quite honest Mrs Kay, I think we should be in there, looking after them.

Blackout and freeze the teachers.

The Shopkeeper (*amidst the chaos*)   'Ere. Put that down. Keep your hands to yourselves.

Girl 2   How much are the Bounties?

The **Shopkeeper** *turns her back and much of the counter contents goes into the* **Kids'** *pockets.*

Shopkeeper   Now just a minute, give me that hand. Come on, put it back.

Kid   Y' big robber.

Girl 1   'Ey you, I haven't robbed nott'n.

Milton   How much are the penny chews?

Shopkeeper   Tenpence, the penny chews are tenpence. (*She clouts a* **Kid**.) Take your 'ands off!

Milton   But they're called 'penny' chews.

Shopkeeper   Yes! They're called penny chews but they cost tenpence each.

Maurice   It's robbery that.

Milton   If the penny chews cost tenpence each don't you think they should be called tenpenny chews?

Shopkeeper   But they're not called tenpenny chews. They're called penny chews and they cost tenpence! Right?

Milton   I hope you realise this represents a serious breach of the Trades Description Act.

Shopkeeper   And I hope you realise that if you don't shut up there'll be a serious breach of your bloody head!

Ronson   D' y' sell chips?

Shopkeeper   NO!

Blackout and freeze the shop.

Mrs Kay *and* **Briggs** *outside the café.*

Briggs   There's not just our school to think of, you know. What about those who come after us? They're dependent on the goodwill of the people who run these places.

Mrs Kay   Considering the profit they make from the kids I don't think they've got too much to complain about.

Kids *are beginning to emerge from the shop/café moaning about the prices and dismissing the place.*

Mrs Kay   Mr Briggs. I didn't ask you to come on this trip.

Briggs   No, but the headmaster did.

Throughout the following song the coach is reassembled. By the end of the song everyone is sat in his or her seat and the coach is on its way again.

Kids (*sing*)
    Penny chews are tenpence in this caff
    Yes penny chews are tenpence in this caff
    They say prices are inflated
    But it's robbery, let's face it
    When penny chews are tenpence, what a laugh

    They're chargin' stupid prices for their sweets
    Yes they're chargin' stupid prices for their sweets
    An' they must be makin' quids
    Out of all poor starvin' kids
    Cause they're chargin' stupid prices for their sweets

    No they shouldn't be allowed to charge that much
    They shouldn't be allowed to charge that much
    It's robbery it's last it's
    Just a bunch of thievin' bastards
    Who think that everyone they meet's an easy touch

    Well it would have cost us more than we have got
    Yes it would have cost us more than we have got
    Why swindle an' defraud it?
    When they know we can't afford it
    It's a good job that we robbed the bleedin' lot!

Colin, *who has been sitting with* **Briggs**, *gets up to check that everything is OK. As he gets near* **Linda**'s *seat her mate* **Jackie** *taps* *her on the shoulder and points him out.* **Linda** *turning and smiling at* **Colin**.

Linda   Sir, are y' comin' to sit by me, are y'?

Jackie   Don't sit by her, sir, come an' sit by me.

Colin   I've got my seat down at the front thanks Jackie.

Linda   Here, sir.

Colin   What Linda?

Linda   Come here, I wanna tell y' somethin'.

Colin   Well go on.

Linda   Ah hey sir. I don't want everyone to hear. Come on, just sit here while I tell y'.

Jackie   Go on sir, she won't bite y'.

Linda   Come on.

Colin *reluctantly sits.* **Jackie***'s head poked through the space between the seats.*

Colin   Well? What is it?

They laugh.

You're not going to tell me a joke are you?

They laugh.

Look Linda, I'll have to go I've . . .

Linda (*quickly links her arm through his and holds him there*)   No sir, listen, listen. She said I wouldn't tell y', but I will. Sir, sir I think you're lovely.

Colin (*quickly getting up*)   Linda! (*And returns to his seat next to* **Briggs**.)

Linda   I told him. I said I would. Oh God he's boss him isn't he eh?

Jackie   Oh go way you. You've got no chance. He's goin' with miss.

Linda   He might chuck her. Might start goin' with me.
Might marry me.

Jackie (*shrieking*)   Oh don't be mental. You'll never get a
husband like sir. You'll end up marryin' someone like your
old feller.

Linda   You're just jealous girl.

Jackie   Get lost.

Linda *turns and dismisses her, stares out of the window and begins to
sing.*

Linda
I'm in love with sir
But sir doesn't care
Cos sir's in love with her
Over there
With the hair
It isn't fair.

She turns to **Jackie**.
If I was the wife of a man like sir
My life would not be full of trouble and care
I'd look forward to the nights and we'd make a perfect pair
Me and sir

I'm in love with sir
But sir doesn't care
Cos sir's in love with her
Over there
With the hair
It isn't fair

If I could marry sir I'd be all right
I wouldn't need to work and we would stay in every night
We'd have some lovely holidays and I would wash his
    collars
Really white

Kids
She's in love with sir
But sir doesn't care

Cos sir's in love with her
Over there
With the hair
It isn't fair

Jackie
You'll be the wife of a man like your dad
He'll disappear when you grow fat
You'll be left with the kids and you'll live in a council flat

Kids
She's in love with sir
But sir doesn't care
Cos sir's in love with her
Over there
With the hair
It isn't fair

Linda
I'm in love with sir

Mrs Kay *is talking to the* **Driver**. *She returns to her seat next to* **Carol**.

Briggs (*to* **Colin** *who is sat next to him*)   You know what Mrs Kay's problem is, don't you?

Colin (*trying to keep out of it*)   Mm?

Briggs   Well! She thinks I can't see through all this woolly-minded liberalism. You know what I mean? All right (**Girls 1** *and* **2**, **Little Kid** *and* **Maurice** *arguing about sweets*, **Briggs** *machine gunning a 'Be quiet' at them*.) I mean, she has her methods and I have mine but this setting herself up as the champion of the non-academics! I mean, it might look like love and kindness but it doesn't fool me. And it doesn't do kids a scrap of good. I think you've got to risk being disliked if you're going to do anything for kids like these. They've got enough freedom at home haven't they? Eh? With their five quid pocket money and telly till all hours, video games and that. Eh? I don't know about you, I don't know about you but to me her philosophy's all over the place. (*Pause*.) Eh?

Colin (*reluctant but having to answer*)   Actually I don't think it's got anything to do with a formulated philosophy.

Briggs   You mean you've not noticed all this anti-establishment, just-let-the-kids-roam-wild, don't check 'em sort of attitude?

Colin   Of course I've noticed. But she's like this all the time. This trip isn't organised on the basis of any profound theory.

Briggs   Well what's the method she does work to then? Mm? Eh? I mean, you know her better than me, go on you tell me.

Colin   Well . . . she, for one thing, she likes them.

Briggs   Who?

Colin   The kids. She likes kids.

Briggs   What's that got to do with it?

Colin (*pause*)   The principle behind this trip is that the kids should have a good day out.

Briggs   And isn't that what I'm saying? But if they're going to have a good and stimulating day it's got to be better planned and executed than this . . .

Briggs *suddenly noticing that they have turned off the expected route.*

What's this? Where are we going? This isn't . . .

Mrs Kay   Oh it's all right Mr Briggs. I've checked with the driver, we thought it might be a good idea if we called in at the zoo for an hour. We've got plenty of time.

Briggs   But, this trip was arranged so that we could visit Conway Castle.

Mrs Kay   Ooh, we're going there as well. I know you're very fond of ruins. Now listen everyone, as an extra bonus, we've decided to call in here at the zoo.

Cheers.

Briggs   But look, we can't . . .

Mrs Kay   Now the rest of the staff will be around if you
want to know anything about the various animals, although
it's not much good asking me because I don't know one
monkey from the next . . .

Briggs   Mrs Kay . . .

Mrs Kay (*ignoring him*)   But, Progress Class, we're very
lucky today to have Mr Briggs with us, because Mr Briggs is
something of an expert in natural history. He's something of
a David Bellamy, aren't you, Mr Briggs? So if you want to
know more about the animals, ask Mr Briggs. Now come on.
Leave your things on the coach.

*The underscoring for 'Who's Watching Who?' begins as the teachers
set up the Zoo and café.*

The **Kids** *spread out in groups around the auditorium as though at
different parts of the zoo.*

Kids (*singing as they move*)
    Sealions and penguins

Drums.

    Swimming in the zoo

Drums.

    What do seals eat?

Drums.

    Pilchard sarnies
    Who's watching who's watching who's watching who?
    Who's watching who's watching who's watching who?

    Centipedes and pythons
    Wriggling at the zoo
    What do snakes eat?
    Wrigleys spearmint
    Who's watching who's watching *etc.*

Middle eight:

    Elephants from Africa, an Aussie Kangaroo
    All flown in on jumbo jets and stuck here in the zoo

The two **Bored girls** *enter and speak with drums underscoring their verse.*

Bored girls
　　It's borin'
　　It's bleedin' borin'
　　The lions are all asleep
　　They're not even roarin'
　　It's just a lod of parrots
　　Bleedin' monkeys an' giraffes
　　It isn't worth a carrot
　　I come here for a laugh

　　But it's borin'
　　It's really borin'
　　We shoulda stayed at school
　　An' done some drawin'
　　A zoo's just stupid animals
　　An' some of them are smelly
　　I think zoos are better
　　When y' watch them on the telly
　　It's borin'
　　Bleedin' borin' . . .

As they close their verse the other **Kids** *take up the song again.*

Kids
　　Coloured birds in cages
　　Do you want to fly away?
　　What do birds eat?
　　Sir, bird's custard
　　Who's watching who's watching *etc.*

Briggs *and a group of* **Kids** *enter and look down into the bear pit.*

Briggs   And a brown bear is an extremely dangerous animal. You see those claws, they could leave a really nasty mark.

Andrews   Could it kill y' sir?

Briggs   Well why do you think they keep it in a pit?

Ronson   I think that's cruel sir. Don't you?

Briggs Not if it's treated well, no. Don't forget, Ronson, that an animal like this would have been born into captivity. It's always had walls around it so it won't know anything other than this sort of existence, will it?

Ronson I'll bet it does.

Girl 2 How do you know? Sir's just told you hasn't he? If it was born in a cage an' it's lived all its life in a cage well it won't know any different will it? So it won't want anything different.

Ronson Well why does it kill people then?

Andrews What's that got to do with it, dickhead?

Ronson It kills people because people are cruel to it. They keep it in here, in this pit so when it gets out it's bound to go mad an' want to kill people. Can't y' see?

Andrews Sir he's thick. Tell him to shuttup.

Ronson I'm not thick. Even if it has lived all its life in there is must know mustn't it sir?

Briggs Know what Ronson?

Ronson Know about other ways of livin'. About bein' free. Sir it only kills people cos they keep it trapped in here but if it was free an' it was treated all right it'd start to be friends with y' then wouldn't it? If y' were doin' nothing wrong to it it wouldn't want to kill y'.

Briggs Well I wouldn't be absolutely sure about that, Ronson.

Andrews Sir's right. Bears kill y' cos it's in them to kill y'.

Girl 1 Ah come on sir, let's go to the Pets Corner.

Andrews No way sir, let's see the big ones.

Briggs We'll get round them all eventually.

Girl 1 Come on then sir, let's go the Pets Corner . . .

Girl 1 and **Girl 2** *go to link* **Briggs'** *arms. He shrugs them off.*

Briggs Now walk properly, properly . . .

Girl 1   Agh hey sir, all the other teachers let y' link them.

Mrs Kay *enters with another group of* **Kids**. *She has got* **Kids** *on either side, linking her arms.*

Mrs Kay   How are you getting on? Plying you with questions?

Briggs   Yes, yes they've been . . . very good.

Mrs Kay   I'm just going for a cup of coffee. Want to join me?

Briggs   Well I was just on my way to the Pets Corner . . .

Andrews   It's all right sir, we'll go on our own.

Mrs Kay   Oh come on, they'll be all right.

Briggs   But can these people be trusted Mrs Kay?

Mrs Kay   They'll be all right. Colin and Susan are walking round. And the place is walled in.

Andrews   Go on sir, you go an' have a cuppa. You can trust us.

Briggs   Ah can I though? If I go off for a cup of tea with Mrs Kay, can you people be trusted to act responsibly?

Kids   Yes sir.

Jimmy   Sir what sort of bird's that sir?

Briggs   Erm. Oh let me see, yes it's a macaw.

Mrs Kay   Come on.

Briggs (*following* **Mrs Kay**)   They're very good talkers.

Mrs Kay *and* **Briggs** *off*.

Kevin   I told y' it wasn't a parrot.

Jimmy (*trying to get the bird to talk*)   Liverpool, Liverpool. Come on say it, y' dislocated sparrow.

Kids (*sing*)
    Mountain lions and panthers
    Leopards in the zoo
    What do lions eat?

Jim ⎫
Kev ⎭ Evertonians

Kids

Who's watching who's watching, who's watching who?
Who's watching who's watching who's watching who?

Mrs Kay *and* **Briggs** *sitting as if in the café, two teas and a couple of cakes.* **Kids** *as though looking through the windows of the café.*

Kids

Teachers in the café
Takin' tea for two
What do they eat

(*Spoken.*) Ogh, chocolate cream cakes!

Briggs *and* **Mrs Kay** *suddenly noticing hungry eyes on their cakes.*

Mrs Kay (*waving them away*)   Ogh go on, go away . . .
shoo . . .

Kids (*dispersing and going off singing*)
Who's watching who's watching who's watching who
Who's watching who's watching who's watching who?

Briggs   Another tea Mrs Kay?

Briggs   Oh call me Helen. Do you know I loathe being called Mrs Kay. Do you know I tried to get the kids to call me by my first name. I told them, call me Helen, not Mrs Kay. They were outraged. They wouldn't do it. So it's good old Mrs Kay again. Oh, no, no more tea thanks.

Briggs   They're really quite interested, the kids, aren't they?

Mrs Kay   In the animals, oh yes. And it's such a help having you here because you know so much about this sort of thing.

Briggs   Well I wouldn't say I was an expert but . . . you know, perhaps when we're back at school I could come along to your department and show some slides I've got.

Mrs Kay   Would you really? Oh Mr Briggs, we'd love that.

Briggs · Well look, I'll sort out which free periods I've got and we'll organise it for then.

Colin *and* **Susan** *approaching*.

The **Kids** *quickly lined up in the sort of orderly queue* **Briggs** *would approve of*.

Susan   Ready when you are.

Mrs Kay   Are they all back?

Susan   It's amazing, we came around the corner and they're all there, lined up waiting to get on the bus.

Mrs Kay   Wonders will never cease.

Briggs   OK. (*Sees the* **Kids**.) Well look at this Mrs Kay, they're learning at last eh? Right, all checked and present? On board then . . .

The **Kids** *go to climb aboard just as an* **Animal keeper**, *all polo-neck and wellies, rushes towards them*.

Keeper   Hold it right there.

Mrs Kay   Hello, have we forgotten something?

Keeper   Are you supposed to be in charge of this lot?

Mrs Kay   Why, what's the matter?

Keeper   Children? They're not bloody children, they're animals. It's not the zoo back there, this is the bloody zoo, here.

Briggs   Excuse me! Would you mind controlling your language and telling me what's going on?

Keeper (*ignores him, pushes past and confronts the* **Kids**) Right, where are they?

Innocent faces and replies of 'What?', 'Where's what?'

Keeper   You know bloody well what . . .

Briggs (*intercepting him*)   Now look, this has just gone far enough. Would you . . .

He is interrupted by the loud clucking of a hen.

The **Keeper** *strides up to a* **Kid** *and pulls open his jacket. A bantam hen is revealed.*

Keeper (*taking the hen, addresses the other* **Kids**)   Right, now I want the rest.

There is a moment's hesitation before the floodgates are opened. Animals appear from every conceivable hiding-place.

Briggs *glares as the animals are rounded up. The* **Kids** *stay in place, waiting for the thunder.*

Briggs   I trusted you lot. And this is the way you repay me. (*Pause as he fights to control his anger.*) I trusted all of you but it's obvious that trust is something you know nothing about.

Ronson   Sir we only borrowed them.

Briggs (*screaming*)   Shut up lad! Is it any wonder that people won't do anything for you? The moment we start to treat you like real people, what happens? Well that man was right. You act like animals, animals.

Mrs Kay   Come on now, take the animals back.

The **Kids** *relieved at finding a way to go. As they move off* **Briggs** *remains.*

Briggs   And that's why you're treated like animals, why you'll always be treated like animals.

Kids (*sing very quietly as they exit*)
  Our day out
  Our day out

Briggs (*alone on stage*)   ANIMALS!

Blackout.

Act Two

Teachers *and* **Kids** *outside Conway Castle.*

Briggs   We'll split into four groups Mrs Kay. Each
member of staff will be responsible for one group. It will take
approximately one and a quarter hours to tour the castle and
at three-fifteen we will reassemble at the coach. Walk round
in twos, and I mean walk! Right, my group, this way . . .

The others going off. The **Kids** *in* **Briggs**' *group following him with
little enthusiasm.*

Briggs (*pointing up at the castle walls*)   Now, those large
square holes just below the battlements: long planks of wood
were supported there and that's where the archers would fire
from if the castle was under attack. Something really
interesting up there is, if you look at that tower, you'll see
that it's not quite perpendicular. What does perpendicular
mean?

Maurice   I don't know.

Milton   Sir, sir . . .

Briggs   Yes?

Milton   Sir, straight up.

Sniggers from the other **Kids**.

Briggs   Are you listening lad? You might just learn
something.

Music intro for 'Castle Song'. **Briggs** *sings:*

> I find it so depressing
> I just can't understand
> Your failure to appreciate
> A thing so fine and grand
> Your heritage, your history

You can touch it with your hand
The Yanks have nothing like it

Milton
'Sir, but they've got Disneyland

Briggs (*spoken*)   Disneyland. (*Sings.*)
That's not the same at all, this is history, this is real
It should make you feel so proud, so thrilled, so awed
Just standing here for centuries, how does that make you
    feel?

Kids
Sir it makes us feel dead bored

Briggs (*music continuing as underscoring*)   Bored! Yes and
you'll be bored for ever; do you want to know why? Because
you put nothing in. You invest in nothing. And if you invest
in nothing you get nothing in return. This way. Come on,
quickly, move.

As **Briggs** *leads his group off,* **Reilly** *and* **Digga** *slip away from it
and get the ciggies out. They hide though when they hear* **Colin**
approaching. **Linda** *and* **Jackie** *are with him.*

Colin (*sings*)
Now though these walls are very thick
In places fifteen feet
Just think how cold it must have been
With no real form of heat
Even in the summertime
It must have been quite cold

Linda
I wonder how they managed, sir
To keep warm in days of old

Tell us sir go on.

Jackie
Tell us everything you know
We want to learn from you sir
Yes we do, ooh ooh
We really think you're great sir

Tell us everything you know
We'd be really brainy sir
If all the teachers were like you

Colin   Well. They'd obviously . . . where's everybody else gone? Where are the others?

Jackie   Sir they kept droppin' out as you were talkin'.

Colin   Oh God!

Linda   Oh it's all right sir, we're dead interested. Y' can keep showin' us around.

Colin (*sighs*)   All right, what was I saying?

Linda   You were tellin' us how they kept warm in the olden days.

Colin   Well for one thing . . . Linda (*Sings.*)
They wore much thicker clothing

Linda
Even damsels in distress?

Colin
I expect they *all* had more sense
Than to walk around half-dressed

Girls
We seen this movie once sir
Where they had some better ways
To keep each other cosy sir
Back in them olden days

Colin (*spoken*)   All right Linda, all right . . .

Girls
Tell us sir go on
Tell us everything you know
We want to learn from you sir
Yes we do, ooh ooh
We really think you're great sir
Tell us everything you know
We'd be really brainy sir
If all the teachers were like you

Linda   Sir it's dead spooky here. Sir I think it's haunted.

She grabs his arm.

Colin   Don't be silly.

She throws her arms around him.

Linda   I'm frightened.

Colin   Don't do that Linda.

Linda   But I'm frightened. (*Holding tight.*)

Jackie (*also grabbing him*)   Sir, so am I.

Colin (*freeing himself*)   Now girls, stop being silly. Stop it!
(*Sings.*)
   There's nothing to be frightened of
   There's no such things as ghosts
   Just look how this position
   Gives a clear view of the coast

Girls
   But we'd rather look at you sir

Colin
   Yes, but girls, you're here to learn

Girls
   Oh sir, you're so impressive when
   You behave so strong and firm
   Tell us sir, go on
   Then we won't be scared at all
   We feel so warm and safe when we're with you, ooh ooh
   We know you will protect us sir
   Cos you're all strong and tall
   And if we can't believe in ghosts
   We can still believe in you

Digga and **Reilly** *lean out unnoticed from their hiding position.*
They touch the **Girls** *who scream and grab* **Colin** *again.*

Linda   It touched me.

Colin   What did?

Linda   Oh it did.

Reilly *and* **Digga** *jeering and running off.*

Colin   God. Come on, girls, come on.

They follow him.

Carol *is sitting on the battlements, looking out over the estuary.
Nearby, on a bench,* **Mrs Kay** *is sitting back enjoying the sun.*

Mrs Kay   Why don't you go and have a look around the
castle, Carol? You haven't seen it yet.

Carol   Miss, I don't like it. It's horrible. I'd rather sit here
with you an' look at the lake.

Mrs Kay   That's the sea.

Carol   Yeh that's what I mean.

Andrews (*runs on and joins them*)   Miss, miss I just thought of
this great idea; miss wouldn't it be smart if we had somethin'
like this castle round our way. The kids wouldn't get into
trouble, would they, if they had somewhere like this to play.

Carol   Miss, we couldn't have somethin' like this round our
way, could we?

Mrs Kay   Why not?

Carol   Cos if we had somethin' like this we'd only wreck it
wouldn't we?

Andrews   No we wouldn't.

Carol   We would. That's why we never have nothin' nice
round our way – we'd smash it up. The corporation knows
that an' so why should they waste their time and money.
They'd give us nice things if we looked after them, but we
don't do we?

Andrews   Miss, d' y' know what I think about it miss?

Mrs Kay   Go on John, what?

Andrews   Miss, miss if all this belonged to us – like it
wasn't the corporation's but it was something that we
owned, well we wouldn't let no one wreck it would we? Eh?

We'd look after it wouldn't we? Defend it. D' y' know what I mean, miss?

Mrs Kay   Yes, I think I do. (**Briggs** *enters.*) What you're saying . . .

Briggs   Right. You two, off. Go on move.

Carol   Sir where?

Briggs   Anywhere girl. Just move. I want to talk to Mrs Kay. Well come on then.

The two **Kids** *reluctantly wander off.* **Briggs** *waiting until they are out of hearing.*

Mrs Kay (*quietly angry*)   I was talking to those children.

Briggs   Yes, an' I'm talking to you, Mrs Kay. This has got to stop.

Mrs Kay   Pardon me. What's got to stop?

Briggs   What! Can't you see what's going on? It's a shambles, the whole ill-organised affair. Just look what they did at the zoo. Look. (*As a group of* **Kids** *run past playing chase and tick.*) They're just left to race and chase and play havoc. God knows what the castle authorities must think. Now look, when you bring children like this into this sort of environment you can't afford to just let them roam free.

Kids *rushing past.*

Briggs   They're just like town dogs let off the leash in the country. My God, for some of them it's the first time they've been further than Birkenhead.

Mrs Kay (*quietly*)   I know. And I was just thinking: it's a shame really isn't it? We bring them out to a crumbling pile of bricks and mortar and they think they're in the fields of heaven.

Briggs   You *are* on their side aren't you?

Mrs Kay   Absolutely Mr Briggs, absolutely.

A couple of **Kids** *shouting to try and hear the echo of their names.*

Briggs   Look, all I want to know from you is what you're going to do about this chaos?

Mrs Kay   Well I'd suggest that if you want the chaos to stop you should simply look at it not as chaos but what it actually is – kids, with a bit of space around them, making a bit of noise. All right, so the Head asked you to come along – but can't you just relax? There's no point in pretending that a day out to Wales is going to be of some great educational benefit to them. It's too late for them. Most of these kids were rejects the day they came into the world. We're not going to solve anything today Mr Briggs. Can't we just give them a good day out? Mm? At least we could try and do that.

Briggs   Well that's a fine attitude isn't it? That's a fine attitude for a member of the teaching profession.

Mrs Kay (*beginning to let her temper go*)   Well what's your alternative? Eh? Pretending? Pretending that they've got some sort of a future ahead of them? Even if you cared for these kids you couldn't help to make a future for them. You won't educate them because nobody wants them educating.

Briggs   Listen Mrs Kay . . .

Mrs Kay   No you listen Mr Briggs, you listen and perhaps you'll stop fooling yourself. Teach them? Teach them what? You'll never teach them because nobody knows what to do with them. Ten years ago you could teach them to stand in a line, you could teach them to obey, to expect little more than a lousy factory job. But now they haven't even got that to aim for. Mr Briggs, you won't teach them because you're in a job that's designed and funded to fail! There's nothing for them to do, any of them; most of them were born for factory fodder, but the factories have closed down.

Briggs   And I suppose that's the sort of stuff you've been pumping into their minds.

Mrs Kay (*laughing*)   And you really think they'd understand?

Briggs   I'm not going to spend any more time arguing with you. You may have organised this visit, but I'm the one who was sent by the headmaster to supervise. Now, either you take control of the children in your charge or I'll be forced to abandon this visit and order everyone home.

Mrs Kay   Well . . . that's your decision. But I'm not going to let you prevent the kids from having some fun. If you want to abandon this visit you'd better start walking because we're not going home. We're going down to the beach!

She walks away.

Colin, round everybody up. Come on everybody, we're going to the beach.

Briggs   The beach?

Kids *and other teachers entering as we hear the intro for a song.* **Mrs Kay** *calling to* **Briggs**.

Mrs Kay   You can't come all the way to the seaside and not pay a visit to the beach.

Kids (*singing to the tune of the 'Mersey Tunnel Song'. As they sing they set up the rocks and the beach*)
    The castle's just a load of stones
    It's borin' and it's dead
    Can't even fire the cannons
    Cos they're blocked off at the end
    So we're goin' to the seashore
    An' miss says we can
    Build a better castle there
    With just the bloody sand

Continue underscoring as **Kids** *begin to whip off shoes and socks,* **Mrs Kay** *doing the same. The* **Bored girls** *firmly keeping their shoes and socks on.*

Bored girls
    It's borin'
    It's bleedin' borin'
    It's only a load of sand
    An' seagulls squawkin'

Bored 1

God, we've been here bloody hours
Can't we go home yet?

Bored 2

Look at the water

Bored 1

Water's borin'
All it does is make y' wet

Both

Yeh it's borin'
Really borin'.

Kids

We're gonna find some thingies
In the pools and in the rocks
We're gonna shout an' run about
Without our shoes and socks

They do until almost as one the immensity of the place hits them. They each stand, transfixed, looking out to sea and squelching their toes in the wet sand. Music slow and wave-like.

The sea's gi-bleedin-gantic
It must be really wide
Cos we can't even see
What's over on the other side

The sound of the ocean.

Driver *running on with a ball.*

Driver   Mrs Kay, all right if I take some of them off for a game of footie?

Mrs Kay   Yes.

Carol (*tugging at* **Mrs Kay**'s *sleeve as some of the* **Kids** *rush off with* **Ronny**)   Miss, when do we have to go home?

Mrs Kay   What's the matter love? Aren't you enjoying yourself?

Carol   Yeh. But I don't wanna go home. I wanna stay here.

Mrs Kay   Carol love, we're here for at least another hour yet. Now why don't you start enjoying yourself instead of worrying about going home.

Carol   Cos I don't wanna go home.

Mrs Kay   Carol love, we have to go home in the end. This is a special day. It can't be like this all the time.

Carol   Why not?

Mrs Kay (*looks at her and sighs. Puts her arm around her*)   I don't know, love. Come on, let's go and play football with the others.

Carol   Nah. (*She breaks away and wanders off.*)

Mrs Kay (*watching her for a moment and then turning to the two* **Bored girls**)   Come on you two; let's go and play football.

Bored 1   Miss what for?

Mrs Kay   What for? Oh, you don't like football. (*Suddenly mimicking them.*) Football's borin', it's dead borin', it's borin' borin' borin'.

They look at her as though she's lost a screw.

Bored 1   We like football.

Mrs Kay   Well come on then. (*Beginning to go.*) Come on.

Bored 2   Miss where?

Mrs Kay (*almost screaming*)   To play football, you said you liked football. Well?

Bored 1   We do on the telly!

Bored 2   Don't like playin' it though. Playin' football's dead . . .

Mrs Kay, *hands outstretched to throttle them both, rushing at them, and the two* **Girls** *suddenly moving. The* **Girls** *being chased off by* **Mrs Kay**.

Colin, **Susan**, **Linda**, **Jackie** *and other* **Girls** *are examining the rock pools.* **Reilly**, **Digga** *and a small group of followers are having* *a smoke behind some large rocks.* **Reilly** *comes out from behind the rocks and shouts over to* **Susan**.

Reilly   All right, miss?

Colin (*quietly*)   Here we go.

Andrews (*to* **Reilly**)   Gis a drag.

Digga   Buy your own.

Andrews   Don't be a rat. Come on.

Reilly *holds out the butt.* **Andrews** *goes to take it but before he can,* **Reilly** *drops it into the sand and treads on it.*

Reilly (*shouting across*)   Y' comin' for a walk with me, miss?

Colin (*standing and shouting back*)   Look I'm warning you Reilly . . .

Susan   Leave it . . .

Colin   I'm just about sick of him.

Susan   Well go over and have a word with him.

Colin   I've tried that but whatever I do I can't seem to get through to friend Brian.

Susan   I wonder if I could.

Reilly (*shouting over*)   What are y' scared of, miss?

Susan (*to* **Colin**)   You go back with the others.

Colin   What are you going to . . .

Susan   Go on . . .

Colin *and the group of* **Girls** *begin to move away.*

Linda   Is miss gonna sort him out, sir?

Jackie   He needs sortin' out doesn't he, sir?

Linda   He's all right really y' know, sir. He's great when y' get him on his own.

Jackie   Oh! An' how do you know?

Linda   I just do.

They go off and **Susan** *begins to walk towards* **Reilly***, slow and determined, staring straight at him, provocative.* **Reilly***'s smile begins to disappear and he gulps for air.* **Susan** *steps straight up to him, pins him against the rocks.*

Susan (*husky*)   Well Brian . . . I'm here.

Reilly   'Ey miss.

Susan   I'm all yours . . . handsome . . . sexy . . . Brian!

Reilly   Don't mess miss.

Susan (*putting her arms around him*)   I'm not messing, Big Boy. I'm very, very serious.

Briggs *suddenly enters, sees what he thinks is happening, turns and exits again.* **Susan** *unaware of him.*

Susan   What's wrong?

Reilly   I was only havin' a laugh, miss.

Susan   You mean . . . don't tell me you weren't being serious, Brian.

Reilly   I was only jokin' with y', miss.

Susan (*dropping the act*)   Now you listen to me Brian Reilly, you're a handsome lad, but I suggest that in future you stay in your own league, instead of trying to take on ladies who could break you into little pieces. All right? We'll leave it at that shall we?

Reilly   Yes, miss.

She smiles at him, touches his arm affectionately and turns to walk away. As she does so a pile of jeering faces appear from behind the rocks where they've been hiding and listening.

Susan (*turning back*)   Clear off all of you. Go and play football or something. I said go!

They do.

Brian.

She motions him to join her. He does.

You know what I was saying about leagues? Well have you ever thought about whose league Linda's in?

Reilly   Linda Croxley? She doesn't fancy me. She's mad about sir. No one else can get a look in.

Susan   I wouldn't be too sure about that. (*Sings.*)
I know you like her
Yes you do, you know you do
I can't be sure but
I think that she likes you.

Reilly   Ah go way, miss. You're nuts.

Susan
Maybe, if you asked her
Out one night, she'd like to go
Anyway, no harm done
The worst thing she can say is 'no'

Reilly   No chance.

Susan
Perhaps you think you'd never stand a chance with her
Maybe never ever get a second glance from her
So where the hell's your confidence
All you need's a bit of nerve

Reilly   I'm no good at . . .

Susan
Don't put yourself down
Can't you see you're not so bad (*She gives him her compact mirror.*)
Take a look at your reflection
There you'll see a handsome lad

Reilly, *smiling and flattered*.

Susan
Perhaps you think you'd never stand a chance with her
Maybe never ever get a second glance from her
So where the hell's your confidence
All you need's a bit of nerve

I know you like her
Yes you do, you know you do
I can't be sure but
I think that she likes you. (*Repeat.*) She likes you.

(*Spoken.*) See you Brian.

Reilly   See y' miss.

He turns and walks to his mates. They begin jeering and laughing but he stands smiling and proud.

Reilly   Well! At least I'm not like you ugly gets. *I* . . . am handsome!

More jeers.

Ronny, **Mrs Kay** *and the footballers rush on playing and* **Reilly** *and the others join the game.*

Mrs Kay (*as* **Reilly** *scores and she gives up being goalie*)   Whoooh. I've had enough, I'm all in.

Maurice   Ah miss, we've got no goalie now.

Mrs Kay   Carol can go in goal. (*To* **Susan** *and* **Colin** *who are just approaching*.) Where is she?

Susan   Who?

Kids *all exit.*

Mrs Kay   Carol, I thought she was with you.

Colin   We haven't seen her for hours.

Mrs Kay   I thought . . . You haven't seen her at all?

Susan   We thought she was here.

Mrs Kay (*looking around*)   Oh, she couldn't, could she?

Susan   Lost?

Mrs Kay   Don't say it. Perhaps he's seen her. (*Shouting across to* **Briggs**.) Mr Briggs . . . Mr Briggs . . .

Briggs *enters.*

Briggs   Is that it then? Are we going home?

Mrs Kay   Have you seen Carol Chandler in the last hour?

Briggs   I thought I'd made it quite plain that I was having nothing more to do with your outing.

Mrs Kay   Have you seen Carol Candler?

Briggs   No, I haven't.

Mrs Kay   I think she may have wandered off somewhere.

Briggs   You mean you've lost her?

Mrs Kay   No. I mean she might have wandered off somewhere!

Briggs   Well what's that if it's not losing her? All I can say is it's a wonder you haven't lost half a dozen of them. (*He turns to go.*)

Colin   Listen Briggs, it's about time someone told you what a berk you . . .

Briggs (*wheels on him*)   And you listen! Sonny! Don't you try to tell me a thing, because you haven't even earned the right. Don't you worry, when we get back to school your number's up, as well as hers (**Mrs Kay**). And you (**Susan**). Yes. I saw what was going on between you and Reilly. When we get back I'll have the lot of you.

Mrs Kay   Would you mind postponing your threats until we find Carol Chandler? At the moment I'd say the most important thing is to find the girl.

Briggs   Don't you mean *try* and find her?

Mrs Kay   Susan, you keep the rest of them playing football. We'll split up and look for her.

They go off in separate directions.

We see **Carol**. *She is standing on a cliff, looking out, waving at seagulls.*

Carol (*sings*)
   Why can't it always be this way?
   Why can't it last for more than just a day?
   The sun in the sky and the seagulls flying by

I think I'd like to stay
Then it could always be this way

Why can't it always be like this?
I can't think of anything back home that I would miss
Suppose there'd be a fuss if I wasn't on the bus
But it really would be bliss
If it could always be like this

Shouting to the seagulls
Seagulls say 'hello'
Wonder how they stay up there so high
Looking at the seashore miles and miles below
Makes me wish that I could fly

Why can't we just stay where we are?
Far far away from the muck and motor cars
If I close my eyes and try and try and try
And wish upon a star
Then we could all just stay where we are

As the song ends, **Briggs** *appears on the cliffs and sees* **Carol**.

Briggs   Carol Chandler, just come here. Who gave you permission to come on these cliffs?

Carol (*moving to the edge*)   No one. (*She turns and dismisses him.*)

Briggs   I'm talking to you Miss Chandler.

She continues to ignore his presence.

Now just listen here young lady . . .

Carol (*suddenly turning*)   Don't you come near me!

Briggs (*taken aback by her vehemence, he stops*)   Pardon?

Carol   I don't want you to come near me.

Briggs   Well in that case just get yourself moving and let's get down to the beach.

Carol   You go. *I'm* not comin'.

Briggs   You what?

Carol   Tell Mrs Kay she can go home without me. I'm stoppin' here, by the sea.

Pause.

Briggs   Now you just listen to me. I've had just about enough today, just about enough and I'm not putting up with a pile of silliness from the likes of you. Now come on!

He starts towards her but she moves to the very edge of the cliff.

Carol   Try an' get me an' I'll jump over.

Briggs *stops in his tracks, astounded and angered.*

Briggs (*shouting*)   Listen you stupid girl, get yourself over here this minute.

She ignores him.

I'll not tell you again!

They stare at each other. It's obvious that she will not do as he bids.

I'll give you five seconds! Just five seconds. One, two, three, four, I'm warning you! . . . Five.

Carol   I've told y', I'm not comin' with y'. I will jump y' know. I will.

Briggs   Just what are you tryin' to do to me?

Carol   I've told y', just leave me alone an' I won't jump. (*Pause.*) I wanna stay here where it's nice.

Briggs   Stay here? How could you stay here? What would you do eh? Where would you live?

Carol   I'd be all right.

Briggs   I've told you, stop being silly.

Carol (*turning on him*)   What are you worried for eh? You don't care do y'? Do y'?

Briggs   What? About you? . . . Listen, if I didn't care, why would I be up here now, trying to stop you doing something stupid?

Carol Because if I jumped over, you'd get into trouble when you get back to school. That's why Briggsy, so stop goin' on. You hate me.

Briggs Don't be ridiculous. Just because I'm a schoolteacher it doesn't mean to say that . . .

Carol Don't lie, you! I know you hate me. I've seen you goin' home in your car, passin' us on the street. An' the way you look at us. You hate all the kids.

Briggs What . . . why do you say that?

Carol Why can't I just stay out here an' live in one of them nice white houses, an' do the garden an' that?

Briggs Look . . . Carol . . . You're talking as though you've given up on life. It sounds as though life for you is ending, instead of just beginning. Now why can't . . . I mean, if that's what you want . . . why can't . . . what's to stop you working hard at school from now on, getting a good job and then moving out here when you're old enough? Eh?

Carol (*she turns and looks at him with pure contempt*) Don't be so bloody stupid. (*She turns and looks out to the sea.*) It's been a great day today. I loved it. I don't wanna leave here an' go home. (*Pause.*) If I stayed it wouldn't be any good though, would it? You'd send the coppers to get me, wouldn't y'?

Briggs We'd have to. How would you survive out here?

Carol I know. (*Pause.*) I'm not goin' back though.

She kneels at the cliff edge, looks over.

Briggs Carol . . . please . . .

Carol Sir . . . you know if you'd been my old feller . . . I would've been all right wouldn't I?

Briggs *slowly and cautiously creeping forward, holding out his hand.*

Briggs Carol, please come away from there.

She looks down over the cliff.

Please.

Carol   Sir . . . sir you don't half look funny y' know.

Briggs (*smiling*)   Why?

Carol   Sir, you should smile more often. You look great when y' smile.

Briggs (*holding out his hand*)   Come on, Carol.

Carol   Sir . . . what'll happen to me for doin' this?

Briggs   Nothing . . . I promise.

Carol   Sir, you're promisin' now, but what about back at school?

Briggs   It won't even be mentioned, I promise . . .

His hand outstretched. She decides to believe him. She reaches out for his hand. As she does, she slips but he manages to lunge forward and clasp her to safety. He stands with his arms wrapped around her.

The other **Kids** *playing football.* **Reilly** *with the ball trying to get past a huge row of defenders.*

Linda (*from the side of the game*)   Go on Brian, go on, go on . . . (*As he scores.*) Yes.

Reilly *letting on to her.*

Mrs Kay (*entering, shaking her head to* **Susan**)   I think we better let the police know.

Susan   Shall I keep them playing . . . (*She sees* **Briggs** *and* **Carol** *enter.*) Oh look . . . he's found her.

Colin   I'll bet he makes a bloody meal out of this.

Susan   It doesn't matter. She's safe, that's the main thing.

Colin   We'd better round them up. It'll be straight home now.

Colin *begins to do so.*

Mrs Kay (*approaching* **Briggs** *and* **Carol**)   Carol where were you?

Carol   On the cliff, miss.

Mrs Kay   On the . . .

Briggs   It's all right Mrs Kay, we've been through all that. Now. If you'll just let me deal with this.

Mrs Kay *putting her arm around* **Carol**.

Mrs Kay   Carol! The worry you've caused. Oh . . . love . . .

Briggs   Come on . . . everyone on the coach.

Driver   Back to the school then?

Briggs   School? Back to school? It's still early isn't it? Anyway – you can't come all the way to the seaside and not pay a visit to the fair.

Music intro begins.

Carol (*rushing to the other* **Kids**)   We're goin' the fair, sir's takin' us to the fair.

Briggs (*turning to* **Mrs Kay** *who still can't believe her ears*)   You never know, Mrs Kay – play your cards right an' I might take you for a ride on the waltzer!

The benches have been formed in a circle to represent a waltzer onto which everyone piles.

All (*sing*)
  We're goin' on the waltzer
  We gonna have some fun
  Gonna get dead dizzy
  Gonna get well spun
  Hold your belly, gasp for air
  Ooh! Ooh feel the wind in your hair

  Sir's on the waltzer
  He's takin' us to the fair

  We're goin' on the dodgems
  And on the ferris wheel
  Going on the ghost train
  Gonna giggle and scream
  Don't know who's scared the most
  Digga or Reilly or the bleedin' ghost

Sir's on the dodgems
He's takin' us to the fair

We've never seen him laugh before
He's not like this in school
It must be something in the air
That makes him play the fool

Candy floss and hot dogs
Gonna get real sick
Look at old Briggsy
In a kiss-me-quick
Big dipper? Yes sir please
Hold on everybody now
Say cheese . . .

Everybody forming into a group for **Mrs Kay**'s *camera. Everyone holding the note on the word 'cheese'.*

In this pause the two **Bored girls** *are apart from the rest of the group.*

Bored 1   What d' y' think?

Bored 2   The fair?

Bored 1   Yeh.

Bored 2 (*considers*)   Borin'!

As everybody leaps back onto the waltzer.

All (*sing*)
Sir's on the waltzer
He's takin' us to the fair

Repeat the middle eight.
Repeat final verse.
Big finish on last line, ending with **Briggs** *being lifted onto shoulders by a group of* **Kids** *and being photographed by* **Mrs Kay**.

Briggs   Last one on the coach pays the fare.

The **Kids** *singing without accompaniment as they re-form the coach.*

Kids
Everywhere we go
Everywhere we go
People wanna know
People wanna know
Who we are
Who we are
So we tell them
So we tell them
We are the Progress
The mighty mighty Progress

The coach re-formed and nearly everyone on board. **Ronson** *running up to the coach and* **Briggs**, *who is standing waiting for him.*

Ronson   Sir, that was great that, it was great.

Briggs   Come on.

Ronson   Sir, can we come again tomorrow?

Briggs   Oh get on the bus, Ronson.

Piano underscore – 'Coming Round The Mountain'.

As **Briggs** *and* **Ronson** *get on board the coach pulls away. Everyone is singing – 'Coming Round The Mountain'.* **Digga** *and* **Jackie** *are sitting together.* **Reilly** *is with* **Linda**, *arm around her.*

Briggs *is sitting on the back seat with the* **Kids**. **Mrs Kay** *stands and takes a picture of* **Briggs** *and the* **Kids**. **Briggs** *still with a cowboy hat he got at the fair.*

Mrs Kay   Say cheese.

Kids
Singin' aya aye yippee yippee aye
Singin' aya aye yippee yippee aye
Singin' aya aye yippee
Me mother's gone the chippy
Singin' aya aye yippee yippee aye

The **Kids** *begin to repeat the next verse but weariness and tiredness overcome them and the song until most of them are asleep or dozing.*

Piano continues underscoring the song.

Briggs *wearing the cowboy hat makes his way along the aisle. When he reaches* **Mrs Kay** *she turns the camera on him. It is as if at that moment the flashlight signals the beginning of a return to reality for* **Mr Briggs***. He becomes conscious of the hat he is wearing and, smiling at* **Mrs Kay** *he removes it and places it on the head of the sleeping* **Carol** *(who clutches hold of her goldfish won at the fair).* **Mrs Kay** *is putting the completed film in packet for processing, she turns to* **Briggs***, indicating the film.*

Mrs Kay   I've got some gems of you in here. We'll have one of these up in the staff room when they're developed.

Briggs   Eh? One of me? What for?

Mrs Kay   Don't worry . . . I'm not going to let you forget the day you enjoyed yourself.

Briggs *(watching her put the film in the envelope)*   Look, erm . . . why don't you let me develop those? I could do them in the lab.

Mrs Kay   I don't know . . . using school facilities for personal use. *(She hands them over.)* Thank you.

Briggs   Have them done as soon as I can.

He sits.

Linda *(to* **Reilly***)*   Are y' glad y' came?

Reilly   Yeh.

Linda   It was great wasn't it eh?

Reilly   It'll be the last trip I go on.

Linda   Why?

Reilly   I'm leavin' in the summer aren't I?

Linda   What y' gonna do?

Reilly   Nothin' I suppose . . . *(He looks out of the window.)* It's bleedin' horrible when y' look at it isn't it?

Linda   What?

Reilly *(nods – indicating the city)*   That. Liverpool.

Linda   Yeh.

'Coming Round The Mountain' underscoring ends as the coach stops.

Briggs   Right. Come on, everybody off.

Cue intro music for 'We Had A Really Great Day Out'.

During the following all the seats of the coach removed.

Kids
    We had a really great day out
    We went to the beach and went daft and ran about
    We went to the zoo
    And the fair and castle too
    And Briggsy let us sing and shout
    Coming back from our day out

Briggs   OK. Everybody off.

Ronny
    That's the end of that one, see y' all take care
    Better get off home now to me wife
    Out tomorrow morning
    No idea where
    It's a funny way of life

Kids
    Thanks Ron, we had a lovely day
    Thanks sir and miss, it was cracker Mrs Kay
    The best we ever had
    Even Briggsy's not so bad
    Never seen him act that way
    He must have had a lovely day

All
    Climbing off the bus now
    Back in Liverpool
    Better get off home now for me tea
    Looking at the streets, the playground and the school
    Seems a long way from the sea

Continue melody as underscoring.

Everybody is now off the coach. **Ronny** *and various* **Kids** *have moved off.* **Reilly** *and* **Linda**, *arms around each other pass* **Mr Briggs**.

Melody of 'We Had A Really Great Day Out' continues to underscore following dialogue.

Reilly   'Night sir. Enjoyed yourself today didn't y' sir?

Briggs   Pardon?

Reilly   I didn't know you was like that sir – all right for a laugh an that. See y' tomorrow sir.

Briggs (*nods goodbye to them then suddenly calls after them*)   Oh . . . Linda.

She stops and turns.

We erm . . . we'll let the uniform go this time. But don't let me catch you dressing like that again on a school outing.

Reilly *and* **Linda** *exit.*

Bored girl 1   Wasn't that a great day?

Bored girl 2   It was cracker. Come on.

They run off.

Mrs Kay   Well that seems to be it. (*She sees* **Carol** *hovering nearby.*) Are you going home Carol?

From off we hear a whistle and **Ronny** *enters.*

Ronny   Erm, excuse me madam, have you lost a small python?

Mrs Kay (*just for a second thinking, as do we, that it might be true*)   What!

From behind his back **Ronny** *produces the goldfish in the plastic bag.*

Ronny (*as he hands it to* **Carol**)   They always forget somethin'.

Mrs Kay   Thanks Ronny.

Ronny   Thanks Helen. Goodnight. (*To others as he exits.*) Bye now. See y'.

Colin
Susan } Goodnight.
Briggs

Mrs Kay Well that's that. I don't know about anyone else but I'm for a drink.

Susan Oh I'll second that.

Colin They'll just be open.

Mrs Kay (*to* **Briggs**) You going to join us?

Briggs Oh . . . well actually I've . . .

Susan Oh come on.

Briggs No, I'd er . . . I'd better not. Thanks anyway. I've got lots of marking to do at home. Thanks all the same.

Mrs Kay Well if we can't twist your arm . . . . Thanks for today.

She turns and leads the others off, failing to see **Carol** *hovering in the shadows.*

Mrs Kay Car's over here.

Mrs Kay, Colin *and* **Susan** *exit.*

Briggs *reaches into his pocket for his car keys. Along with the keys he brings out the package containing the film. He stands, looking at the package, unaware of the* **Kids: Reilly, Andrews, Jackie, Carol, Digga, Maurice, Ronson, Milton, Linda, Little Kid, Bored girls** *and every other one of them, appearing individually from behind him and watching him.*

Carol *walks forward out of the shadows as* **Briggs** *suddenly makes his decision and exposes the roll of film. He turns and sees* **Carol**, *watching him along with all the other* **Kids. Carol** *moves off as if to home. From off we hear:*

Parent Carol! Where the friggin' hell have you been? Just get in this bloody house.

Kids: *to the same tune as 'We Had A Really Great Day Out' but note use of repeated (or double middle eight) melody.*

As **Briggs** *slowly walks past them all.*

No one can take this time away
No matter what they cannot take the day
No one can steal
Something you just feel
And although the picture fades
No one can take this time away

Just as **Briggs** *is about to exit,* **Carol** *enters and for a brief moment they are face to face before* **Briggs** *moves off.* **Carol** *takes her place in the tableau, amongst the other kids.*

Note the double eight.

Someone said the pictures
Just didn't turn out right
Someone said the shutter had been closed
Someone said the camera
Was pointing at the light
And the film had been exposed

But who needs a picture
Pictures always fade
Get lost or just get stuck behind a drawer
And I can always find
A picture in my mind
Of some far distant shore

No one can take this time away
No matter what they do no matter what they say
We couldn't give a shit 'cos it was

(*Spoken*:)
Brilliant
                    Magic
                            Fit!
And although the picture fades

But instead of it being the last line of this verse, the following becomes the first *line of a reprised first verse, sung by all.*

No one can take this time away
No matter what they cannot take the day

No one can steal
Something you just feel
And although the picture fades
No one can take this time away.

Curtain.

Music for the Play

WE'RE GOIN' OUT

2 KIDS

'Hia Les' We're Goin' Out.

+ 2 KIDS **+ MORE**

Just For The Day, Go-in Off Somewhere Far Aw-ay Out To The Country.

ALL

Maybe To The Sea, Me Mam Says I Can Go If It's Free The

Sky Is Blue, The Sun's Gonna Shine Better Hurry Up Cos It's Near-Ly Nine

This Is A Day That's Just For Us We're Goin' Out. — On A Bus.

MRS KAY'S PROGRESS CLASS

CUE: MR BRIGGS 'THAT'S WHY THE GOVERNMENT HIRED ME'   SUNG AS ROUND

① ②

Mis-ses Kay's Progress Class We're The Ones Who Never Pass

We're Go-in Out. Off With Mis-ses Kay We're Goin' Out To-Day

BOSS OF THE BUS

CUE: DRIVER 'MISS IS NOT THE DRIVER OF THIS BUS . . . I AM!'

BOSS OF THE BUS (continued)

INSTRUCTIONS ON ENJOYMENT

<u>N.B.</u> 'THEY'LL BE NO SHOUTING' IS DIALOGUE AND RETURNS TO STRICT TEMPO
AFTER BRIGGS 'NO SIR' FROM 'TO ENJOY THIS TREAT
DIALOGUE TO END

WE'RE OFF

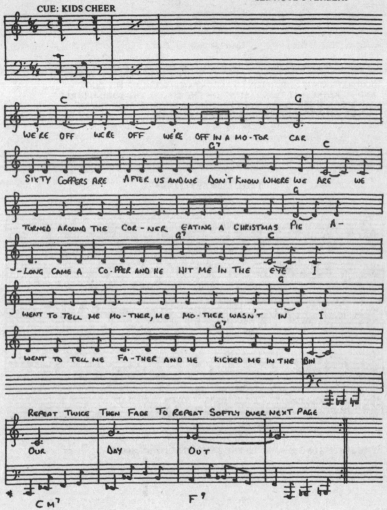

*SEE NOTE OVERLEAF

LOOK AT THE DOGS

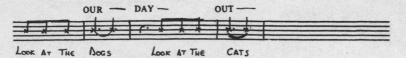

OUR — DAY — OUT —

LOOK AT THE DOGS   LOOK AT THE CATS

CONTINUE DIALOGUE IN RHYTHM WITH 'OUR DAY OUT' MELODY TO FADE.
*THE RIFF IN THE LEFT HAND USED AS ACCOMPANIMENT TO 'OUR DAY
OUT' REFRAIN IS ALSO USED TO ACCOMPANY 'LOOK AT THE DOGS'
AND TO REPRESENT TIME PASSING ON THE COACH. THE BORING GIRLS
CAN SPEAK THEIR VERSE OVER IT AND THE CHORDS, ALSO SHOWN,
CAN BE USED TO UNDERSCORE THE TOILET STOP.

THE MERSEY TUNNEL

*SEE NOTE

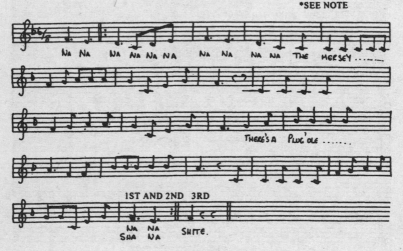

*THE BEACH SONG IS SUNG TO THE SAME MELODY AS ABOVE

STRAIGHT LINE

N.B. FOLLOW NOTES IN SCRIPT

STRAIGHT LINE (2)

2ND TIME TO

2ND TIME (Thing They'll Never Look)

(1.) TUR-NING SOUR

It's

AL-RIGHT EVERY BO-DY THERE WILL . . . .

STRAIGHT LINE (3)

AL -

Come On Get In Line, Get In Line Do What You're Told   For A
2(BETTER THAN A RABBLE)

D   E   A

Straight Line   is   a   Wonderful Thing To Behold.

B   E   A

PENNY CHEWS

Penny Chews are ....

F   C   F   F[7]

B[b]   B[b]M   F   C   F

I'M IN LOVE WITH SIR

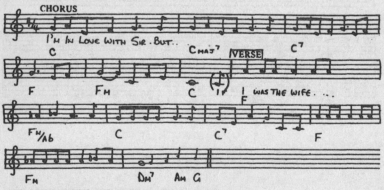

CHORUS

I'm In Love With Sir . But..

C   Cmaj[7]   VERSE   C[7]

F   FM   C   if   I was the wife. ...
                              F

FM/Ab   C   C[7]   F

FM   DM[7]   AM   G

N.B. SONG BEGINS AND ENDS UNACCOMPANIED

ZOO SONG

*SEE NOTES

*A JUNGLE RHYTHM SHOULD PREVAIL THROUGHOUT, NO OTHER
ACCOMPANIMENT IS NECESSARY BUT COULD BE TRIED.

*THE CHANTING OF THE PHRASE 'WHO'S WATCHING WHO' AT THE
BEGINNING AND THE BORED GIRLS VERSE CAN BOTH BE SPOKEN OVER
A SUITABLE RHYTHM. THE DRUMS CAN ALSO BE USED QUIETLY BEHIND
DIALOGUE SECTIONS.

CASTLE SONG

CASTLE SONG (2)

N.B. MUSIC CONTINUES BEHIND DIALOGUE

I KNOW YOU LIKE HER

WHY CAN'T IT ALWAYS BE THIS WAY

AND: WE HAD A REALLY GREAT DAY OUT

N.B. FOR 'WE HAD A REALLY GREAT DAY OUT' USE CHORDS MORE RHYTHM –
CALLY & PLAY 3RD VERSE AS GENTLE INSTRUMENTAL BEHIND DIALOGUE UNTIL
DRIVER SINGS 'THAT'S THE END OF THAT ONE' TO TUNE OF 'SHOUTING AT THE
SEAGULLS', THEN CAROL SINGS 'WHY CAN'T IT ALWAYS BE LIKE THAT' TO VERSE
TUNE, THEN INSTRUMENTAL VERSION TO END OF PLAY. TRY TO REACH PIANO
LINE IN BAR 8 AS CAROL & BRIGGS PASS ON STAGE.

FAIRGROUND SONG

INTRO

AS MANY BARS OF STRAIGHT ROCK & ROLL
AS IT TAKES TO SET BENCHES

VERSE

F WE'RE GOING ON THE   WALTZER

Bb GONNA GET ....   F

F   C OR A7   Bb   C7

CHORUS

F SHE'S ON THE ... D ..   G   C7   F

MIDDLE 8

Bb WE'VE NEVER SEEN HIM .. ....   F

MIDDLE 8

Bb   C PLAY THE FO—OL ......

EVERYWHERE WE GO

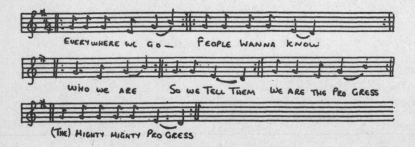

EVERYWHERE WE GO —   PEOPLE WANNA KNOW

WHO WE ARE   SO WE TELL THEM WE ARE THE PRO GRESS

(THE) MIGHTY MIGHTY PRO GRESS

Stags and Hens

Stags and Hens was first produced at the Everyman Theatre, Liverpool, in October, 1978, with the following cast:

Linda	Anne-Louise Wakefield
Maureen	Barbara Peirson
Bernadette	Cecily Hobbs
Carol	Donna Champion
Frances	Lola Young
Dave	
Robbie	Philip Donaghy
Billy	Christopher Martin
Kav	Chris Darwin
Eddy	Edward Clayton
Peter	Richard Clay Jones
Roadie	

Directed by Chris Bond
Designed by Billy Meall

Stags and Hens was subsequently produced in London at the Young Vic in July 1984 with the following cast:

Maureen	Eithne Browne
Bernadette	Noreen Kershaw
Carol	Gilly Coman
Frances	Kate Fitzgerald
Linda	Ann Miles
Robbie	Nick Maloney
Kav	Graham Fellows
Billy	Ray Kingsley
Eddy	Matthew Marsh
Peter	Peter Christian
Roadie	Andrew Secombe
Dave	Vivian Munn

Directed by David Thacker
Décor by Shelagh Killeen

Author's Note
Although the use of music is not specified in the text, I envisage that in production, as the main doors are opened and closed, we would hear snatches of the music being played in the dance hall.

References to media people – e.g. Rod Stewart, Mick Jagger etc. can be updated.

W.R.

Act One

The Ladies and Gents in a Liverpool dance hall. Evening. Stevie Wonder's 'Superstition' is playing. The song fades and we hear, coming in over it, the sound of girls singing.

Girls (*off*)
    She's gettin' married in the morning
    Ding dong the bells are gonna chime
    Pull out his chopper
    Oogh what a whopper
    Get me to the church on time . . .

The **Girls** *come into the Ladies.* **Linda**, *the obvious subject of their song, goes straight into a WC and closes the door. The remaining* **Girls** *begin to make-up.*

Maureen (*crying*)   Congratulations Linda. Congratulations.

Bernadette   What's up with you now?

Maureen   I don't know.

Bernadette   Cryin'! On a hen night! It's supposed to be a happy night.

Maureen (*bawling*)   I am happy. I'm very happy . . . for Linda.

Carol (*calling out to* **Linda**)   We're all happy for y' Linda. Ogh Lind, you lucky sod!

Frances   Just imagine Lind, after tomorrow you'll have your own flat, your own feller. You'll be a married woman.

Bernadette   You'll have your own front room, your own Hoover, your own telly.

Maureen (*crying*)   Your own husband . . .

Carol   Agh yeh. He's great Dave isn't he? He's a great feller. He's really dynamic isn't he?

Frances   He's good lookin'.

Bernadette   An' he's a worker isn't he? I mean he's not like some of them is he?

Carol   They wouldn't lift a finger some of them, would they?

Bernadette   Her feller's not like that though, is he?

Carol   I'll bet he helps in the house an' that. I'll bet y' he does.

Bernadette   Some fellers wouldn't, would they? My feller doesn't. Wouldn't lift a bloody finger. He wouldn't get out that chair if the roof was comin' through. Idle, y' know, that type! The kids call him the reluctant plumber . . . never does a tap!

Frances   Her Dave won't be like that though.

Carol   Agh no, Dave'll be great in the house.

Maureen   I'll bet he even helps when the little ones come along. (*She cries.*)

Frances   Will you shut it!

Bernadette   For Christ's sake Maureen, tonight's supposed to be a celebration, not a wake.

Maureen   I am celebrating. I'm celebrating for Linda. It's just . . . just that I wish it was me . . .

Frances   Well never mind Maureen . . . your turn'll come.

Maureen(*brightening*)   D' y' think so? D' y' really think so?

Frances   Yeh . . . you'll be all right. You've just got to meet the feller who appreciates your sort of looks.

Maureen   What sort of looks?

Frances   Well y' know sort of er, y' know . . . (*Looking round for assistance.*) er . . .

Carol (*calling*)   Agh God . . . I'm so happy for y' Lind.

Bernadette   I can't wait t' see her in church tomorrow.

Carol   Agh I'll bet she looks lovely in white as well. Have y' seen her dress Mo?

Maureen   When I was round there last week her mum said she'd show it me. But I couldn't bring meself to look. I would have cried. I cry very easily.

Frances   We wouldn't have known.

Carol   I saw it. Oh it's gorgeous, y' know, just off the shoulder.

Frances   It's the new length, isn't it?

Carol   Y' know, with the lace, across here Mo.

Frances   The back's lovely isn't it Carol?

Carol   Oh the back's superb. It's got no back. Haven't you seen it Berni?

Bernadette   No . . . I like to save it for the actual day. I like to get me first glimpse of it in church.

Carol   Agh that's nice isn't it eh? That's really nice Bern.

Bernadette (*calling*)   We're all so happy for y' Linda.

Frances   What makes it really special is that it's Linda.

Carol   Ogh I know. I always thought Linda'd be the last one to get married, if she ever got married at all. Oh not 'cos she isn't eligible. She is, she's very eligible.

Bernadette   She could have been a model if she'd wanted to.

Carol   Ogh I know. No I'm not saying that. What I mean is . . . Linda was always like sort of independent wasn't she? Y' know what I mean?

Murmurs of agreement.

Like she wouldn't take things seriously would she? An' then she just announces that she's gettin' married. An' she's not in the club or anythin' like that, is she?

Bernadette   Love, Carol. Love changes you. Love makes you grow up.

Carol   Tch. Ah . . . I'm glad. I'm so glad for y' Linda.

Bernadette   I know she'll be very happy with Dave. Now it'd be a different matter if it was someone like my feller she was marryin'! Man? My feller? He's an apology! I said to him, last night, I was feelin' a bit turned on, y' know, an' he's lyin' there, snorin' again; that type he is, y' know, head hits the pillow an' he's straight asleep. I looked at him, lyin' there an' I said to him, I said . . . 'Hey, it's a bloody good job they didn't have the Trades Descriptions Act when they christened you Dick!'

The **Girls** *laugh.*

Frances   Go away Berni. The poor feller's probably worn out with you. You'd be moanin' about not gettin' enough if y' were married to Rod Stewart.

Bernadette   You what? 'Ey I bet me an' Rod'd get on like a house on fire.

Carol   Oh imagine bein' married to someone like Rod Stewart. You'd have your own big house, servants, a swimming pool, all the clothes y' wanted.

Maureen   It might all look glamorous Carol, but fame has its drawbacks though.

Bernadette   Eh, I'd risk it. Wouldn't you Carol . . . whoa, spit on me Rod!

Maureen   No, but honestly Berni, it's true y' know . . . the price of fame is a big one.

The **Girls** *shriek.*

Maureen   What? . . . What's up Oh 'ey . . . y' know I didn't mean it like that . . . that's awful . . . eh . . . look, I've smudged me eye now . . . I've got half an eye on me nose . . .

Frances Oh come here. (*She does her make-up for her.*)

Carol 'Ey . . . what y' drinkin' tonight?

Maureen I'm goin' on brandy an' Babychams. I could drink them all night.

Frances Yeh, an' y' probably will knowin' you.

Carol You wanna try Pernod an' black, Mo. It's great.

Frances Y' don't wanna drink too much tonight. Save y'selves for tomorrow.

Carol The fellers won't be doin' that will they?

Bernadette Y' can bet they'll be pourin' it down them like it's goin' out of fashion.

Maureen Where are they havin' the stag night?

Frances Dave wouldn't tell Linda where they were goin'.

Carol I'll bet they've gone to a stag club, watchin' those films . . .

Bernadette Tch. An' here's us come to a borin' dance.

Carol Go way Berni. We don't wanna be watchin' blue films.

Bernadette 'Ey, you speak for yourself.

Maureen What are they like Carol?

Carol Horrible. All sex.

Bernadette Great!

Carol They're not like *Emmanuelle* Mo, that's a lovely film. But with the blue films it's just sex, y' know for the sake of it. With *Emmanuelle* it's like beautiful an' romantic, all in slow motion, now that's how sex should be. All soft an' in colour.

Bernadette That's how it should be Carol, but it never is love.

Carol It can be. With the right man it can. I'm not interested in fellers who want to make sex. I want a feller who makes love, not a feller who makes sex.

Maureen   I just want a feller.

Bernadette   Y' know when my feller was young –

Frances   Young? Christ Berni he's only about thirty-two now, isn't he?

Bernadette   Yeah, but I'm talking about young inside; I mean he might be young on the outside, but he's a geriatric inside. No, when me an' him were first married we went on a holiday to Devon. We went the pictures one night and saw this film where this couple kept goin' down to the shore and making love –

Maureen   Ogh . . . I seen that . . . it's great – all the little waves are lappin' over them aren't they, an' the sun's settin', an' all the music an' that . . . It's a great film that . . .

Bernadette   Really beautiful. Magic. So when it was over we come out the pictures an' me an' my feller walked down to the beach, an' honest to God it was just like the film, y' know, deserted it was, the beach. An' the sun was sinkin' into the horizon. There was nothin' but us an' the sound of the sea, just softly lappin' the beach.

Carol   Agh isn't that lovely. It sounds like paradise.

Bernadette   That's what it was like . . . honest. That's just how I felt, like I was standin' on the edge of paradise. (*She pauses.*) An' my feller's got his arm around me, an' he sort of squeezed me an' he said, I'll always remember it, y' know what he said?

All the **Girls** *are wide-eyed in anticipation, shaking their heads.*

'Well are y' gettin' them off or what?'

The **Girls** *laugh.*

Frances   'Ey . . . it'd be great on the films that wouldn't it? Imagine Ryan O'Neal to Ali McGraw? "Ey girl, d' y' fancy a legover?'

Laughter from the **Girls**.

Bernadette Y' see Carol, it's only half of it y' see in the films. I'll tell y' another thing the film didn't mention: the bloody sand gets everywhere!

Maureen (*laughing with the rest of them*)   Agh we're having a great time aren't we? Aren't we eh?

Bernadette We were gonna stay down there in Devon. We didn't though. But y' wanna hear my feller. He's always goin' on about movin' down there – y' know if we go out together an' he has a few jars y' can't shut him up about Devon. I say to him, 'Well let's do it, come on, let's go' . . . but he wakes up the next day and pretends he never said it. I suppose we'll live and die round here.

Carol It's a dump isn't it eh? It's like this place – Christ look at it. Why didn't we go to a club?

Frances Linda wanted to come here. It's her hen night, she chooses where we go.

Carol Why did she choose here though? God it's dyin' on its feet this place.

Frances There's a group on after the disco though, isn't there? She said she wanted to dance to live music not just to records.

Carol I hate groups, they're not half as good as the records. What have they got a group for?

Frances They tryin' t' bring some life back t' the place.

Bernadette It's dyin' this place is.

Frances It's dead.

Carol They'd have to do more than just stick a group on after the disco if they wanted this place to come alive again.

Bernadette It's like everythin' else round here Carol, the life's just drainin' away from the place, but no one ever does anythin' about it. It's like round our way, y' know what they do if a wall's fallin' down – they give it a coat of paint. They do.

Carol   Well I think we should've gone to a club.

Frances   Well we can do that afterwards. But Linda wanted to come here first.

Maureen   'Ey . . . wouldn't it be awful if the fellers turned up as well?

Carol (*shocked*)   Oh God Maureen don't say things like that. If Linda saw Dave on her weddin' night, that'd be it, y' know.

Maureen   I know . . . that's what I'm sayin' – y' marriage would be doomed to perpetual bad luck if y' saw your feller the night before.

Bernadette   'Ey . . . maybe that's what happened to me eh?

Frances   What's she doin' in there anyway? (*She bangs on the WC door.*) Linda . . .

No answer.

Linda! Linda are you comin' out of there?

Linda   No!

We see the foyer doors swing open, **Robbie,** **Billy** *and* **Kav** *are struggling to get the legless* **Dave** *into the Gents.*

Robbie (*to* **Billy**)   Hold the door. Just hold the door will y'.

He does so.

Kav   Jesus!

They get him through the swing doors which **Billy** *continues to hold open.*

Billy   No . . . y' see the problem is that y' not manœuvring him right. You've got to manœuvre correctly. Yeh.

Kav   I'll manœuvre you in a minute.

Billy   What?

Dick   What y' doing?

Billy   I'm holdin' the door like y' said. Yeh.

Robbie   We're in now, dickhead! Come here will y'? Get hold.

*He lets **Billy** take his place. He looks down at the stain on his trousers, holds open the door to the Gents. They begin to get him in.*

Robbie   Agh look at that. Jesus! Curried bleedin' chicken all over me.

Kav   It's disaster for you Robbie. Disaster.

Robbie *begins to help get **Dave** into the Gents.*

Kav   An' that little one was givin' you the big eye on the way in.

Billy   It's all physics y' see. I read about it. Yeh.

Robbie   Was she? Which one?

Kav   Know that little one in the cloakroom?

Robbie   That little one? Looks like Bianca Jagger?

Kav   Yeh . . . that's the one.

Robbie   Was she givin' me the eye?

*They try to get **Dave** into the WC.*

Billy *(as they do so)*   No, see . . . he's a dead weight . . . you've got to take that into account. Yeh.

Robbie   I thought she was givin' me the eye, that one.

Kav   Y' can forget now though can't y'? You've got no chance with spewed curry all over y'. Y'll stink all night like a Chinese chippy.

Robbie   All right, all right. I'll wash it off. Come on, get him sorted out, then I can get me kecks clean.

They get him into the WC.

Where's Eddy? he should be here givin' us a hand.

Kav   He went the bar.

Robbie   As long as he's not tryin' to chat up that little Bianca one.

Kav   No way, I know what Eddy's like. He never chats tarts.

Billy   He gets one when he wants one though. Yeh.

Kav   Yeh, but he doesn't chat them up. He just waits till the end of the night, sees one an' says 'Come here you'! An' they do y' know. But he won't waste his time chattin' them up.

Robbie   He'd have no chance anyway. Not with competition from me. See me when I get out on that floor. They can't take their eyes off me.

Kav   They will when they smell that spewed curry all over y'.

Robbie (*to* **Billy**)   That's you that soft lad! Gettin' us to go the Chinese before we start drinkin' instead of afterwards.

Billy   No y' wrong there Robbie. Yeh. See, I said we should go to the Chinese first 'cos it puts a linin' on y' stomach.

Robbie   Yeh. An' it's put a linin' all over my suit as well!

Kav   Come on . . . lift him so his head's over the bowl.

Billy (*as they struggle with* **Dave**)   I didn't know Robbie. I didn't know he'd start drinking Black Velvets. An' he'd been on double Southern Comforts before that y' know. I said to him 'That's a lethal combination that Dave.' Yeh.

Robbie   Come on . . . lift him . . . an' keep him over that side. If he gets me other leg I'm done for!

They manage to get him arranged. We see only his legs sticking out. They stand back.

Billy   You wanna put your fingers down your throat Dave.

Robbie   You wanna stick y' fingers down your throat. An' keep them there. Give us all a rest.

Billy   I'm only tellin' him Robbie. 'Cos if he got it all up he could start drinkin' again. He's not gonna have much of a stag night if he spends it all in here, is he?

Kav (*looking at* **Dave**)   'Ey it's a good job his tart can't see him now isn't it?

Robbie She'd just laugh, her, she's mental.

Kav She's a good laugh though isn't she? She's all right Linda is.

Robbie She drinks as much as him y' know. I was goin' out with this crackin' tart once, y' know, nice, smart girl she was. We went out on a foursome with Dave an' his tart. I got the first round in, asked them what they were havin'. This girl I'm with she said er, a Babycham or a Pony or somethin', y' know, a proper tarts' drink. Know what Dave's tart asked for eh? A pint of bitter! That's dead true that, she wasn't jokin'. I was dead embarrassed. I'm out with this nice girl for the first time an' Dave's tart's actin' like a docker.

Kav She is a laugh though isn't she?

Robbie Laugh. The one I was with, she never came out with me again after that. I said to Dave after, fancy lettin' your tart behave like that. 'She's always the same,' he said. 'But she'll settle down when she's married.' I wouldn't take the chance.

Billy They do calm down Robbie. Women, y' can't get a laugh out of them once they've turned thirty.

Kav (*beginning to draw on the wall*) I like Linda.

Robbie (*wetting paper towels and beginning to try a repair job on his trousers*) What y' doin' Kav?

Kav Just me name. (*He is beginning an elaborate scroll which is intended to form his name.*)

Billy (*watching*) 'Ey that's dead good that. Yeh. I didn't know you could do that Kav. It's good that isn't it? (*He watches for a moment.*)

Kav *suddenly crosses it all out.*

Kav Agh . . .

Robbie He's a good artist Kav is.

Billy 'Ey don't cross it out. It's dead good that. Yeh.

Kav It was crap.

Billy   I thought it was cracker.

Kav   Useless. Y' shoulda seen the stuff I did in the Top Rank Suite. What was it like Robbie?

Robbie   Didn't y' see that Billy? It was smart that was. Y' know he did a big drawin', didn't y' Kav, on the back of a bog door, covered the whole door it was . . .

Kav   Took me weeks to do that y' know. Every time we went the Top Rank I spent longer in the bogs than I did on the dance floor.

Robbie   It was like abstract wasn't it? Not like that stupid abstract stuff though – y' could see picture in it couldn't y' Kav?

Kav   Even Eddy said that was good, didn't he? But then we went in there one week an' they'd had the painters in to paint out all the writin' in the bogs. They stippled all over me picture with Artex an' put up a sign saying they'd prosecute anyone found defacin' the place.

Billy   How d' y' draw like that eh?

Kav   I dunno. It's dead easy. I just do it.

Billy   I wish I could draw like that . . . don't you Robbie.

Robbie   Too right. I'd spend all day drawin' me own porny pictures.

Billy   Ogh I can do them . . . gis y' pencil Kav. Yeh. (*He takes the pencil and begins drawing on the wall.*)

Robbie (*inspecting his trousers*)   Ah . . . look at that. It's gonna take ages to dry now.

Billy   There's no rush anyway. We can't just leave Dave here can we?

Robbie   On y' bike. He'll be all right. We can keep nippin' in to have a look at him. Where's Eddy anyway? He should be here. Dave's his best mate.

Kav   Eddy doesn't like it when y' get pissed. It gets him narked.

Billy Eddy never gets legless himself though does he? It's 'cos he's captain of the team. He thinks he should set an example.

Kav He's dead professional Eddy, isn't he? An' he's dead serious about his football. He's dead serious about everythin'.

Robbie It's only Sunday League though isn't it? I mean it's not professional football is it?

Kav Don't let Eddy hear y' say that.

Robbie (*showing his trousers to* **Kav**) That look all right or what?

Kav (*non-committal*) It's all right.

Billy Y'll never get that off properly with water Robbie. Y' need petrol. Yeh.

Robbie Well I'll tell y' what . . . why don't you sod off down the garage an' get a can!

Billy What? No, listen. If there were still petrol lighters you'd be OK wouldn't y'? It's all gas though now isn't it? See that's an example of where technology makes significant advances an' losses at the same time.

Robbie Yeh that's just what I was thinkin'.

Billy No listen, I read about it. See if they still had petrol lighters you'd be able to take the cotton wool out an' clean your kecks with it wouldn't y'? Yeh. You wouldn't be stinkin' of curry then.

Robbie Yeh. I'd just be stinkin' of friggin' petrol wouldn't I?

Billy No. It'd evaporate. Yeh.

Robbie I wish you'd bleedin' evaporate! (*He notices* **Billy**'s *drawing.*) What the fuck's that?

Billy It's a tart. With nothin' on! Yeh.

Kav She's got no arms or legs!

Billy   I know.

Robbie   An' where's her head?

Billy   I don't do heads. I only do the important bits. I'm a primitive!

Robbie   You're a fuckin' idiot. Y've given her three tits!

Billy   Where?

Robbie (*pointing*)   There!

Billy   That's her stomach.

Kav   Well why's it got a nipple on it?

Billy   That's not a nipple – that's a belly button.

Robbie   Anyway soft lad, who told y' heads weren't important? The way a tart looks, her face an' that . . . it's dead important. There's nothin' better than a beautiful girl.

Billy   They're all the same when y' get down to it though aren't they?

Robbie   Get lost. When y' get married y' spend longer looking at them than y' do screwin them, don't y'? I'll tell y' la, when I get married she'll be a cracker my missis will, beautiful.

Kav   She might be a cracker when y' get married to her Robbie but she won't stay that way.

Robbie   She bleedin' will!

Kav   Go 'way Robbie. Y' know what the tarts round here are like; before they get married they look great some of them. But once they've got y' they start lettin' themselves go. After two years an' a couple of kids, what happens eh? They start leavin' the make-up off don't they, an' puttin' on weight. Before y' know where y' are the cracker y' married's turned into a monster.

Eddy *enters through the double doors and heads for the Gents.*

Robbie   My missis isn't gonna be like that. If any tart of mine starts actin' slummy she'll be booted out on her arse. A woman has got a responsibility to her feller. No tart of mine's gonna turn fat.

Billy   I like a bit of weight. Somethin' t' get hold of.

Eddy *enters. He goes straight to the urinal.*

Kav   What's the talent like out there Eddy?

Eddy   I don't know about the talent. The ale's last!

Billy   Yeh, y' know why that is Eddy? Eh? It's 'cos it's pumped up with top pressure.

Eddy   Is that right?

Billy   Yeh. I'm a real ale man I am.

Eddy   Whose smart idea was it to come here? We coulda stayed in the pub.

Robbie   There's no talent in the pub Eddy.

Billy   CAMRA. Y' know, the Campaign for Real Ale. I support that. I've got a badge.

Robbie (*giving up the cleaning attempt*)   What am I gonna do? That little Bianca one's gonna be all over me in half an hour. What's she gonna say if she can smell curry everywhere?

Kav   Tell her it's the latest aftershave.

Eddy   'Madras: For Men'.

Robbie   'Ey yeh . . . 'Things happen to a feller who uses Madras for Men.'

Kav   Yeh. Instead of gettin' y' oats y' get chicken biryani.

Robbie   No danger. I'm on I am. See her givin' me the eye did y'?

Kav   Yeh . . . it was me who told y'!

Eddy   Tarts! Women!

Billy (*laughing*)   He's always on about tarts him, isn't he Eddy?

Eddy   Y' know your problem Robbie . . . y' were born with y' brains between y' legs.

Kav *and* **Billy** *laugh.*

Robbie   That's not a problem.

Eddy   Isn't it?

Robbie   What's wrong with likin' the women eh Eddy?

Eddy (*looking in at* **Dave**)   Look at him! You'll end up like him Robbie. See him, he's the best inside player I've ever seen. But it's all over for him. Well, it will be after tomorrow.

Robbie   Christ Eddy, he's gettin' married, not havin' his legs sawn off.

Eddy   You just watch him over the next few months. I've seen it before. Once they get married the edge goes. Before long they start missin' one odd game, not turnin' up. You mark my words. The next thing is they stop playin' altogether. They have t' take the kids out on a Sunday, or they go down the club at dinnertime, drinkin'. Or they just can't get out of bed 'cos they've been on the nest all night. Nah . . . it's the beginnin' of the end for him.

Billy (*approaching* **Eddy**)   I'm not gonna get married Eddy, I'm stayin' at home with me mam.

Kav   Don't you think that woman's suffered enough?

Billy   I'll still be there, playin' in defence, when I'm forty Eddy. Yeh. I keep meself fit I do.

Eddy   I know y' do Billy. Y' not like Robbie are y'? Robbie's a tarts' man. You'll end up like Dave you will, Robbie.

Robbie   Ah give it a rest will y' Eddy. Sunday League football isn't the be all and end all is it? This is supposed to be a stag night, not a pre-match pep talk.

Eddy   Who the fuck are you talkin' to? I'll remember that Robbie, I'll remember that when I'm pickin' this week's team.

Billy (*after a pause*)   Are y' droppin' him Eddy?

Kav   Are y' Eddy?

Robbie   I don't care!

Eddy   Don't y'? Not even when there's an American Scout gonna be watchin' us?

Kav   Watchin' our game Eddy? On Sunday?

Billy   I'm at the top of me form y' know Eddy. Yeh.

Kav   An American Scout Eddy?

Eddy   There's talent scouts from America combin' this country lookin' for potential.

Kav   'Ey . . . we'll be without Dave. Dave won't be playin' on Sunday, will he?

Eddy   That's his hard luck isn't it? If he wants t' be in Spain when we've got a scout watchin' us, that's his hard luck!

Robbie   Ah come on Eddy . . . let's get out there . . . listen to a few sounds, it's great when the music's playin'. Come on, have a few jars an' a laugh an' that.

Eddy snorts and turns away.

Robbie   Look Eddy, I'm set up already with a smart little one, just like Bianca Jagger, isn't she Kav? She's bound to have a crackin' mate with her, Eddy. I'll have the little Bianca one, you take her mate.

Eddy   What? Spend all night chattin' up some dumb tart, two hours of sufferin' her talkin' an' drinkin' and dancin', just to get a poke at her. Sod off.

Billy (*at* **Robbie***'s shoulder*)   I'll take her mate for y' Robbie.

Robbie   On y' bike! You're a bleedin' liability you are.

Billy   Well. You always go after the smartest tarts in the place. I get nervous with that type.

Robbie   I've told y' haven't I? Always go for the crackers. Loads of fellers make that mistake, they see really smart tarts an' they think they've got no chance. But it's the opposite. If a tart looks really good, an' y' can see she's spent hours gettin' herself to look somethin' special it's 'cos she wants someone to tap off with her.

Billy　But I just get shy Robbie.

Kav (*to* **Billy**)　Come on. Me an' you it is. But listen . . . no standin' at the side of the floor all night. When I say go in, we go in . . . right?

Billy　All right.

Robbie　Come on.

The three of them move towards the door.

Eddy　'Ey.

They stop.

Hold on!

Pause.

Where youse goin'?

Robbie　What Eddy?

Eddy　What about him? (*He indicates* **Dave**.)

Robbie　What about him?

Eddy (*after a pause*)　Just gonna leave him here are y'?

The three of them, on the spot, look at each other.

Eddy　He's our mate isn't he?

Kav　Course he is Eddy.

Robbie　Yeh.

Eddy　An' y' just gonna leave him here are y'? Y' gonna leave him like this while y' go off listenin' to cheap music an' chasin' tarts?

Robbie　Ah 'ey Eddy . . .

Eddy　Ah 'ey what? Y' just gonna fuck off on y' mate when he's incapable, needs lookin' after.

Pause. **Eddy** *looks at them.*

Kav   He'll be all right Eddy.

Eddy   That's loyalty for y' isn't it?

Pause.

Robbie   Well you look after him Eddy! We've had our turn. Christ we got him in here didn't we? Look, spewed curry all over me best suit.

Eddy   Haven't you heard of loyalty?

Pause. They can't move.

Go on then . . . piss off. I'll look after him. I'm stayin' in the bar. I'll keep nippin' in to see that he's all right.

Pause.

Go on . . . sod off!

They don't move.

It's last out there anyway. All it is is music, fuckin' music.

Billy   I like music Eddy.

Eddy   You would wouldn't y'. 'Cos y' fuckin' soft, like them! Go on then, get out here, an' listen to it.

Pause.

Kav   What's wrong with music Eddy?

Eddy   (*after a pause, looking at them*)   Y' know what music does don't y'?

Robbie   It makes y' feel good Eddy.

Eddy   Makes y' feel good! Makes y' go soft.

Pause. **Eddy** *looks at them.*

Robbie   Come on Eddy, come with us. Dave'll be all right.

Kav   There's a live group on after, Eddy.

Eddy   (*turning to look into the WC*)   Is there? I'll bet they're shite as well!

Robbie   They're not a local band Eddy. They're up from London. They'll be good.

Eddy　They didn't look like Londoners to me. I just saw them comin' in. They looked local. I thought I recognised one of them.

Robbie　Nah . . . That'll be from off the telly Eddy. They're big league this lot, honest.

Eddy　What d' y' want me t' do Robbie? Rush off home for me autograph book?

Robbie (*to the others*)　Tch . . . agh . . . come on . . .

They turn and go into the corridor. **Eddy** *follows them.*

Kav　Y' comin' with us Eddy?

Eddy　Nah – it's a stag night isn't it? Y' know what y' do on a stag night don't y'?

Kav　What Eddy?

Eddy　Get pissed!

They exit from the corridor.

Carol (*shouting*)　Linda . . . are you comin' out?

Linda (*after a pause*)　No!

Bernadette　Linda . . . Linda love . . . why not?

Linda　Because, Berni love . . . you are getting right up my fucking nose!

Carol　Linda d' you really think that's appropriate language for a bride-to-be?

Bernadette　Take no notice of her Carol . . . she doesn't mean it. They all go a bit funny when they're gettin' married. She's probably just havin' a little cry to herself. They do that on the night before.

Carol (*whispering*)　Agh yeh. Agh . . .

Maureen (*leaning in, joining the whispering*)　What?

Carol　She's havin' a little cry. Did you Berni, did you cry the night before you got married?

Bernadette　No love. I've just been cryin' ever since!

Maureen (*to* **Frances**)   Come here . . . Frankie come here
. . . leave her . . . she's just havin' a little cry to herself . . .
Agh.

Frances   Cryin' . . . what for?

Maureen   Frances! She's crying for what she'll be losing
tomorrow.

Frances (*laughing*)   Oh 'ey Maureen, she lost that years
ago, just like the rest of us.

Maureen   No . . . I didn't mean that. But y' do give
something up when y' get married don't y'? You give up
bein' a girl when y' get married.

Frances   What d' y' turn into instead – a feller? Her Dave's
not gonna be too happy about that tomorrow night is he?

Maureen (*slow*)   What?

Frances (*banging on the WC door*)   Linda . . . come on . . .
the night's gonna be over.

Maureen   Frances . . . leave her with her thoughts as a
single girl. Come here. (*Whispering.*) What have y' bought for
them?

Frances   Weddin' presents y' mean?

Maureen   Shush! Yeh. I thought I'd go for something
functional. I mean it's nice having pictures an' ornaments
but y' can't do anything with them can you? Apart from
looking at them!

Bernadette   What have y' bought them then Mo?

Maureen (*delighted*)   A pair of barbecue chairs! In saddle
brown.

Frances (*aghast*)   What are they?

Maureen   Barbecue chairs. Y' know for in the summer
when you have friends round for a barbecue.

Frances   Oh that'll be very functional Maureen. They'll
have a great time with a barbecue in a block of flats six floors
high!

Maureen   Oh . . . oh . . . 'ey . . . (*Thinking*.) But they will have a balcony won't they?

The others look at each other in disbelief.

No . . . I don't mean they'll be able to have a barbecue on the balcony. But they'll be able to sit out there won't they?

Frances   An' watch the sun go down on the other blocks of flats!

Maureen   I'll tell her that they're balcony chairs. She won't know the difference will she? I'll tell her they're balcony chairs.

Carol   We all clubbed together in work. We got them a coffee percolator. Y' know for real coffee.

Bernadette   Ah that'll be nice Carol. They'll be able to sit an' have coffee when their friends come round.

Frances   Or when they're sittin' out on the balcony! What have you got them Berni?

Bernadette   My feller knows someone at work who makes antique furniture, they're great. I've got them a coffee table in antique.

Frances   Christ I hope they like coffee! I've got them a coffee set!

Maureen   Ah that'll be really swish that, won't it? They will like coffee Frances. You might drink tea when you're at home with your mum, but when you become a couple you drink coffee together. An' that's worked out really lovely hasn't it? Ah . . . just think . . . they'll be able to sit at Bernadette's coffee table, drinking coffee out of Carol's percolator in the coffee cups that you gave them, sittin' on my balcony chairs. Agh. It'll remind them of us won't it? ·

Frances   They'll never be able to forget us Mo. (*She knocks on the WC door.*) Linda!

Bernadette   Oh come on Linda love . . . all the good-lookin' lads'll have gone home if they think I'm not here.

Robbie *and* **Billy** *burst through the double doors and into the Gents.*

Robbie The bitch . . . the stuck-up bitch . . .

Billy (*checking out* **Dave**) All right Dave. Yeh. She was dead fuckin' humpety anyway! She was destroyed when you got in close.

Robbie I've told you three times haven't I? What d' y' want me t' do, write it out for y'?

Billy But I couldn't hear y' in there, with the music an' that . . . go on, what did she say?

Robbie She said – 'I never dance with men in suits.'

Billy Is that what she said?

Robbie I thought she was jokin' at first, y' know, comin' on with the laughs an' that. I give her a big smile an' said to her, 'I'll tell y' what love, if y' don't like suits why don't we go back t' your place an' y' can take it off for me.'

Billy (*laughing*) Did y'? What did she say?

Robbie She walked away. She walked away from me. What's wrong with suits, eh? Cost sixty-five quid this did, from Hepworths. No rubbish goes on my back. The stuck-up cow. She doesn't look like Bianca Jagger anyway. She looks more like Mick Jagger. I told her though. Should've heard me Billy . . . classic it was: 'Eh love,' I said, 'I don't waste my time on tarts who don't appreciate quality.'

Billy Is that what you said Robbie?

Robbie Too right. . . ! 'This suit, this suit,' I said, 'cost every penny of sixty-five notes.' See her face did y'? See her face when I told her that?

Billy Yeh Robbie. An' she said 'You were robbed.'

Robbie (*stung*) I thought you said you couldn't hear!

Eddy *enters the corridor.*

Billy I couldn't hear what you said Robbie. I heard what she said though.

Robbie   Well y' wanna get y' friggin' ears tested don't y' 'cos she never said that.

Billy   She did Robbie, I was standin' —

Eddy *comes into the Gents.*

Robbie (*as* **Eddy** *enters*)   All right Eddy. We were just keepin' an eye on Dave for y'.

Eddy   Good lad.

Robbie   Doin' y' a favour.

Eddy   Yeh . . . Kav's doin' the same for you out there!

Robbie   What?

Eddy   Know that tart who keeps givin' you the elbow, that really smart-lookin' one, Kav's dancin' with her. She's all over him as well!

Robbie   I don't care, I wasn't interested anyway . . . she was destroyed.

Eddy *laughs.* **Robbie** *heads for the door.*

Robbie (*to* **Billy**)   Come on.

Robbie *and* **Billy** *go into the corridor, then exit.*

Eddy   Go on then . . . go on . . . piss off. Piss off t' y' dancin'. An' y' music. Music . . . bleedin' music makes me wanna spew! Eh Dave . . . is that what made you spew, the music eh (*Laughing.*) music! (*He produces a quarter bottle and takes the cap off.*)

In the Ladies. The WC door opens. **Linda** *stands in the door frame.*

Linda   'But if we do not change, tomorrow has no place for us.' It says so . . . on the wall in there. (*She goes to the mirror and simply pushes her hair into place.*)

Carol   Tch. There must have been a students' dance here. No one with sense'd write somethin' like that.

Maureen   They write dead stupid things don't they, students.

Carol   I went to a dance once, y' know at the students' union. Y' should have seen the bogs, they were full of writin'. An' it was last. Y' couldn't understand any of it. Honest.

Bernadette   What was it like?

Carol   Y' know all dead soft stuff. Somethin' about God bein' a woman. It was terrible. An' this thing that said 'A woman needs a fish like a feller needs a bike', y' know really stupid stuff like that.

Bernadette   An' the bloody tax my feller pays to keep them students. Wouldn't y' think with all them brains they'd write somethin' sensible on the bog wall.

Frances   Take no notice of her, Berni. There were some really good things. There was this great thing, it said 'Love is blind, marriage is an institution, who wants to live in an instutute for the blind.'

Maureen   God Frances . . . that's wicked . . . don't say things like that.

Linda   Come on . . . let's go.

Frances   You haven't done y' make-up.

Linda   I can't be bothered. Come on.

Frances   Y' not goin' into a dance without y' make-up on!

Linda   Why not?

Bernadette   We'll wait for y' Linda . . . go on, do y' make-up. Y' don't wanna look a mess.

Frances (*taking* **Linda**'s *arm*)   Come on. I'll do it for y'. Be quicker then.

Linda (*turning away*)   Tch. I'll do it meself then. Go on, you lot have waited long enough. Go on, I'll see y' in there. (*She takes out her make-up.*)

Carol   Linda, we're y' mates aren't we? It's your hen night. Y' don't think we'd desert y' do y'?

Linda   Y' not deserting me. I'll come an' find y' when I'm ready.

Bernadette We never leave someone behind. We only go out when we're all ready.

Carol We stick together.

Linda Why don't y' all come on me honeymoon?

Bernadette We would Linda love, but I'm afraid if I was there, you wouldn't get a look in.

The **Girls,** *apart from* **Linda,** *laugh.*

Linda Look . . . I am a big girl now y' know. I can find me way out of the Ladies an' into the dance.

Bernadette Linda . . . it's your hen night, we stick with you.

Linda Yeh, until some feller wants t' take you outside. Then you'll be off like a flash.

Bernadette Well . . . you've got to get a bit of fresh air haven't you?

Linda Is that what you call it?

Bernadette With some of them that's what it feels like!

Shrieks from the **Girls.**

Linda Well you'd better watch out tonight, Berni. You're gonna have a bit of competition.

Bernadette Ooh. Tch. Who from?

Linda Well y' don't think I'm gonna end my hen night stuck in the bar like some old married woman do y'? I'm gonna get out on that floor an' forget about everythin' else. I'm gonna get real legless. If it's a last fling then that's what I'm gonna make it.

Frances Well y' better get a move on or your last fling'll be already flung. Come here, let me do it. Go on, you lot go . . . y' can be gettin' the drinks in.

Carol Yeh . . . come on then . . . what y' havin'?

Frances Get us a port an' lemon. What d' y' want, Linda?

Maureen Come on, let's go then.

Linda Get me a pint of bitter.

Bernadette Linda love, no come on. A joke's a joke. I've seen you do that before love and we all think it's a good laugh. But not tonight. It's a hen night you're on, not a stag night. Now come on, something a bit more lady-like.

Linda All right, I'll have a pint of mild!

Bernadette Oh sod off . . .

Carol We'll get y' a Snowball Linda, y' like them.

Linda All right. With a nice little cherry on the top.

Bernadette Come on. We'll be in the bar.

Carol We'll just have a drink an' listen to the sounds till you come out . . .

Bernadette Ogh . . . come on. Give us some music. Music, music, music. It's an aphrodisiac to me.

Linda Bromide'd be an aphrodisiac to you.

Bernadette Too right . . . ooogh . . . come on girls . . .

They go into the corridor and exit.

Frances *is fixing* **Linda**'s *hair and make-up.*

Frances It's great the way music gets to y' though, isn't it? Y' can come to a disco or a dance an' be feelin' really last. But once y' walk into the music it gives y' a lift doesn't it? Makes y' feel special.

Linda Yeh. (*After a pause.*) I get lost in music I do.

Frances Yeh I do that.

Linda I become someone else when the music's playin'. I do y' know.

Frances Yeh I'm like that.

Linda D' y' know if it wasn't for music I wouldn't be gettin' married tomorrow.

Frances (*laughing*)   Oh don't be stupid Linda. You're nuts sometimes. Y' are y' know.

Linda   I'm not bein' stupid. We were dancin' when he asked me to marry him. 'When A Man Loves A Woman' it was. I heard this voice in my ear, like it was part of the music, sayin' 'Will y' marry me?' So I said yeh. I would've said yeh if I'd been dancin' with Dracula's ugly brother.

Frances   Linda stop bein' soft.

Linda   When the music stopped I looked up an' there was Dave, beamin' down at me, talkin' about gettin' married an' I'm wonderin' what he's on about, then I remembered. An' the next thing y' know I'm here, tonight.

Frances   Linda!

Linda   Oh come on, hurry up an' get me hair done. All I wanna do is get out there an' dance the night away. There mightn't be another opportunity after tonight.

Frances   Linda, you're gettin' married, not gettin' locked up! There y' go. (*She begins putting her implements away*.)

Linda (*looking at herself in the mirror*)   Y' do get frightened y' know. I mean if it was just gettin' married to Dave it'd be OK, he's all right Dave is. But it's like, honest, it's like I'm gettin' married to a town.

Frances   To a what?

Linda   It's not just like I'm marryin' Dave. It's like if I marry him I marry everythin'. Like, I could sit down now an' draw you a chart of everythin' that'll happen in my life after tomorrow.

Frances (*looking at her*)   D' y' know something Linda, you're my best mate, but half the time I think you're a looney!

Linda (*going into an exaggerated looney routine*)   I am . . . (*She plays it up*.)

Frances (*laughing*)   Linda . . . don't mess y' hair up . . .

Linda (*quickly knocking her hair back into place, preparing to leave*)   Well . . . look at it this way, after tomorrow I'll have me own Hoover, me own colour telly an' enough equipment to set up a chain of coffee bars.

They go into the corridor and exit.

In the Gents, **Eddy** *is taking a swig from the bottle.*

Eddy (*laughing*)   'Ey, Dave . . . d' y' wanna drink? (*He laughs.*) 'Ey, can't y' hear me Dave? Jesus . . . you wouldn't hear if a bomb went off would y'? It's your own fault Dave. Y' can't blame me lad. It's all your own fault. Y' don't have to drink do y'. See, y' don't have to do anythin'. (*He pauses.*) The US, Dave, an' you coulda' been comin' with me . . . you should've been comin' with me. Not with a wife though. Y' can't travel when there's too much baggage weighin' y' down. (*He pauses.*) She's OK your tart. She's all right. But round here, if y' get married Dave, y' trapped then. It's the end. Y' don't go anywhere, y' just stay forever in this fuckin' dyin' dump. It's hard to get out anyway Dave, you know it is. Look at all the scouts who've seen our team. But I'm still here aren't I eh? It's hard to go. But once y' get married round here, y' never gonna go at all. You've got t' fuckin' leave y'self free Dave so that when the time comes y' can be off without a word to anyone. Y've got t' leave yourself free like me. I can go anywhere Dave, anywhere, at any time. There's nothin' holdin' me down. (*He pauses.*) But if you don't wanna come with me, if you wanna get married to some tart, well you do it. Yeh you do it! Mate? Soft get . . .

Robbie *and* **Billy** *enter from the foyer and go towards the Gents.*

Eddy *goes to take a swig from the bottle.* **Robbie** *and* **Billy** *enter.* **Eddy** *quickly hides the bottle in his pocket.* **Billy** *stands at the door.* **Robbie** *goes to the urinal.*

Robbie   All right Eddy. (*He sees* **Billy** *holding the door.*) Come in an' close the bleedin' door will y'?

Billy (*entering*)   What have we come in here for? We told them we'd see them in the bar. Yeh.

Robbie   Yeh . . . soft lad . . . we told them that 'cos we wanted t' get rid of them didn't we?

Billy   Did we? Mine was nice!

Robbie   Nice? Shoulda seen her Eddy, she could have had the star part in *Jaws*.

Eddy   Where's Kav?

Robbie   What?

Billy   We saw him goin' out the back with that one who looks like Bianca Jagger.

Robbie   I hope he gets a dose.

Eddy (*moving to the door*)   I'm goin' the bar. (*Snorting.*) Soft gets . . .

Billy   Are you pissed Eddy?

Eddy (*wheeling and grabbing him*)   Have you ever seen me pissed?

Billy   No Eddy.

Eddy   No Eddy . . . I don't get pissed. I'm not like you. I'm not like him . . . I don't get pissed.

Billy   No Eddy, what I meant was –

Robbie   Shut up Billy . . .

Eddy   Yeh, shut it. Soft arse! (*He pushes him away and goes to the door.*) Look after Dave. I'm goin' the bar.

Eddy goes into the corridor and exits.

Billy   I think he is a bit pissed y' know Robbie.

Robbie   Well there's no need to go tellin' him is there? Eddy thinks he never gets pissed. I've seen him in a state loads of times. But I never tell him.

Billy   Well why doesn't he just say, y' know, that he's pissed?

Robbie   I don't know, do I? He just likes to pretend, y' go along with him, don't y'? It's like he pretends that one day he's gonna play big league football. Y' just go along with him.

Kav *enters. Sheepish.*

Kav   I'm sorry Robbie.

Robbie (*all innocence*)   What about Kav? What's up son?

Kav   Y' know.

Robbie   What? What?

Kav   I'm sorry about gettin' off with your little Bianca one. It wasn't my fault though, honest, she was —

Robbie   Did you get off with her? Christ y' didn't did y'? Did you hear that Billy?

Kav   What? What's wrong?

Robbie   Ah no . . . you'll be all right though, y' didn't go outside with her did y'?

Kav   Yeh . . . round the back, why?

Robbie   Yeh, but y' didn't slip her one, did y'?

Kav   Yeh . . . she couldn't get out there fast enough.

Robbie   Ogh Kav, Kav . . .

Kav   What's up?

Robbie   Come on Kav. Why d' y' think I gave her the knock back?

Kav   What?

Robbie   Tommy Stevens told me didn't he? That one who looks like Mick Jagger's got the clap! Come on Billy . . . those two'll be up in the bar now. Ogh . . . wanna see these two we've tapped off with Kav, stunners. What they like Billy?

Billy   Y' wanna see them Kav. Ugliest boots y' ever saw in y' —

Robbie   Go way soft lad . . . take no notice of him, he's blind.

A coughing from the WC takes them over to **Dave**.

Robbie   That's it Dave, go on get it up.

Billy   It might be a gold clock. Yeh.

Kav   Don't y' think we better get him sobered up? It's his stag night isn't it?

Robbie   Christ you're considerate all of a sudden aren't y'? I'll bet y' weren't thinkin' of him when y' were round the back gettin' a dose off that tart.

Kav   I haven't got a dose. You were just messin' . . .

Robbie   You wait an' see pal. You wait.

Kav   Go away. Come on . . . let's try an' make him get it all up.

Robbie   Ah leave him. Christ it's not a proper stag night if the groom's conscious.

Billy   It's bad luck if the groom's sober the night before he gets married, yeh.

Robbie   That's right that is. Me dad told me. He was sober on his stag night an' look what happened to him the next day!

Kav   What?

Robbie   He married me mother! All right, come on, just get him right over the bowl an' he'll be OK.

In the corridor **Peter** *enters, carrying a pint. Passing him, carrying cable, is the* **Roadie**.

Peter   Have y' cracked it?

Roadie (*southern accent*)   Have we fuck. Every socket we try's an antique. What a bleedin' dump. Every socket I try just blows.

Peter   Keep tryin'.

Roadie   I'll keep tryin' but I'm tellin' y' it'll be a miracle if you get on tonight. What a place. What a fuckin' town.

Peter 'Ey dickhead, I'll have you know you're talkin' about my home town.

Roadie Yeh . . . an' I can see why y' left it now. Where y' goin'?

Peter There's no bogs workin' backstage.

Roadie See . . . see what I mean? Will I be glad when this one's over.

Peter Get lost. You'd be moanin' about the state of the plug sockets if we were playin' the bleedin' Hollywood Bowl.

Roadie I'll tell you what Peter mate, after this place I'll never complain about a plug socket again.

Peter Well comin' here's done some good then!

Roadie Huh!

The **Roadie** *exits.*

Peter *goes into the Gents, pint in hand, smoking, goes into the urinal. He leans back and looks at what the fellers are doing.*

Peter All right lads. Christ he's in a state isn't he?

They look at him.

What's up with him, one over the eight?

Robbie No, it's his hobby, lookin' down bogs!

Peter (*laughing*) No accountin' for taste eh?

They stand and look at him. He zips up and returns the gaze.

Kav 'Ey, d' y' get paid for wearin' boots like that?

Peter What? (*Laughing.*) Good aren't they? (*He shows them off.*) Like them?

Billy They look like tarts' boots to me.

Peter They are tarts' boots. Good though aren't they?

Robbie (*laughing*) Tarts' boots.

Billy I wouldn't even wear them if I was a tart!

Peter (*walking through them and getting a look at* **Dave**)   What's he been drinkin'?

Robbie (*aggressively*)   Y' what?

Peter   You deaf?

Robbie   What the fuck d' you wanna know what he's been drinkin' for?

Peter   It's one of me hobbies, gettin' to know what people drink.

Billy   He's been on Black Velvets an' Southern Comfort.

Peter   Ah. That type is he? Subtle palate?

Kav   Listen you – who the fuck d' y' think you're talkin' to?

Peter   Kavanagh isn't it? Erm . . . Tony Kavanagh.

Kav   How the fuck d' you know my name? How does he know my name? Listen you, you just . . . (*Pointing.*) Hold on . . . 'ey . . . it is, isn't it it is! You used to live round our way didn't y'?

Robbie   Ogh fuck. It's you isn't it?

Peter   I hope so.

Billy   Who is it?

Kav (*excited*)   You know . . . you know him . . . er hold on, hold on, don't tell me . . . it's erm . . . erm.

Peter   Peter.

Kav   That's it, that's it . . . I knew it was . . .

Robbie   'Ey, you're famous aren't y'?

Kav   Are you with this group tonight? 'Ey . . . they're famous . . .

Billy   Who is it?

Kav   'Ey . . . I always said you were dead good on that guitar y' know, I did didn't I Robbie? Here, look, that's Robbie. Y' remember Robbie don't y'?

Peter   Hia Robbie.

Kav An' Billy . . . y' remember Billy don't y', Billy Blake?

Peter Erm . . .

Kav Ah y' do . . . y' must do . . . his mam an' your mam were mates . . . remember . . .

Peter Oh yeh . . . all right erm . . .

Billy Who is he?

Kav Christ, is that really you? Look at y' now! An' you used to be just like us! Tch. 'Ey, here's Dave. Y' remember Dave don't y'? (*He leads him over.*)

Peter Er, no I think er . . .

Kav Ah y' do. You remember Dave. (*Shouting.*) 'Ey Dave, Dave, wake up . . . look who's here Dave! Dave'll be sick at missin' y'.

Peter Maybe that's the best thing eh?

Kav (*laughing, too much*) Still kept your sense of humour eh? Great. (*He looks at him.*) I can't believe it.

Robbie What y' doin' playin' in a dump like this?

Peter It's work isn't it?

Kav (*to anyone*) Gis a piece of paper, where's a piece of paper? (*He goes into the WC.*)

Robbie You're on the radio an' the telly an' that, aren't y'?

Peter Now an' then.

Robbie An' y' come back playin' in dives like this.

Peter It's only one gig. It was arranged before the single happened.

Robbie Well y' should've told them to fuck off. Y' don't wanna belittle y'selves do y', playin' holes like this when y' famous. Live in London now do y'?

Peter Yeh.

Robbie What's it like?

Peter   It's all right man, it's OK.

Robbie (*looking at him*)   I'll bet it's fuckin' great!

Peter (*smiling*)   It's OK.

Robbie (*looking at him*)   Jesus!

Peter   Small world eh?

Kav (*coming out of the WC with the bog paper*)   I'm sorry about the paper, I couldn't find any other . . . (*He offers pencil and paper.*)

Peter   Ah come on man, you don't want . . .

Kav   Put, erm . . . 'To Kav – an old mate.'

Peter   Look man, for Christ's sake you don't want me to do this . . .

Kav   You're jokin' aren't y'? Of course I do . . .

Peter   Look, for Christ's sake I used to live just down the road from you . . .

Kav   I know. I'm gonna show that to people.

Peter *looks at him.* **Billy** *comes out of the WC with a piece of paper, joins the queue.* **Peter** *signs.*

Robbie   'Ey is it true what they say about the tarts, y' know, the groupies.

Peter   A bit of it. Most of it's fiction.

Robbie   I'll bet it's not. Jesus I bet you can have anythin' y' want can't y'?

Kav (*looking at his piece of paper*)   Ogh . . . look at that!

Peter *takes* **Billy**'*s paper, signs it.*

Robbie   'Ey, what sort of a car d' y' drive now?

Peter   I haven't got one. Listen, what you lads doin' these days?

Robbie   Fuck all, us. Eh, have y' got a big house in London?

Peter   A flat. What, y' all on the dole?

Kav   Nah, we work.

Robbie   Got a big house in the country have y'?

Peter   What sort of work's that then?

Kav   Listen, we don't wanna talk about us, it's dead borin'. We just fuckin' work. Go on, tell us all about you. Tell us all about the, y' know, the thingy, an', what it's like an' all about it.

Peter   Go 'way. What d' y' wanna hear about me for?

Kav   Listen Peter. You're someone who's made it. We're proud of you. We are.

Billy *has been studying his piece of bog paper.*

Billy   Who is he?

Robbie   Can't you read?

Peter   Look lads . . . I've gorra go. We haven't even got the gear set up yet. Gotta tune up an' that . . .

Robbie   Aren't y' gonna come an' have a bevvy with us?

Peter   We're not even set up yet.

Kav   What about afterwards, y' know after the gig?

Peter   Yeh, maybe . . . that's a possibility. See y' lads. 'Ey, look after the Southern Comfort King won't y'?

He goes into the corridor and exits.

Kav   See y' Peter.

Robbie   Tarar.

Billy (*looking up from his paper*)   'Ey . . . that was Peter Taylor! Ogh . . . he's famous. Yeh.

Robbie   Imagine comin' back to this dive when y' as big as he is. See his boots. They were smart weren't they?

Billy   I'm gonna get a pair of them.

Robbie   They wouldn't look the same on you.

Billy   Why won't they?

Robbie   They just won't.

Kav   They'll be custom-made anyway.

Robbie   Y' wouldn't get nothin' like that round here.

Kav   Christ . . . the way he must live eh?

Robbie   I'll be his tarts never grow old, do they?

Billy   Boots like that'd suit me.

Kav   I'll bet he's never bored is he? An' he used t' live near us!

Eddy *enters*.

Kav   Eddy . . . Eddy guess what?

Eddy   I know! Dave's tart's out there!

Others   What?

Eddy   I've just seen her now. She's out there, dancin'!

Blackout.

Act Two

Bernadette *and* **Carol**, *laughing, enter the Ladies.*

Bernadette   Ogh . . . God! Did y' see the state of him. An' he was serious. He tried to get off with me! He was all of four foot nothin'.

Carol   What about his mate? He was smaller. An' he had acne. (*Disgusted.*) Oogh, God the thought: four foot nothin' an' spotted all over. He was like a walkin' Eccles cake. Oogh . . .

Bernadette   At least you got rid of him after the first dance.

Carol   I had to Berni. He made me feel ill; honest I hate ugly people. I feel sorry for them like, but no, I had to get rid of him. You should have given yours the elbow straight away.

Bernadette   Didn't y' see me tryin'? 'Are you stayin' up?' he says to me. All three foot six of him starin' up at me. I said 'I don't know about stayin' up, don't y' think y' better sit down before y' get trodden on.

Carol (*shrieking*)   Y' didn't . . . Berni . . . Y' could have hurt his feelings.

Bernadette   Y' jokin'. He didn't have any feelings. He just ignored everythin'. He wouldn't take no for an answer. I said to him, 'Look son, I'll let y' into a secret, it's no use tryin' it on with me, I'm a lesbian . . .'

Carol   Berni . . .

Bernadette   It did no good. 'That's all right,' he said, 'I like a challenge.' By this time I'm dancin' away again, hopin' no one'd see me with him. And honest to God, he's so small he kept gettin' lost. I'm just walkin' away when he appears again. 'Goin' for a drink are we?' he says, I said to him, ''Ey you'd better run along, Snow White'll be lookin' for you.' 'Ey, he didn't get it though. 'Oh I'm sorry,' I said, 'but I thought you were one of the Seven Dwarfs.' He started laughin' then, y' know, makin' out he's got a sense of humour. 'Oh yeh,' he says, 'I'm Dozy,' I said 'You're not friggin' kiddin' . . .'

Carol *and* **Bernadette** *laugh.*

Bernadette   I'm walkin' away an' he's shoutin' after me. ''Ey I'll see y' in the bar, I'll be in the bar.' I said 'Yeh, an' that's the best place for you, along with every other pint that thinks it's a quart!'

Frances *enters.*

Carol   Frankie . . . have y' been in the bar?

Frances   Yeh.

Carol   Is there a spotted midget in there?

Frances   Ogh him? He's destroyed isn't he? An' his mate, just been tryin' to chat me up.

Bernadette   Well the two-timin' sod!

Frances   Three-timin'. He's chattin' Mo up now.

Carol   Ogh God.

Frances   She's made up!

Carol   Go way!

Frances   She's just standin' there, beamin' down at him with big dreamy eyes. Mind you that might be the Pernod. She's had five in the last half-hour.

Bernadette   She'll need a bottle full if she's takin' him on.

Maureen *well away, enters. She's singing the chorus of 'Dancing Queen'.*

Maureen   Whoa . . . hia . . . I feel great! . . . great! That's how I feel . . . great . . . I feel really . . . beautiful . . .

Frances   I thought you were off with someone.

Maureen (*laughing*)   Big John Wayne. . . !

Frances   I thought it was all set up Maureen.

Maureen   He said, he did, he said to me . . . 'D' y' wanna drink?' So, so I said, 'Yeh, a double Pernod!'

Carol   Tch. Maureen!

Maureen   He said, 'On y' bike.' 'On y' bike,' he said, 'y' can have half a lager an' like it.' Honest, cheeky get; he said 'I'm not made of money y' know.' So I said (*Laughing.*) an' I was dead made up with this, I said to him, 'Listen you, to make you out of money would only cost about three an' a half pence!' (*Laughing.*) An' he got all dead narked then, an' said he was fed up 'cos people had been takin' the piss all night. So y' know what I said, I told him to go for a swim in his half of lager!

She laughs and goes into the song again. Raucous, pitched too high. The others join in.

Linda *enters. She joins in the singing.*

Maureen   We're havin' a good time, aren't we? Aren't we eh? We're all havin' another good time. Ogh sometimes . . . sometimes I feel so happy. Linda . . . Linda, are you havin' a good time?

Linda   Great Mo.

Frances   God, can't y' tell she is? Haven't y' seen her, she hasn't stopped dancin' since she got out there . . .have y' Linda?

Linda   I love this y' know. I love it when we're all out together an' havin' a laugh. It's good isn't it? It's great.

Bernadette   Y' can't beat it when there's a crowd of y'.

Linda   Come on . . . let's all go out an' have a dance together . . .

Frances   Come on yeh, we'll have a line out . . .

Carol   Agh yeh . . .

Linda   An' if any fellers try to split us up we'll tell them to sod off . . .

Frances (*as she leaves*)   Come on . . .

Maureen (*as she leaves*)   I feel a bit sick . . .

Bernadette   Come on . . . (*Pushing* **Maureen**.) Get out . . . you'll be all right . . .

They all go down the corridor. Someone begins the 'Dancing Queen' chorus, they all sing.

In the Gents, the fellers are all as at the end of Act One.

Eddy   Talk about a rope round y' neck . . .

Kav   Yeh, but what I'm tryin' to tell y' Eddy is who's been *here*!

Eddy   She's not even married to him yet, an' she's spyin' on him! Couldn't she leave him alone eh? Couldn't she leave him with his mates on his last night?

Kav   Eddy . . .

Robbie   She won't know Dave's here Eddy. She'll just be here for the dancin'.

Kav   Eddy guess –

Eddy   Dancin', yeh, she's dancin' all right. I just seen her from the balcony, dancin' round with all different fellers, the bitch!

Robbie   Come on Eddy, it's only dancin'.

Eddy   Is it? An' what about him? (*He indicates* **Dave**.)

Robbie   Christ Eddy, she's only dancin', isn't she?

Kav   Forget her Eddy . . . listen, y' know who's been here eh? Guess who's been standin' on that very spot you're standin' on.

Billy   Y' should've seen his boots Eddy. Custom-made, yeh.

Kav   Go on Eddy, guess, guess who?

Eddy I don't fuckin' know do I?

Kav Peter Taylor.

Eddy Who?

Kav You know Peter Taylor. Remember? He used to live round our way, played the guitar. He's with this group that's on tonight. He's famous Eddy.

Eddy Famous?

Billy He's got these great boots Eddy. I'm gonna get a pair. Yeh.

Kav You'll be able to see him after, Eddy. He's gonna have a drink with us, y' know after the gig.

Eddy After the what?

Kav The gig. That's what they call it Eddy, when they play somewhere.

Billy He's a real star y' know Eddy.

Eddy I thought I told you to look after Dave.

Billy We have done Eddy.

Robbie (*to* **Dave**)   All right Dave? OK?

Billy (*going across to join* **Robbie**)   All right Dave? Yeh.

Kav Ah he's fantastic Eddy, not stuck up or anythin' y' know. (*He brings out his autograph.*) Look Eddy.

Eddy *takes it.*

Kav See what it says Eddy . . . 'To Kav – an old mate' an' that's his name there.

Billy (*coming over with his autograph paper*)   He did one for me Eddy, look. Yeh.

Eddy *takes it and looks at it.*

Billy I'll bet he'll do one for you Eddy. Yeh. If y' ask him.

Eddy What are these?

Billy   Yeh, it's dead hard to read at first Eddy, I couldn't read it at first but look it says . . .

He goes to point at the paper. **Eddy** *turns away, holding up the paper.*

Eddy   This? What's this?

Billy   We didn't have an autograph book Eddy.

Eddy   You big soft tarts!

Kav   What Eddy?

Eddy   Kids get autographs. Are you little kids?

Kav   No Eddy, but he's famous!

Eddy   On y' bike! (*He crumples up the paper.*) Famous!

He goes to the WC, throws the paper down the pan and flushes it.

Kav (*transfixed*)   Eddy, what have y' done?

Eddy (*coming out*)   What have I done?

Robbie (*from the bog*)   You've just flushed Dave's head, Eddy.

Eddy   Do it again. It might sober him up.

Kav   Eddy! That was my autograph!

Billy   An' mine. But y' couldn't read it anyway.

Kav   Eddy, that was my fuckin' autograph!

Eddy (*swiftly grabbing him*)   Who the fuck d' y' think you're talking to? (*He glares him into submission.*) Y' don't get autographs from people like him! He's just a fuckin' nomark!

He glares at **Kav** *who stares back, helpless.* **Eddy** *lets him go.*

Eddy   Y' don't wanna waste y' time Kav. See, it's people like you Kav, runnin' around after people like him that make them what they are. You're as good as he is! Did he ask you for your autograph? Did he?

Kav (*quietly*)   No.

Eddy   No. You wanna keep your dignity you do. You're as good as him. You could do that, what he does if you wanted to. You can do anythin' he can do. We all can. We can do anythin' we want to do, anythin'. He's nothin' special, so don't belittle y'self beggin' for a scrawlin' on a piece of bog paper. We can all write our names y' know. Here, here, give me that pencil. Give it me!

Kav *does so.*

Eddy   Look, look, it's dead easy y' know. You want an autograph? I'll give y' a fuckin' autograph . . . here. (*He writes his name in huge letters on the wall.*)

Kav   It was great meetin' him though. Wasn't it Robbie?

Robbie   It was all right.

Billy   Gis a go Eddy, Eddy . . . I'm gonna do my autograph. I am. I'm gonna do mine bigger than yours Eddy. Yeh.

Robbie   He's no bleedin' big shot is he? Hasn't even got a car.

Billy (*doing his name*)   Y' shoulda seen the stupid boots he had on Eddy, y' know, tarts' boots.

Robbie (*taking out a felt-tip pen and doing his own name*)   He's nothin' special, anyone could do what he does.

Kav   Oh yeh. Anyone could do it. That's why later on, whilst he's standin' up on the stage with all the coloured spotlights on him, you'll be down on the floor, dancin' in the dark with all the other nomarks.

Eddy (*snatching the pencil from* **Billy**)   Gis that. (*He offers it to* **Kav**.) Go on!

Kav   What?

Eddy   Put y' name up.

Kav (*after a pause*)   I don't want to Eddy.

Eddy   Why?

Kav   There's no point is there?

Eddy   The point, Kav, is that our names are up there. Where's yours?

Kav   What?

Eddy   Your name has got to be up there!

Kav   Why?

Eddy . So they can be seen, that's why. So that everyone'll know we've been here.

Kav   They'll only paint it out. They always do.

Eddy   Let them, we'll come back an' do it again.

Kav   Then they'll stipple over the walls so y' can't write on them.

Eddy   So. We'll come back again, an' carve our names out, won't we? I've told y' Kav, we can do anythin'. (*He pauses.*) Write y' name.

Kav *looks at* **Eddy**.

Robbie   Go on Kav. I wouldn't mind, but he can write better than any of us.

Eddy   Come on Kav. I want y' t' do it for me. Y' know the way y' do it in fancy scrolls an' that, that's clever that is Kav. You do it. For us. Come on.

Kav (*taking the pencil; after a pause*)   All right Eddy.

Eddy   Agh . . . good lad Kav.

Kav (*stepping up to the wall, looking at their writings*)   Who taught you lot t' write? Look at the state of that.

Eddy   You show us how it should be done Kav.

Kav (*beginning to write*)   Go on, youse lot go. It'll take a bit of time this. Go on, I can keep me eye on Dave, Eddy.

Eddy   Come on . . . (*He goes into the corridor.*)

Robbie (*following with* **Billy**)   Y' gonna go for a dance Eddy?

Eddy   Nah.

Billy   Why not Eddy?

Eddy   'Cos I'd rather just watch youse make fools of yourselves.

They exit.

As **Kav** *is doing his name, we see* **Bernadette** *and* **Carol**, *followed by* **Maureen**, *come through the doors.*

Bernadette   Well the inconsiderate swines.

Carol   Tch.

Maureen   What's up?

Carol (*as they enter the Ladies*)   You saw them didn't y'?

Maureen   Who? Oh me head . . .

Carol   Robbie Smith's here. An' Billy Blake.

Maureen   Oh he's nice him, Billy Blake isn't he?

Carol   Tch. God Maureen, that's not the point is it?

Maureen   What?

Bernadette   Maureen love, if Billy Blake an' Robbie Smith an' them are here, who else must be here?

Maureen   Dave! Dave? Oh God . . . get Linda in, get Linda in here quick . . .

Carol (*pulling her back from the door*)   Come here, Frances has gone to tell her . . .

Bernadette   We'll just have t' go somewhere else.

Carol   Tch. I was dead made up when I first saw Robbie, I really fancy him.

Bernadette   Fancy him or not Carol, we can't take the risk, for Linda's sake.

Carol   Oh God I know, I'm not sayin' we should take the risk, Berni.

Maureen   If she sees her Dave tonight that's it y' know. Her marriage has had it.

Bernadette   We'll go somewhere else. We'll have to.

Maureen   My mum knew a couple who saw each other the night before they got married an' y' know what happened eh?

Bernadette   What?

Maureen   The next day, in church, they were standin' y' know in the archway, havin' their picture taken. And the archway collapsed on them. Killed outright, an' that's true that.

Carol   That was in the paper wasn't it?

Maureen   Yeh, the picture was in the paper wasn't it? Y' know, just a pile of stones, Berni.

Bernadette   There was this woman by us y' know, she got an emerald engagement ring . . .

Carol   Go 'way . . .

Maureen   Did she take it off for the weddin'?

Bernadette   Everyone told her . . .

Carol   Y' should never wear green at a weddin' should y'?

Bernadette   Everyone told her. But she wouldn't listen, thought she knew best, that type y' know, thought she could make her own rules . . .

Carol   Y' can't can y'?

Bernadette   'Ey she wouldn't learn though, Carol. A couple of years later she got married again, an' y' know what colour her dress was?

Carol   Green?

Maureen   Tch.

Bernadette   Everyone told her. I believe her mother was distraught about it. But she wouldn't listen, tried to make out that things like that didn't matter.

Maureen   What happened Berni?

Bernadette   Heart attack wasn't it? Three months married an' her feller had a cardiac arrest. Gone, finished!

Carol   I'll bet she was sorry after that . . .

Bernadette   No, that's not the end of it. She got married again didn't she?

Carol   God, y' wouldn't think a feller'd take a chance on her, would y'?

Bernadette   She was told, time an' again she was told, everyone told her. An' she said all right, y' know no green this time . . .

Carol   I'll bet her feller was relieved wasn't he?

Bernadette   They get to the church an' she hasn't got a patch of green, anywhere.

Maureen   Oh thank God for that! Did they live, y' know, happily an' that?

Bernadette   Yeh, for ten minutes. As she was walkin' out the church she slipped, knocked her head on one of the gravestones. Dead!

Carol   Go 'way.

Maureen   But there was no green, Berni.

Bernadette   No, there was no green Mo, but as they picked her up, what did they see? Pinned to her dress?

Maureen   What?

Bernadette   An opal brooch!

Maureen   Agh. . . !

Linda *enters, led by* **Frances**. *They head for the Ladies.*

Carol   Tch, when y' think about it, gettin' married's a terrible liability y' know.

Maureen   Never wear an opal unless it's y' birth-stone.

Carol   She was askin' for trouble though, that one, wasn't she Berni?

Bernadette   Thought it didn't matter, y' see. Thought she could make up her own rules.

Linda *and* **Frances** *enter*.

Linda   For Christ's sake Frances. What's wrong with you lot? If y' wanted to talk to me why didn't y' come out there? Come on, I wanna get back t' the dancin'.

Bernadette   Linda love, we've got to go somewhere else.

Linda   What's wrong with here?

Carol   Give us y' cloakroom tickets, I'll go 'n' get the coats an' make sure it's all clear.

Linda   What's wrong?

Bernadette   Nothing. Apart from the fact that the man you're marryin' is here tonight.

Linda   Who? Dave? Where?

Frances   He's here, somewhere. We've seen all his mates.

Linda   Well?

Bernadette   Well what?

Linda   Well why do we have to go?

Bernadette   Linda! You cannot see your future husband on the eve of your wedding!

Linda   Who says so?

Carol   Linda, you see your Dave tonight an' your marriage is doomed.

Linda   Ogh . . . Carol. Get lost will y' . . .

Maureen   Linda, d' you want to end up under a pile of stones?

Linda (*laughing*)   What?

Bernadette   We don't want to go Linda. This is for your sake love. We're only thinkin' of you Linda.

Carol   You can't afford to see Dave tonight, Linda.

Linda Y' don't really believe that do y'?

Carol Linda. Y've got to believe it, 'cos it's true.

Linda Y' do don't y'? You really believe it.

Bernadette Yes, an' so should you. Now come on, let's have your cloakroom ticket, we'll get the coats an' –

Linda (*to* **Frances**) You don't believe this do y'? Eh?

Frances Well y' don't do y' Linda? Y' don't see each other the night before y' get married.

Linda For Christ's sake. Come on!

Bernadette Linda, we don't want to see you put your future in jeopardy.

Linda (*looking at them; after a pause*) If it wasn't for the fact that you're my mates, an' have been for a long time, I'd say you were all certifiable! (*She stares at them.*) Why don't y' do what y' *want* t' do? Why don't y' do what you think you should do? But y' won't will y'? That's the biggest sin of all to you lot isn't it? You'll just keep on doin' what you're told to, won't y'?

Bernadette Nobody tells me what to do Linda. I do whatever I want to do.

Linda Oh do y'? Well look Berni, you came here tonight to get off with a feller. Well there's loads of them out there. Come on, come on out an' get one . . .

Bernadette I could do Linda. I could. But for your sake –

Linda For my sake? Look, just forget about my sake, will y'? (*She opens the door.*) Now come on, all of y' come on, now . . .

She holds the door for them. They make no move.

Well, sod off then!

She turns and goes out. In the corridor she leans against the wall, takes out her cigarettes, lights one.

Bernadette   Well if you ask me I say she's not been herself all night.

Frances   But that's what she's like Berni. How long have I been her mate eh? An' I've seen her, she can be like this y' know . . .

Bernadette   It's the pressure isn't it? I know what's goin' through her mind.

Carol   Yeh but if she's actin' like this now Berni, imagine what she'll be like tomorrow.

Bernadette   What we've got to do is to stop her doin' anythin' stupid, whether she wants to or not.

Frances   I say we go an' see the fellers. Tell them to go somewhere else.

Carol   They won't though will they? Y' know what fellers are like.

Frances   We were here first weren't we? Sod it. I'll go an' see if I can find Eddy Ainsworth. He'll tell them what to do. If he says leave they will do.

Frances *goes out to the corridor. In the Ladies they pass around fags, smoking, thinking. In the corridor . . .*

Linda (*as* **Frances** *passes*)   Frances . . .

Frances *tries to ignore it.*

Linda   Frankie. . . !

Frances (*turning*)   What?

Linda (*after a pause*)   Forget it.

Frances   Listen Linda . . . I don't know what's wrong with you tonight but you can't half be an awkward bitch . . .

Linda *turns away.* **Frances** *continues on down the corridor and out through the doors.*

From the other end of the corridor we see **Peter** *and the* **Roadie** *enter.*

Roadie Well I'll try this and I'm tellin' y', if it don't work we've had it. We might as well throw the gear back in the van an' piss off.

Peter Not play at all?

Linda *looks up, with recognition.*

Roadie Well y' can't play without power can y'? You show me how t' get some power out to the –

Linda Hello . . .

Roadie (*thinking it's for him*)   Hello darlin', what y' doin' eh?

Linda (*passing him*) 'Ey.

Peter (*looking at her, with recognition*)   Christ! 'Ey . . . Jesus . . . come here . . .

He hugs her, she breaks away smiling and looking at him.

Roadie (*going down the corridor*)   What the fuck. I wish I was famous . . .

He exits.

Linda (*looking at him*)   Well the state of you!

Peter What d' y' mean?

The **Roadie** *sticks his head through the doors.*

Roadie 'Ey . . . an' don't be long. You're on in a minute . . .

Peter I thought you said y' couldn't get any power!

Roadie I will now!

The **Roadie** *exits.*

Peter (*of his gear*)   Like it do y'?

Linda Where d' y' get y' boots?

Peter (*camp*)   Tch. Chelsea Girl . . .

Linda (*laughing*)   They're great . . .

Peter Did y' know we were on?

Linda   No. How long have y' been with this lot?

Peter   'Bout a year. Just out for a bop are y'?

Linda   Sort of.

Peter   Christ, I would have thought you'd given up comin' to this sort of place.

Linda   Same could be said for you.

Peter   Nah . . . it's different for me isn't it? I'll never grow up.

She laughs.

Anyway, it's work isn't it? I don't come out of choice. (*He laughs.*) How are y'?

Linda   All right. How are you?

Peter   I'm OK. Lovely. Tch. I'm all right.

Linda (*looking at him*)   The state of y'.

Peter   I thought y' liked it.

Linda   I do but y' don't wanna go out like that round here. Y'll get locked up.

Peter   I know. We went over the road for a pint before. Should have heard them in there . . . 'All right cowboy' they kept shoutin'. 'Where's Tonto then?' (*He laughs.*) I dunno . . .

Linda   Well what d' y' expect if y' come round here in women's boots?

Peter (*grabbing her in a mock headlock*)   Agh . . . (*He turns it into a hug.*) You know better than that. (*He holds her and looks at her. Shaking his head.*) I can't believe it.

Frances *comes through the corridor doors.* **Linda** *pulls away from* **Peter**. **Frances** *clocks it. She goes into the loo, closes the door, leans on it.*

Peter   Isn't that whatshecalled, your mate?

Linda   Frances.

Peter Frances, that's right. How is she?

Linda All right.

Peter 'Ey it's great to see y' y' know.

Linda It's great to see you. I suppose.

Peter Suppose? Tch. I'll say tarar an' go an' tune up if you like.

Linda Go on then.

Peter Come off it. Fancy a dance?

Linda With you?

Peter No, with Tonto! Who d' y' think?

Linda I didn't think fellers from famous groups went dancin', I thought they kept themselves apart from the rabble.

Peter They do usually. But you're special rabble!

Linda Tch. Oh such flattery. Or was it an insult?

Peter (*leading her along the corridor*) Come on. What's the dance up here these days? Still do the twist?

Linda The Foxtrot actually . . .

Peter Oh is it actually . . .

They go through the doors.

Frances *moves from the outer door, through the inner door into the Ladies.*

Carol What did they say?

Bernadette Well?

Carol Are they goin' Fran?

Frances No.

Carol Tch. Fellers.

Frances Listen. Guess whose group it is that's playin'?

Bernadette Y' what?

Frances   Peter Taylor. It's his group . . .

Bernadette   We don't wanna know about a group Frances, we wanna know –

Frances   Berni! The thing is Berni, in this group there's a feller called Peter Taylor. An' him an' Linda only had a thing goin' for about two years didn't they?

Carol   You what?

Frances   They're right outside this door, now, arms round each other . . .

Bernadette   Oh . . . so that's why she wanted to come here is it?

Frances   Well we don't know that, Berni . . .

Carol   Oh come off it, Frances.

Bernadette   Look Frances, if she went out with him for that long she's bound t' know what group he's playin' in . . . there's a poster outside isn't there?

Carol   I wondered why Linda wanted to come to a dump like this. Well fancy doin' somethin' like this, on y' weddin' night . . .

Maureen   God . . . no good'll come of this . . . I'm tellin' y' I know . . .

Frances   Look . . . she is only talkin' to him . . .

Bernadette   Yes, an' we all know where talk leads . . .

Maureen   Don't Berni . . . don't . . .

Carol   Y' don't see ex fellers the night before y' gettin' married do y'?

Frances   She could just have bumped into him y' know . . .

Bernadette   Well we can soon find out can't we Frances? We'll get her in here . . . (*She goes out to the corridor.*)

Frances (*sighing*)   Ogh Christ . . .

Carol I knew we shoulda gone the Top Rank . . . I knew we shouldn't have come here.

Bernadette *comes in.*

Bernadette Where did you say she was?

Frances Just outside.

Bernadette Well she's not there now . . .

Carol Well where is she?

Bernadette How do I know? But I'll tell y' what, if y' ask me she's up to no good. That girl is playin' with fire. We're her mates, I reckon we better sort out a way to stop her gettin' burnt . . .

Maureen Oh God . . . (*Beginning to cry, she rushes into the WC.*)

Frances For God's sake Maureen shut it will y' . . .

Maureen (*frantic*) Why can't everything be nice?

Bernadette Who said everything won't be nice Maureen?

Maureen (*crying*) No good'll come of this . . . You mark my words . . . you see . . .

Bernadette Maureen . . . we'll sort it out, don't worry. Everything will be nice Maureen. There's a wedding tomorrow; there'll be a nice cake and a nice service, nice bridesmaids, nice presents. And a nice bride and groom. But Mo, we've just got to see that Linda doesn't do anything silly. We're her mates Mo. What are mates for eh? Eh?

Maureen *comes out of the WC.* **Bernadette** *puts her arm round her.*

Bernadette Everything will be nice love. We'll look after her . . . don't worry. Come on . . . everything'll be very nice.

The **Girls** *go into the corridor as* . . .

Billy *and* **Robbie** *come through the doors.*

Robbie All right girls?

Bernadette Come on girls . . .

Carol (*stopping*) Hia Robbie . . .

Robbie All right . . . er . . . Carol isn't it?

Carol (*flattered*) Tch . . . y' good at names aren't y'?

Robbie I'm good at most things Carol!

Bernadette (*from the door*) CAROL!

Carol Got t' go. See y' tomorrow eh Robbie . . . at the weddin' . . .

She dashes off through doors, following the others.

Billy You're on there Robbie. I could tell. Yeh . . .

Robbie Don't fancy it much though . . .

Billy Don't y'?

Robbie Nah. I'd screw it though. Come on . . . hurry up or them other two'll have gone. 'Ey they're crackers those two aren't they?

Billy Yours is, Robbie. Yeh . . .

Robbie Dead ringer for Britt Ekland isn't she? Whoa. Come on . . .

They enter the Gents. **Kav** *is putting the finishing touches to an impressive drawing of his own name.*

Robbie Ogh . . . look at that . . .

Billy That's dead smart that Kav.

Kav It's all right isn't it?

Robbie Yeh. 'Ey . . . y' wanna see these two we've tapped off with. Mine looks just like Britt Ekland, doesn't she Billy?

Billy Yeh. Mine looks just like Rod Stewart. That's great that, Kav . . .

Robbie Come on Billy . . . what y' moanin' for? She's all right that one. Don't you go doin' a bunk on her will y'? I'm knackered with the Britt Ekland one if you give her mate the elbow.

Billy I can't stand her though, Robbie. That's smart, Kav.

Robbie What's wrong with her?

Billy She's destroyed.

Robbie Well it's dark in there isn't it? Keep her out the light an' no one'll notice her hunchback. Ah come on Billy . . . I'd do the same for you wouldn't I eh? Wouldn't I Kav? I'm your mate aren't I?

Billy Yeh.

Robbie Well, I'm askin' y' to do me a favour.

Kav Robbie's right y' know Billy. You stand by y' mates an' they stand by you, don't they?

Maureen, Carol and **Frances** *come through the corridor doors and into the Ladies.* **Bernadette** *follows them.*

Billy Yeh. All right.

Robbie Good lad . . . come on . . . 'ey, it's smart that Kav. Eddy'll be made up with y'.

Kav (*as they leave*) Yeh . . . I'm gonna tell him.

Bernadette *enters the Ladies just before the fellers come into the corridor and exit.*

Bernadette Well the brazen . . . ogh . . . did you see it . . . did y' see it?

Maureen Dancin' . . . like that, with him . . .

Frances An' ignored her mates.

Maureen She was dancin' like she was stuck to him wasn't she?

Bernadette She's makin' a spectacle of herself she is.

Carol An' it wasn't even a slowy was it?

Bernadette Y' don't dance like that to a fast record unless you've got one thing in mind. It's written all over them what they've got in mind.

Maureen What Berni?

Bernadette   Come on Maureen. It's patently obvious.

Carol   God, he's got a cheek that feller hasn't he eh, comin' round here, dancin' like that. He must have no shame that feller.

Linda *enters through the corridor and heads for the Ladies.*

Bernadette   Well I think she's immoral, I do. There's no excuse for that sort of behaviour. Not on the night before y' gettin' –

Linda *enters. Immediate silence. She walks through them and into the WC, closing the door.*

Bernadette   Linda . . . Linda!

Linda (*from the WC*)   What Berni?

Bernadette   Linda, don't y' think you're bein' a bit inconsiderate?

Linda (*all sweetness*)   Why's that Bern?

Bernadette   I could say 'improper' Linda, but I won't. There is moderation y' know Linda.

Linda (*from the WC*)   Why don't y' tell me what's botherin' y' Bern?

Bernadette   Do you really think you should be carryin' on like this, with a stranger, the night before your weddin'?

Linda (*from the WC*)   He's not a stranger . . . he's someone I know very well. You could call him an intimate friend, Berni . . .

Bernadette   Don't you try and take the piss out of me Linda.

The WC flushes, the door opens and **Linda** *crosses to the basin.*

Linda   Berni . . . I'm dancing, that's all.

Carol   Yeh, but y' used to go out with him didn't y' Linda?

Linda   Yes Carol, I did.

Carol   Well don't y' think that makes it worse?

Linda (*drying her hands*)   No Carol, I don't think it makes it anything. I am dancin', with someone I used to go out with. I like him. I like him very much as it happens. An' I think it's got sod all to do with you, or you or you or any of you.

Bernadette   Have you forgotten that tomorrow you an' Dave will be standing in that church, getting married?

Linda *finishes drying her hands, goes to the door, opens it, turns and looks at them.*

Linda   An' what makes you think I'm still going ahead with it?

Linda *goes into the corridor and exits.*

Maureen   I knew it . . . I told you . . . I knew it . . . what did I say?

Carol   God, I'm supposed to be a bridesmaid an' everythin' . . .

Maureen   I'm gonna be sick, I am, I'm gonna be sick. What am I gonna do with the barbecue chairs?

Bernadette   This is gettin' out of hand this is.

Frances   What we gonna do?

Bernadette   Y' know who y' can blame for this don't y', eh? This is Peter Whatsisname's doing isn't it?

Carol   What we gonna do though Berni?

Bernadette   Well if y' ask me Carol I reckon the sooner she gets away from that Peter feller and comes to her senses the better it'll be for everyone.

Frances   She's makin' a fool of herself.

Bernadette   She's makin' a fool of everyone. I think the fellers should know about this. I think they've got to be told . . .

Carol   Don't tell Dave, Berni . . .

Bernadette   I won't have to tell him if she carries on flauntin' herself out there. He'll see it for himself soon enough. No, come on, we'll tell the others . . .

They begin to exit into the corridor.

Frances   What y' gonna say Berni?

Bernadette   I'll tell them what she told us . . . that the weddin's off!

They go into the corridor and exit through the doors.

Peter *and* **Linda** *enter as if from the bandroom.* **Peter** *is carrying a pint.*

Linda   Does that mean you won't be able to play?

Peter   Doesn't look like it.

Linda   Ah I was lookin' forward t' seein' y'.

Peter   It's not our fault. All the wiring's lethal. Every time they connect to a socket it blows. The place is fallin' to bits.

Linda   It's like everythin' else round here. It's dyin' this place is. Didn't y' notice?

Peter   Huh. I didn't think I'd see y' y' know. I thought you would have left by now.

Linda   Left for where?

Peter   Nowhere in particular. I just didn't think you'd stay round here.

Linda   An' what's wrong with round here?

Peter   Come on, y' just said yourself it's dyin'.

Linda   Well, that's no reason to leave is it?

Peter   I just never thought this place'd be big enough for you.

Linda   Get lost!

Peter (*laughing*)   I'm not takin' the piss, honest. I'm serious.

Linda   Tch.

Peter   You should've come to London when I went. You should've come with me.

Linda   I couldn't, could I?

Peter   Wouldn't.

Linda   All right, wouldn't.

Peter   Why?

Linda   I didn't (*Camping it.*) erm, love you enough. (*After a pause.*) I didn't half like you a lot though.

Peter (*camping it*)   You always were a smooth-talking bitch Linda.

She smiles.

Anyway, I didn't necessarily mean with me in that sense. What y' gonna do then, settle down here?

Linda   I might.

Peter (*shaking his head*)   Tch.

Linda   'Ey, it might have escaped your notice but there are a lot of people who like livin' in this town.

Peter   Including you?

Linda   Yes.

Peter   Why?

Linda   Oh sod off you. Just 'cos you live in London now it doesn't give you the right to come back up here an' start tellin' us we're all peasants y' know. We do know where London is. I mean it's only two and a half hours away on the train. Christ you'd think you'd gone to the other end of the world to hear you talk. It's only a train ride away.

Peter (*laughing*)   Not when you've only got a single ticket.

Linda   Comin' up here, tellin' everyone what to do.

Peter   I'm not tellin' you what to do.

Linda   You think you can tell anyone what to do just 'cos you can get away with wearin' women's boots . . .

Peter (*laughing*)   You do what you like. I'm not tellin' you. Stay around here if y' want to Linda. Have y' kids an' keep y' mates an' go dancin' an' go to the pub an' go to the shops an' do all those things you used to tell me you hated doing.

Linda *goes to reply. Can't.* **Peter** *is waiting for her.*

Linda   Get lost you! Well, I was young then. I mean y' do hate all those things when y' young, don't y'?

Peter   An' how old are y' now?

Linda   Twenty-two.

Peter   A twenty-two year old geriatric.

He looks at her. She at him.

Linda   You're a bastard y' know.

Peter   I know. I'm a selfish shitty bastard because I did what I wanted to do. I did the worst thing possible y' know, what I wanted to.

Linda   An' why do y' think I should get out?

Peter   Come on lovely; because you want to! Because while you're doin' all this number you hate it. Y' do it, but while you're doin' it you hate it. You want out of it.

Linda   D' y' know somethin'? You are the most arrogant big-headed . . .

Peter   I know. But I'm right aren't I?

Linda   No. You're just so arrogant, you think you're . . . that you're right.

Peter *smiles and shakes his head at her.*

Linda   Think what you like. It doesn't matter.

Peter (*after a pause*)   Why don't y' jack it in up here? When we finish tonight we're in the van and away – Scotland tomorrow, Newcastle on Sunday, day off on Monday, on to Norwich, Southampton, couple of gigs in Devon. Then back to London. Come with us.

Linda   I gave you your answer a couple of years ago.

Peter   But then I was askin' you to come with me. This time, lovely, I'm just offerin' you a lift. You can get off wherever you want.

Linda   I never accept lifts off strange men.

Peter   Yeh. Well you should.

Linda   Oh should I? God has spoken has he? Listen, Mr Knowall . . . it'd be great wouldn't it, speedin' through Scotland with a second-rate band when there's a hundred an' twenty guests stood in the church tomorrow waitin' to see me get married.

Peter (*after a long pause; looking at her*)   We are not a second-rate band.

Linda *laughs. He puts his arm round her.*

Peter   Honestly?

Linda   Yeh. Why d' y' think I came here tonight? It's the hen night.

Peter (*baulking*)   Hen night! What? D' y' want us to play 'Congratulations' for y'? Or d' y' prefer 'Get me to the church'?

Linda   Neither. Just give us a kiss.

He does so. She looks at him, hugs him, breaks away, turns to the door of the Ladies.

Linda   Thanks for lettin' me have me last fling with you.

Peter   Hey.

She stops.

D' y' love him?

Linda   Accordin' to me mates I do. (*She opens the door.*)

Linda   Hey . . . do you?

Linda (*stopping*)   What's it to you Peter?

Peter   I'm tryin' to understand why you're stayin'.

Linda   Look . . . don't you listen? I've told y', I'm gettin' married tomorrow.

Peter   I wasn't askin' about that.

Linda (*smiling at him*)   Tarar Peter. (*She enters the Ladies.*)

He stares at the closed door for a moment before turning and going into the Gents. He heads for the urinal, sees **Kav**'*s drawing, stops to look at it. In the Ladies,* **Linda** *goes into the WC.*

The corridor doors fly open, **Eddy** *leading the others.*

Robbie   An' the weddin's off is it Eddy?

Eddy   You're jokin' aren't y'? She might fuckin' say it's off. But no one makes a laughin' stock of my mate.

Billy   Too right. Yeh.

Eddy   Thinks she's some sort of clever tart does she? We'll fuckin' sort her out. An' we'll sort out her fancy feller as well.

Robbie   The fuckin' cheek of him – comin' up here an' nabbin' Dave's tart. He thinks he can just take whatever he wants, doesn't he?

Eddy   He'll think again when we've finished with him. We wanna get him in here, right, away from the rest of his posin' mates . . . Look Billy you go down the back an' see if y' can.

Peter *having finished in the bog and taken another look at* **Kav**'*s drawing opens the door of the Gents. He sees them.*

Peter   All right lads?

Eddy *blocks his exit, the others supporting him, crowding* **Peter** *back into the Gents.*

Eddy   No sunshine, it's not all right is it?

Peter   What?

Eddy   In there. Go on.

Peter   Look the –

Eddy   In.

Peter *backs into the Gents. They stand looking at him.*

Peter   Well?

Eddy   You what? You just shut it. (*He looks at him.*) Are you a tart?

Peter *looks back, sighs. Pause.*

Eddy   'Ey I asked you a question.

Peter   No. I'm not a tart.

Eddy   Well why have y' got tarts' boots on?

Peter (*after a pause*)   I like them.

Eddy   I don't!

Peter   No. Well . . .

Eddy   I don't like you either.

Peter   Yeh. Yeh I'd gathered that.

Eddy   Oh had y' now?

Peter   Well . . .

Eddy (*after a pause; pointing*)   You've been dancin' with our mate's tart.

Peter   What?

Robbie   While he's fuckin' lyin' sick in there.

Peter (*glancing at the WC*)   Look, I didn't know she was anythin' to do with −

Eddy   You've been messin' around with Dave's future missis.

Peter   Now hold on −

Eddy   NO! You just hold on! Comin' back here. Posin' all over the place. You can't just walk over us. Think y' someone special don't y'? Eh? You think y' can fuckin' do things that we can't, don't y'? Well I'll fuckin' show you what we can do . . .

Peter *backs away.* **Eddy** *grabs him, turns him and forces him to face* **Kav**'*s drawing.*

Eddy   That's what we can do! Look at it. Look.

Peter   I'm lookin'.

Eddy   Good.

Robbie   That's fuckin' clever that is.

Peter   I know.

Eddy   Oh do y'?

Peter   Who did it?

Kav   Me.

Eddy (*to* **Kav**)   Shut it.

Peter (*to* **Kav**)   It's good.

Eddy   We can do anythin'. (*He pushes him away*.)

Peter   Yeh. (*To* **Kav**.) D' y' go to Art School?

Robbie (*laughing*)   Art School! Listen t' the stupid get . . .
(*He laughs.*)

Eddy (*laughing*)   'Ey Kav . . . y' could be an artist you
could! (*Laughing.*) Picasso Kavanagh . . .

Robbie   Kav the artist . . . (*Camp.*) Oogh can I hold y'
brush for y' ducky?

Eddy *and* **Billy** *laugh*.

Kav (*joining the laughter*)   Art School! The only artist I
wanna be is a piss artist.

They laugh.

Peter (*to* **Kav**)   You stupid cunt!

Eddy *wheels and grabs him.*

Eddy   Don't you . . . don't you dare! I'm gonna tell you
somethin' for your own good – don't you come round here
with your music, y' fuckin' music. Don't you come makin'
people unhappy! Understand? We'll be watchin' you. You go
near Dave's tart again an' your fuckin' number's up. Right?

Peter   Yeh. Whatever you say.

Eddy   She's our mate's tart. We look after our mates. We stick with them. (*He leans in close.*) You left this town. Y' walked out. You've got no claims here. You left this town, so when you've finished tonight just fuck off out of it! (*He pushes him away.*) Get out!

Peter *starts to go.*

Billy (*shouting*)   An' don't come back. Y' big poufter.

Peter *stops in the corridor and shakes his head. In the Ladies,* **Linda** *comes out of the WC and washes her hands.*

Eddy   Right, come on. Let's find his tart.

They leave the Gents.

As they do so, the **Roadie** *enters and sees* **Peter**.

Roadie   It's no good, Pete, the bleedin' place is −

Peter (*walking as if to the bandroom*)   Good. Come on, let's get the gear packed and piss off.

Eddy *and the others approach the corridor doors.*

As they do, **Bernadette** *and the girls come through.*

Bernadette   We can't find her, Eddy . . .

Eddy   We will. Come on.

The fellers exit.

The ladies continue on their way to the Ladies.

Bernadette (*watching* **Eddy** *go*)   Ogh . . . I wish y'd find me Eddy.

Carol   D' y' fancy him Berni?

Bernadette   I wouldn't say no to an hour with him. Come on.

They enter the Ladies.

Linda   What you doin' here? Why aren't y' out dancin'. There's not a lot of fellers left y' know Berni.

Bernadette   You should be ashamed of yourself. (*Aside to* **Maureen**.) Go an' tell Eddy she's here.

Linda   Why should I Berni?

Maureen *goes into the corridor and exits.*

Carol   Ignore your mates Linda. We don't matter to you, do we Linda?

Linda   For God's sake, what y' on about now?

Bernadette   Look Linda, you just listen to us for a minute.

Linda   Tch . . . yes sir!

Carol   See, see. Well don't listen Linda. Be selfish. You be a selfish bitch.

Linda (*after a pause*)   All right. Go on. I'm listening . . .

Bernadette   Listen to me Linda. Now I've been married quite a few years Linda. You're forgettin' that I've been through what's happening t' you. I understand.

Linda   Well? Go on.

Bernadette   Linda, there isn't one woman who doesn't have doubts the night before she gets married −

Linda   Berni −

Bernadette   Now don't interrupt me Linda! Every woman has doubts. But that's all they are, doubts. Y' don't act on feelin's like that. Just because you've got some doubts it doesn't mean you can go rushin' into the arms of some ex-boyfriend an' then disappear with him −

Linda (*slightly warning*)   Berni −

Bernadette   What would happen if every woman did that eh? Who'd be married today if we all took notice of how we feel? Eh? Eh?

Linda   Berni. Can I get a word in now?

She looks at them all. Their intensity is too much for her. She laughs.

We see the fellers come through the corridor doors, led by **Eddy**.

Robbie   Eddy, don't be daft . . . we can't go in there . . .

Carol   See . . . see . . .

Linda   Look Carol . . . look, all of y'. For your information I've got no intention of –

Eddy *knocks the door open, points at* **Linda**.

Eddy   Right you, out. Now!

Carol   She won't listen Eddy. (*Glancing out to the corridor.*) Hia Robbie.

Eddy *and* **Linda** *stare at each other.* **Robbie** *and the others hesitate outside the Ladies.*

Robbie   Come on Eddy, we can't go in there . . . It's the Ladies.

Eddy (*to* **Linda**)   Get outside I said!

Carol   I've told y' Eddy. She won't listen.

They stare at each other.

Eddy   All right, all right. Stay in here. I'll stay as well. (*To the others.*) Get in here.

They can't.

It doesn't bother me y' know. I don't care that it's the fuckin' Ladies – rules mean nothin' to me! (*To the others.*) I said get in here!

Reluctantly they do so.

Robbie   Come on Eddy . . . let's get out . . . we can't stay in here . . .

Kav   Eddy, we're in the women's bogs . . . come on . . .

Eddy   You stay where y' are. What does it matter where it is. Y' don't worry about names on doors do y'? Names on doors don't bother me. I go where I wanna go. (*He turns to* **Linda**.) Now you just listen to me. You might be Dave's tart, yes. But I'm his mate. I'm his best mate. He's our mate. You might try an' treat him like shite but we don't.

Linda *glares.*

Carol   Eddy's right y' know Linda . . . you are makin' a terrible show of Dave.

Eddy   Goin' round tellin' people y' not marryin' him – you! (*Pointing at her.*) Don't you treat a man like that – understand? You just learn a bit of respect an' loyalty an' don't you go tellin' no one that y' not marryin' Dave. 'Cos you are. Tomorrow!

Linda   Piss off little man!

She quickly turns and goes into the WC, closing the door. **Eddy,** *fast, bangs it open and grabs her.*

Eddy   Don't . . . just fuckin' don't . . . you! Now you listen to what I'm sayin' girl. You play awkward friggers with me, you do it once more tonight an' I'll get that posin' bastard you've been dancin' with an' I'll break every finger he's got. Did you hear me, eh? We've already seen him. He's been warned. And so have you. Did you hear me?

Linda   Yes. All right. Yes. OK . . .

He lets go of her but stays close.

Eddy (*quietly*)   He's crap y' know. (*He pauses.*) He can't even play the guitar. (*He pauses.*) Y' think he's good don't y'? Well he's not. (*He pauses.*) I know about guitars. I play the guitar. Chords I play. G and F an' D minor.

Robbie   Come on Eddy . . . if we're seen in here . . .

Eddy   Y' don't wanna be impressed by him girl. He's all show. I could've been in a group. A famous group. I play the guitar. (*He backs out of the WC, turns to the other women.*) She's all right now. She's come to her senses. Haven't y' eh?

Linda (*dumb*)   Yeh.

Kav   Come on Eddy, this is the Ladies.

Robbie   Come on . . .

Eddy   Right. (*To* **Linda**.) See y' in church! Come on.

They go into the Gents.

Eddy   Come on. (*He begins running a bowl of water*.) Get him over here, lets get him sorted out. I've had enough of this place. We're goin' the club.

They begin to try and sober **Dave** *up by dousing his head in water*.

Carol   Eddy was right wasn't he Linda?

Linda   Yeh. Yeh.

Bernadette   Oh Lind . . . Linda . . . thank goodness you've come to your senses.

Frances   I'm always tellin' y' about your moods aren't I Lind?

Maureen *comes through the corridor doors and heads for the Ladies*.

Bernadette   Well I'm glad it's all been sorted out . . .

Carol   Ah yeh. (*Arms around her*.) Come on now Linda eh? I didn't mean anythin' harsh that I might have said, Lind. All friends now eh?

Maureen *rushes in*.

Maureen   What's happenin'?

Bernadette   It's all right Mo. Everything's fine now.

Maureen   Ah I'm glad. Hia Lind.

Bernadette   Now we can get back to havin' a good night, eh?

Maureen   'Ey, listen the group's not gonna be playin'.

Frances   Why?

Maureen   I dunno. They just announced it. There's not enough power or somethin', for their equipment.

Bernadette   'Ey, I bet I could put a bit of power in their equipment, eh?

The **Girls**, *apart from* **Linda**, *laugh*.

Eh Lind?

Linda (*smiling*)   Yeh.

Frances   What we gonna do now?

Carol   Why don't we go somewhere else?

Frances   What does Linda want to do?

Bernadette   Linda only wanted to come here 'cos there was live music. If there isn't gonna be any she won't mind movin' on. Will y' Linda?

Carol   Let's go to a club.

Maureen   Ah shall we eh?

Bernadette   Come on eh. Eh Lind?

Linda   If you like.

Carol   I'll go get the coats. Hurry up. We'll get a taxi before the pubs start emptyin'.

Carol *goes into the corridor and exits.*

The others start preparing to go. In the Gents . . .

Kav   Come on Dave . . . Dave . . . we're goin' down the club . . . have another bevvy . . .

Billy   We'll have t' get in before eleven y' know. Yeh.

The ladies leave the loo. They approach the corridor doors. As they do so, **Carol** *comes through with coats. They begin preparing themselves to leave.* **Linda** *leans on the wall, slightly apart from the rest of them.*

Eddy   Sod it. Come on. Let's get him out. We'll get a taxi.

Frances   I'll go see if there's any taxis passin' . . .

She goes through the doors.

Bernadette (*to* **Linda**)   All right love?

Linda   Feel a bit sick.

Bernadette (*to the others*)   That'll be all the drink. Don't worry love, you'll be OK tomorrow. Be all right on the big day.

The door to the Gents opens. The fellers come into the corridor, carrying **Dave**.

Bernadette   Linda . . . close your eyes.

Linda *does as ordered.* **Maureen** *crosses to her and turns her to face the wall.*

Maureen   Turn this way Lind. Y' can't be too safe. God Linda . . . count y'self lucky y' can't see him. What a state.

Robbie (*as they approach*)   All right girls.

Carol   Hia Robbie.

Bernadette   'Ey . . . don't bring him here. We don't want tomorrow's bride seein' tomorrow's groom.

Kav   He can't see anythin'.

Robbie   He's blind.

Carol   Hia Robbie . . .

Robbie   Here . . . put him down here till we get a cab . . . he'll be all right.

They put him down, propping him against the wall. **Robbie** *leaves the others to it and shoots across to* **Carol**.

Robbie   'Ey, I was hopin' I might get a dance with y'.

Carol (*almost overcome*)   Were y'?

Robbie   Who's er . . . lookin' after y'?

Carol   No one.

Robbie   No one? Y' mean no one's lookin' after a lovely young thing like you? (*He puts his arm around her.*) We'll have t' do somethin' about that won't we?

Frances *enters*.

Frances   There's no taxis anywhere.

Eddy (*looking at* **Robbie**)   I'll er, I'll go see if I can see one . . .

Bernadette   Need a hand Eddy?

Eddy   What (*He looks at her.*) Yeh. All right then.

Eddy *and* **Bernadette** *exit*.

Maureen *beaming at* **Billy** *who doesn't know where to put himself.* **Kav** *goes up to* **Robbie** *who is now necking with* **Carol**.

Kav   Eh Robbie . . . y' were only jokin' weren't y'?

Robbie (*breaking*)   What?

Kav   Y' were only jokin' . . . about the clap? Weren't y'?

Robbie   Yeh. (*Aside.*) Sod off will y' . . .

Kav   What?

Robbie (*breaking again; indicating* **Frances**)   Go on.

Kav *goes across to* **Frances**.

Frances   There's no taxis.

Kav   I know. It's terrible isn't it? Can't get one anywhere.

Frances   Your name's Kav isn't it?

Kav   Me real name's Tony. But they call me Kav.

Frances   Oh.

Kav   Hey.

Frances   What?

Kav   Come here.

She does.

Frances   What?

Kav   Give us a kiss.

Frances   Tch. Sod off.

Kav   Come here. (*He gets a grip.*) Come on.

He kisses her. She responds. Throughout the above, **Maureen** *has been edging along the wall to* **Billy**. *She is now next to him. He tries to ignore it.*

Maureen   Hia.

Billy (*not looking*)   Hello. (*He coughs.*)

Maureen   I see everyone's made friends!

Billy   Yeh.

Maureen   Has anyone ever told you you've got come-to-bed eyes?

Billy   I don't think so.

Maureen   Well you have y' know.

Billy   Have I? Yeh.

Maureen   Tch . . . you're a real smooth-talker you, aren't y'?

She goes to walk away. He quickly grabs her and starts necking with her. **Linda** *turns and opens her eyes. Looks at the scene before her. Looks at* **Dave**. *She crosses to him, bends down to him and quietly shakes him.*

Linda (*quietly*)   Look at me . . . look at me . . . come on . . . just look once . . . come on. (*She shakes him.*) Look at me! . . . (*She shakes him roughly.*) I said look at me!

Carol   Linda what y' —

Robbie   Come here. (*He starts necking again.*)

Carol   But she's —

Robbie   He can't see anythin' he's well away . . . come here . . .

They begin necking again.

Linda   Yes . . . that's it . . . that's it . . . (*She holds his brief gaze, drops him back against the wall. She stands.*)

Bernadette *enters, linking arms with* **Eddy**.

Linda *begins to walk down the corridor to the toilets.*

Bernadette   You all right Linda?

Linda   Yeh. I'm all right. Stay there. I'm just gonna be sick.

Bernadette (*to* **Eddy**)   Wait here. (*She starts to go after* **Linda**.)

Linda (*turning and pointing; vicious*)   I said stay there!

Bernadette (*stopped by the force of it*)   Linda!

She starts to approach . . . **Linda** *backs away.*

266 Stags and Hens

Bernadette I'm only coming to look after you love. You don't wanna be all on your own when y' sick.

Linda Stay there . . . don't come near me . . . I'm warnin' y' . . .

Bernadette (*hurrying forward*) Now Linda don't start this . . .

Linda *goes to enter the Ladies. Instead, she looks across the corridor, rushes into the Gents.*

Bernadette Linda! That's the Gents, Linda . . . Linda come out . . . y' can't go in the Gents . . . She's gone into the Gents . . . (*To* **Eddy**.) I can't go in there – you go in, see if she's all right . . .

Eddy She'll be all right.

Bernadette Linda! (*She goes to the door, gingerly opens it and calls through.*) Linda . . .

Throughout the above: **Linda** *goes into the Gents. She tries the large window. It is reinforced glass, no way out. She goes into the WC. She comes out looking for something to break the window. She sees the towel dispenser and smashes it off the wall. She goes into the WC, closes the door and bolts it. There is a crash of glass.* **Linda** *exits.*

Bernadette *goes into the Gents. She tries the WC door.*

Bernadette Eddy . . . Eddy . . . come here . . .

He does so as she is trying to force the lock.

Bernadette Eddy, Eddy quick . . . get that open.

Eddy *puts his shoulder to it a few times. It flies open.* **Bernadette** *goes in.*

Bernadette She's gone . . . she's friggin' gone . . . she's in that van . . . quick Eddy, quick past the front . . .

Cursing, **Eddy** *rushes out into the corridor.*

Bernadette (*as he goes*) Fuck . . .

Eddy *exits through the double doors.*

Bernadette *looks out of the window.*

Bernadette   Y' won't do it Eddy . . . y' won't . . . she's gone . . . you're too late Eddy . . .

Kav (*prompted by* **Eddy** *rushing out*)   'Ey, come on . . . Eddy must have got a taxi. (*He looks through the doors.*) Come on there's a couple comin' . . .

Carol   Quick . . . oogh quick come on . . . someone stop them . . . come on . . .

Maureen   Berni . . . Berni . . . come on . . .

Bernadette *slowly walks up the corridor.*

Carol   Come on Berni we've got taxis . . . we're goin' the club with the lads, come on . . .

Bernadette   Where's Eddy?

Carol   He must be in the taxi . . . come on . . . get Linda . . . come on . . .

Carol *exits with the others.*

Bernadette   Carol, Carol hold on . . .

Bernadette *exits.*

Shouting from outside. It's garbled but as it dies away we hear **Eddy**.

Eddy (*off*)   Bastards . . . come back . . . bastards.

He enters, panting for breath.

Bastards. (*He sees* **Dave**, *walks down to him, stands getting his breath back.*) They've bailed out on us Dave. They've left us. (*Starting to pick him up.*) They've all gone Dave. She's gone. She's fuckin' gone Dave. The bitch. (*He gets* **Dave** *standing.*) Well fuck them all. (*He starts to carry* **Dave** *towards the doors.*) They've gone. She's gone. Well y've got no baggage weighin' y' down. There's nothin' holdin' us back now Dave. We can go anywhere.

He carries him through the doors.

Blackout.

Educating Rita

Educating the Author

I was born in Whiston, which is just outside Liverpool. They talk funny in Whiston. To a Liverpudlian everyone else talks funny. Fortunately, when I was five my mum and dad moved to Knowsley, into an estate full of Liverpudlians who taught me how to talk correctly.

My dad worked in a factory (later, having come to hate factory life, he got out and bought a chip shop) and my mother worked in a warehouse; in those days there was a common ritual called employment. I went to school just down the road from my grandma's mobile grocer's (it was in an old charabanc which had long since lost any chance of going anywhere but everyone called it the mobile).

In school I learned how to read very early. Apart from reading books I played football and kick-the-can and quite enjoyed the twice-weekly gardening lessons. We each had a plot and at the end of the summer term we could take home our turnips and lettuces and radish and stuff. We used to eat it on the way. Our headmaster (Pop Chandler) had a war wound in his leg and everyone said it was 'cause of the shrapnel. When we went to the baths (if he was in a good mood) he'd show us this hole in his leg. It was horrible. It was blue. We loved looking at it.

Other than reading books, gardening, playing football and looking at shrapnel wounds I didn't care much for school. I watched the telly a lot. Never went to any theatres or anything like that. Saw a show at the village hall once but it was all false. They talked funny and got married at the end. I only remember it 'cause I won the raffle, a box of fruit, with a coconut right in the middle. When we opened it the coconut stunk. It was bad.

When I was eleven they sent me to a secondary school in Huyton. Like all the other Knowsley kids I was frightened of Huyton. There were millions of new houses there and flats, and everyone said there were gangs with bike chains and broken bottles and truck spanners. What everyone said was right; playtime was nothing to do with play, it was about survival. Thugs roamed the concrete and casually destroyed anything that couldn't move fast enough. Dinner time was the same only four times as long.

If you were lucky enough to survive the food itself you then had to get out into the playground world of protection rackets, tobacco hustlers, trainee contract killers and plain no-nonsense sadists. And that's without the teachers!

Anders his name was, the metalwork teacher. All the other kids loved metalwork. First thing we had to do was file a small rectangle of metal so that all the sides were straight; this would then be name-stamped and used as a nameplate to identify each kid's work. I never completed mine. After a matter of weeks other kids had moved from making nameplates to producing anything from guns and daggers to boiler-room engines while it was obvious that I was never going to be able to get the sides of my piece of metal straight. Eventually it was just a sliver, a near-perfect needle, though not straight. I showed it to him, Anders; I couldn't hide it from him any longer. He chucked it in the bin and wordlessly handed me another chunk of metal and indicated that I had to do it again and again and again until I did it *right*! And I did, for a whole school year, every metalwork lesson, tried and failed and with every failure there came a chunk of metal and the instruction to do it again. I started to have terrible nightmares about Anders. It's the only time I can remember feeling real hatred for another human being.

After another year I moved schools, to Rainford where it used to be countryside, where they all talked funny, where the thugs were rather old-fashioned, charming even. Whereas in Huyton you could be bike-chained to bits without warning, in Rainford the thugs observed some sort of manners: 'Ey you, does t' want t' fight wi' me?' You could still get hurt, of course, and some of the teachers were headcases; but there were no sadists, metalwork was not on the curriculum, there were fields and lawns in place of concrete playgrounds and compared to Huyton it was paradise. We even had a long lesson every week called 'silent reading'; just enter the classroom and pick up a book, start reading and as long as you made no noise you were left completely alone with your book. I remember clearly, during one of these lessons, locked into a novel, the sun streaming through the windows, experiencing the feeling of total peace and security and thinking what a great thing it must be to write books and create in people the sort of feeling the author had created in me. I wanted to be a writer!

It was a wonderful and terrible thought – wonderful because I sensed, I knew, it was the only thing for me. Terrible because how could I, a kid from the 'D' stream, a piece of factory fodder, ever change the course that my life was already set upon? How the hell could I ever be the sort of person who could become a writer? It was a shocking and ludicrous thought, one that I hid deep in myself for years, but one that would not go away.

During my last year at school they took us to a bottle-making factory in St Helens, me and all the other kids who were obviously factory types. I could feel the brutality of the place even before I entered its windowless walls. Inside, the din and the smell were overpowering. Human beings worked in there but the figures I saw, feeding huge and relentlessly hungry machines, seemed not to be a part of humanity but a part of the machinery itself. Those men who were fortunate enough to not have to work directly with the machinery, the supervisors, foremen I suppose, glared, prodded, occasionally shouted. Each one of them looked like Anders from the metalwork class.

Most of the kids with whom I visited that place accepted that it was their lot to end up in that place. Some even talked of the money they would earn and made out that they couldn't wait to get inside those walls.

But in truth, I think they all dreaded it as much as I. Back in school I stared at the geography books I hadn't read, the history pages and science I hadn't studied, the maths books (which would still be a mystery today, even if I'd studied them from birth), and I realised that with only six months' schooling to go, I'd left it all hopelessly too late. Like it or not I'd end up in a factory. There was no point in trying to catch up with years of schoolwork in a mere six months. And so I didn't. The months I had left were spent sagging school and going to a dark underground club every lunchtime. It was called the Cavern and the smell of sweat in there was as pungent as any in a factory, the din was louder than any made by machines. But the sweat was mingled with cheap perfume and was produced by dancing and the noise was music, made by a group called the Beatles.

One afternoon in summer I left the Cavern after the lunchtime session and had to go to the Bluecoat Chambers to sit an examination, the result of which would determine how suited I was to become an apprentice printer. I didn't want to be an apprentice printer; I wanted to be back in the Cavern. I did the exam because my dad thought it would be a good thing. I answered the questions on how many men it would take to lift three tons of coal in seven hours if it took one man two minutes to lift a sack of coal on a rainy day etc. And I wrote the essay of my choice (titled 'A Group Called The Beatles'). And I failed.

At home there were conferences, discussions, rows and slanging matches all on the same subject – me and the job I'd get. Eventually my mother resolved it all. She suggested I become a ladies' hairdresser! I can only think that a desire to have her hair done free must have clouded her normally reasonable mind. It was such a bizarre suggestion that I went along with it. I went to a college for a year or so and pretended to learn all about hairdressing. In reality most of my time was spent at parties or arranging parties. It was a good year but when it ended I had to go to work. Someone was actually prepared to hire me as a hairdresser, to let me loose on the heads of innocent and unsuspecting customers. There were heads scalded during shampooing, heads which should have become blonde but turned out green, heads of Afro frizz (before Afro frizz had been invented) and heads rendered temporarily bald. Somehow, probably from moving from one shop to another before my legendary abilities were known, I survived. For six years I did a job I didn't understand and didn't like. Eventually I even had my own small salon and it was there that on slack days I would retire to the back room and try to do the one and only thing I felt I understood, felt that I could do: write.

I wrote songs mostly but tried, as well, to write sketches and poetry, even a book. But I kept getting interrupted by women who, reasonably enough on their part, wanted their hair done. It dawned upon me that if ever I was to become a writer I had first to get myself into the sort of world which allowed for, possibly even encouraged such aspiration. But that would mean a drastic change of course. Could I do it? Could I do something which those around me didn't understand? I would have to break away. People would be puzzled and hurt. I compromised. I sensed that the world in which I would be able to write would be the academic world. Students have long holidays. I'd be able to spend a good part of the year writing and the other part learning to do a job, teaching perhaps, which would pay the rent. I wasn't qualified to train as a teacher but I decided to dip my toe in the water and test the temperature. I enrolled in a night class for 'O' level English Literature and passed it. To go to a college though, I'd need at least five 'O' levels. Taking them at night school would take too long. I had to find a college which would let me take a full-time course, pack everything into one year. I found a college but no authority was prepared to give me a maintenance grant or even pay my fees. I knew I couldn't let the course go, knew I could survive from day to day – but how was I going to find the money to pay the fees? The hairdressing paid nothing worth talking of.

I heard of a job, a contract job in Ford's, cleaning oil from the girders high above the machinery. With no safety equipment whatsoever and with oil on every girder the danger was obvious. But the money was big.

I packed up the hairdresser's and joined the night-shift girder cleaners. Some of them fell and were injured, some of them took just one look at the job and walked away. Eventually there were just a few of us desperate or daft enough to take a chance.

I stayed in that factory just long enough to earn the fees I needed; no extras, nothing. Once I'd earned enough for the fees, I came down from the girders, collected my money and walked away. I enrolled at the college and one day in September made my way along the stone-walled drive. The obvious difference in age between me and the sixteen-year-olds pouring down the drive made me feel exposed and nervous but as I entered the glass doors of Childwall College I felt as if I'd made it back to the beginning. I could start again. I felt at home.

Willy Russell

Educating Rita was first performed on 10 June 1980 at the Royal Shakespeare Company Warehouse, London, with the following cast:

Frank   Mark Kingston
Rita   Julie Walters

Directed by Mike Ockrent
Designed by Poppy Mitchell

Educating Rita subsequently transferred to the Piccadilly Theatre, London, and the cast changed several times during a long run. It was also filmed with Michael Caine as Frank and Julie Walters as Rita directed by Lewis Gilbert.

Act One

Scene One

A room on the first floor of a Victorian-built university in the north of England.

There is a large bay window with a desk placed in front of it and another desk covered with various papers and books. The walls are lined with books and on one wall hangs a good print of a nude religious scene.

Frank, *who is in his early fifties, is standing holding an empty mug. He goes to the bookcases and starts taking books from the shelves, hurriedly replacing them before moving on to another section.*

Frank (*looking along the shelves*) Where the hell . . . ? Eliot? (*He pulls out some books and looks into the bookshelf.*) No. (*He replaces the books.*) 'E'. (*He thinks for a moment.*) 'E', 'e', 'e' . . . (*Suddenly he remembers.*) Dickens. (*Jubilantly he moves to the Dickens section and pulls out a pile of books to reveal a bottle of whisky. He takes the bottle from the shelf and goes to the small table by the door and pours himself a large slug into the mug in his hand.*)

The telephone rings and startles him slightly. He manages a gulp at the whisky before he picks up the receiver and although his speech is not slurred, we should recognise the voice of a man who shifts a lot of booze.

Yes? . . . Of course I'm still here . . . Because I've got this Open University woman coming, haven't I? . . . Tch . . . Of course I told you . . . But darling, you shouldn't have prepared dinner should you? Because I said, I distinctly remember saying that I would be late . . . Yes. Yes, I probably shall go to the pub afterwards, I shall need to go to the pub afterwards, I shall need to wash away the memory of some silly woman's attempts to get into the mind of Henry James or whoever it is we're supposed to study on this course

. . . Oh God, why did I take this on? . . . Yes . . . Yes I
suppose I did take it on to pay for the drink . . . Oh, for God's
sake, what is it? . . . Yes, well – erm – leave it in the oven . . .
Look if you're trying to induce some feeling of guilt in me
over the prospect of a burnt dinner you should have prepared
something other than lamb and ratatouille . . . Because,
darling, I like my lamb done to the point of abuse and even I
know that ratatouille cannot be burned . . . Darling, you
could incinerate ratatouille and still it wouldn't burn . . .
What do you mean am I determined to go to the pub? I don't
need determination to get me into a pub . . .

There is a knock at the door.

Look, I'll have to go . . . There's someone at the door . . .
Yes, yes I promise . . . Just a couple of pints . . . Four . . .

There is another knock at the door.

(*Calling in the direction of the door.*) Come in! (*He continues on the
telephone.*) Yes . . . All right . . . yes . . . Bye, bye . . . (*He
replaces the receiver.*) Yes, that's it, you just pop off and put
your head in the oven. (*Shouting.*) Come in! Come in!

The door swings open revealing **Rita**.

Rita (*from the doorway*)   I'm comin' in, aren't I? It's that
stupid bleedin' handle on the door. You wanna get it fixed!
(*She comes into the room.*)

Frank (*staring, slightly confused*)   Erm – yes, I suppose I
always mean to . . .

Rita (*going to the chair by the desk and dumping her bag*)   Well
that's no good always meanin' to, is it? Y' should get on with
it: one of these days you'll be shoutin' 'Come in' an' it'll go on
forever because the poor sod on the other side won't be able
to get in. An' you won't be able to get out.

Frank *stares at* **Rita** *who stands by the desk.*

Frank   You are?

Rita   What am I?

Frank   Pardon?

Rita   What?

Frank (*looking for the admission papers*)   Now you are?

Rita   I'm a what?

Frank *looks up and then returns to the papers as* **Rita** *goes to hang her coat on the door hooks.*

Rita (*noticing the picture*)   That's a nice picture, isn't it? (*She goes up to it.*)

Frank   Erm – yes, I suppose it is – nice . . .

Rita (*studying the picture*)   It's very erotic.

Frank (*looking up*)   Actually I don't think I've looked at it for about ten years, but yes, I suppose it is.

Rita   There's no suppose about it. Look at those tits.

He coughs and goes back to looking for the admission paper.

Is it supposed to be erotic? I mean when he painted it do y' think he wanted to turn people on?

Frank   Erm – probably.

Rita   I'll bet he did y' know. Y' don't paint pictures like that just so that people can admire the brush strokes, do y'?

Frank (*giving a short laugh*)   No – no – you're probably right.

Rita   This was the pornography of its day, wasn't it? It's sort of like *Men Only*, isn't it? But in those days they had to pretend it wasn't erotic so they made it religious, didn't they? Do *you* think it's erotic?

Frank (*taking a look*)   I think it's very beautiful.

Rita   I didn't ask y' if it was beautiful.

Frank   But the term 'beautiful' covers the many feelings I have about that picture, including the feeling that, yes, it is erotic.

Rita (*coming back to the desk*)   D' y' get a lot like me?

Frank   Pardon?

Rita   Do you get a lot of students like me?

Frank   Not exactly, no . . .

Rita   I was dead surprised when they took me. I don't suppose they would have done if it'd been a proper university. The Open University's different though, isn't it?

Frank   I've – erm – not had much more experience of it than you. This is the first O.U. work I've done.

Rita   D' y' need the money?

Frank   I do as a matter of fact.

Rita   It's terrible these days, the money, isn't it? With the inflation an' that. You work for the ordinary university, don't y'? With the real students. The Open University's different, isn't it?

Frank   It's supposed to embrace a more comprehensive studentship, yes.

Rita (*inspecting a bookcase*)   Degrees for dishwashers.

Frank   Would you – erm – would you like to sit down?

Rita   No! Can I smoke? (*She goes to her bag and rummages in it.*)

Frank   Tobacco?

Rita ⁻ Yeh. (*She half-laughs.*) Was that a joke? (*She takes out a packet of cigarettes and a lighter.*) Here – d' y' want one? (*She takes out two cigarettes and dumps the packet on the desk.*)

Frank (*after a pause*)   Ah – I'd love one.

Rita   Well, have one.

Frank (*after a pause*)   I – don't smoke – I made a promise not to smoke.

Rita   Well, I won't tell anyone.

Frank   Promise?

As **Frank** *goes to take the cigarette* **Rita** *whips it from his reach.*

Rita (*doing a Brownie salute*)   On my oath as an ex Brownie. (*She gives him the cigarette.*) I hate smokin' on me own. An' everyone seems to have packed up these days. (*She lights the cigarettes*.) They're all afraid of gettin' cancer.

Frank *looks dubiously at his cigarette*.

Rita   But they're all cowards.

Frank   Are they?

Rita   You've got to challenge death an' disease. I read this poem about fightin' death . . .

Frank   Ah – Dylan Thomas . . .

Rita   No. Roger McGough. It was about this old man who runs away from hospital an' goes out on the ale. He gets pissed an' stands in the street shoutin' an challengin' death to come out an' fight. It's dead good.

Frank   Yes. I don't think I know the actual piece you mean . . .

Rita   I'll bring y' the book – it's great.

Frank   Thank you.

Rita   You probably won't think it's any good.

Frank   Why?

Rita   It's the sort of poetry you can understand.

Frank   Ah. I see.

Rita *begins looking idly round the room*.

Frank   Can I offer you a drink?

Rita   What of?

Frank   Scotch?

Rita (*going to the bookcase*)   Y' wanna be careful with that stuff, it kills y' brain cells.

Frank   But you'll have one? (*He gets up and goes to the small table*.)

Rita   All right. It'll probably have a job findin' my brain.

Frank (*pouring the drinks*)   Water?

Rita (*looking at the bookcase*)   Yeh, all right. (*She takes a copy of* Howards End *from the shelf.*) What's this like?

Frank *goes over to* **Rita**, *looks at the title of the book and then goes back to the drinks.*

Frank   *Howards End*?

Rita   Yeh. It sounds filthy, doesn't it? E.M. Foster.

Frank   Forster.

Rita   Oh yeh. What's it like?

Frank   Borrow it. Read it.

Rita   Ta. I'll look after it. (*She moves back towards the desk.*) If I pack the course in I'll post it to y'.

Frank *comes back to the desk with drinks.*

Frank (*handing her the mug*)   Pack it in? Why should you do that?

Rita *puts her drink down on the desk and puts the copy of* Howards End *in her bag.*

Rita   I just might. I might decide it was a soft idea.

Frank (*looking at her*)   Mm. Cheers. If – erm – if you're already contemplating 'packing it in', why did you enrol in the first place?

Rita   Because I wanna know.

Frank   What do you want to know?

Rita   Everything.

Frank   Everything? That's rather a lot, isn't it? Where would you like to start?

Rita   Well, I'm a student now, aren't I? I'll have to do exams, won't I?

Frank   Yes, eventually.

Rita   I'll have to learn about it all, won' I? Yeh. It's like y' sit there, don't y', watchin' the ballet or the opera on the telly an' – an' y' call it rubbish cos that's what it looks like? Cos y' don't understand. So y' switch it off an' say, that's fuckin' rubbish.

Frank Do you?

Rita I do. But I don't want to. I wanna see. Y' don't mind me swearin', do y'?

Frank Not at all.

Rita Do you swear?

Frank Never stop.

Rita See, the educated classes know it's only words, don't they? It's only the masses who don't understand. I do it to shock them sometimes. Y' know when I'm in the hairdresser's – that's where I work – I'll say somethin' like, 'Oh, I'm really fucked', y' know, dead loud. It doesn't half cause a fuss.

Frank Yes – I'm sure . . .

Rita But it doesn't cause any sort of fuss with educated people, does it? Cos they know it's only words and they don't worry. But these stuck-up idiots I meet, they think they're royalty just cos they don't swear; an' I wouldn't mind but it's the aristocracy that swears more than anyone, isn't it? They're effin' an' blindin' all day long. It's all 'Pass me the fackin' grouse' with them, isn't it? But y' can't tell them that round our way. It's not their fault; they can't help it. (*She goes to the window and looks out.*) But sometimes I hate them. God, what's it like to be free?

Frank Ah. Now there's a question. Will you have another drink? (*He goes to the small table.*)

Rita (*shaking her head*) If I'd got some other tutor I wouldn't have stayed.

Frank (*pouring himself a drink*) What sort of other tutor?

Rita Y' know, someone who objected to swearin'.

Frank How did you know I wouldn't object?

Rita I didn't. I was just testin' y'.

Frank (*coming back to the desk and looking at her*)   Yes. You're doing rather a lot of that, aren't you?

Rita   That's what I do. Y' know, when I'm nervous.

Frank (*sitting in the swivel chair*)   And how am I scoring so far?

Rita   Very good, ten out of ten go to the top of the class an' collect a gold star. I love this room. I love that window. Do you like it?

Frank   What?

Rita   The window.

Frank   I don't often consider it actually. I sometimes get an urge to throw something through it.

Rita   What?

Frank   A student usually.

Rita (*smiling*)   You're bleedin' mad you, aren't y'?

Frank   Probably.

Pause.

Rita   Aren't you supposed to be interviewin' me?

Frank (*looking at the drink*)   Do I need to?

Rita   I talk too much, don't I? I know I talk a lot. I don't at home. I hardly ever talk when I'm there. But I don't often get the chance to talk to someone like you; to talk at you. D' y' mind?

Frank   Would you be at all bothered if I did?

She shakes her head and then turns it into a nod.

Frank   I don't mind. (*He takes a sip of his drink.*)

Rita   What does assonance mean?

Frank (*half-spluttering*)   What? (*He gives a short laugh.*)

Rita   Don't laugh at me.

Frank   No. Erm – assonance. Well, it's a form of rhyme. What's a – what's an example – erm – ? Do you know Yeats?

Rita   The wine lodge?

Frank   Yeats the poet.

Rita   No.

Frank   Oh. Well – there's a Yeats poem, called 'The Wild Swans at Coole'. In it he rhymes the word 'swan' with the word 'stone'. There, you see, an example of assonance.

Rita   Oh. It means gettin' the rhyme wrong.

Frank (*looking at her and laughing*)   I've never really looked at it like that. But yes, yes you could say it means getting the rhyme wrong; but purposefully, in order to achieve a certain effect.

Rita   Oh. (*There is a pause and she wanders round.*) There's loads I don't know.

Frank   And you want to know everything?

Rita   Yeh.

Frank *nods and then takes her admission paper from his desk and looks at it.*

Frank   What's your name?

Rita (*moving towards the bookcase*)   Rita.

Frank (*looking at the paper*)   Rita. Mm. It says here Mrs S. White.

Rita *goes to the right of* **Frank**, *takes a pencil, leans over and scratches out the initial 'S'.*

Rita   That's 'S' for Susan. It's just me real name. I've changed it to Rita, though. I'm not a Susan any more. I've called meself Rita – y' know, after Rita Mae Brown.

Frank   Who?

Rita   Y' know, Rita Mae Brown who wrote *Rubyfruit Jungle*? Haven't y' read it? It's a fantastic book. D' y' wanna lend it?

Frank   I'd – erm – I'd be very interested.

Rita   All right.

Rita gets a copy of Rubyfruit Jungle *from her bag and gives it to* **Frank**. *He turns it over and reads the blurb on the back cover.*

Rita   What's your name?

Frank   Frank.

Rita   Oh. Not after Frank Harris?

Frank   Not after Frank anyone.

Rita   Maybe y' parents named y' after the quality. (*She sits in the chair by the desk.*)

Frank *puts down* Rubyfruit Jungle.

Rita   Y' know Frank, Frank Ness, Elliot's brother.

Frank   What?

Rita   I'm sorry – it was a joke. Y' know, Frank Ness, Elliot's brother.

Frank (*bemused*)   Ah.

Rita   You've still not got it, have y'? Elliot Ness – y' know, the famous Chicago copper who caught Al Capone.

Frank   Ah. When you said Elliot I assumed you meant T.S. Eliot.

Rita   Have you read his stuff?

Frank   Yes.

Rita   All of it?

Frank   Every last syllable.

Rita (*impressed*)   Honest? I couldn't even get through one poem. I tried to read this thing he wrote called 'J. Arthur Prufrock'; I couldn't finish it.

Frank   'J. Alfred'.

Rita   What?

Frank   I think you'll find it was 'J. Alfred Prufrock', Rita. J. Arthur is something else altogether.

Rita   Oh yeh. I never thought of that. I've not half got a lot to learn, haven't I?

Frank (*looking at her paper*)   You're a ladies hairdresser?

Rita   Yeh.

Frank   Are you good at it?

Rita (*getting up and wandering around*)   I am when I wanna be. Most of the time I don't want to though. They get on me nerves.

Frank   Who?

Rita   The women. They never tell y' things that matter. Like, y' know, doin' a perm, well y' can't use a strong perm lotion on a head that's been bleached with certain sorts of cheap bleach. It makes all the hair break off. But at least once a month I'll get a customer in for a perm who'll swear to God that she's not had any bleach on; an' I can tell, I mean I can see it. So y' go ahead an' do the perm an' she comes out the drier with half an inch of stubble.

Frank   And what do you do about it?

Rita   Try and sell them a wig.

Frank   My God.

Rita   Women who want their hair doin', they won't stop at anythin', y' know. Even the pensioners are like that, y' know; a pensioner'll come in an' she won't tell y' that she's got a hearin' aid: so y' start cuttin' don't y'? Next thing – snip – another granny deaf for a fortnight. I'm always cuttin' hearin' aid cords. An' ear lobes.

Frank   You sound like something of a liability.

Rita   I am. But they expect too much. They walk in the hairdresser's an' an hour later they wanna walk out a different person. I tell them I'm a hairdresser, not a plastic

surgeon. It's worse when there's a fad on, y' know like Farrah
Fawcett Majors.

Frank   Who?

Rita   Far-rah Fawcett Majors. Y' know, she used to be
with *Charlie's Angels*.

Frank *remains blank*.

Rita   It's a telly programme on ITV.

Frank   Ah.

Rita (*wandering towards the door*)   You wouldn't watch ITV
though, would y'? It's all BBC with you, isn't it?

Frank   Well, I must confess . . .

Rita   It's all right, I know. Soon as I walked in here I said
to meself, 'Y' can tell he's a Flora man'.

Frank   A what?

Rita   A Flora man.

Frank   Flora? Flowers?

Rita (*coming back to the desk*)   No, Flora, the bleedin'
margarine, no cholesterol; it's for people like you who eat
pebble-dashed bread, y' know the bread, with little hard bits
in it, just like pebble-dashin'.

Frank (*realising and smiling*)   Ah – pebble-dashed bread.

Rita   Quick? He's like lightnin'. But these women, you see,
they come to the hairdresser's cos they wanna be changed.
But if you want to change y' have to do it from the inside,
don't y'? Know like I'm doin'. Do y' think I'll be able to do
it?

Frank   Well, it really depends on you, on how committed
you are. Are you sure that you're absolutely serious about
wanting to learn?

Rita   I'm dead serious. Look, I know I take the piss an' that
but I'm dead serious really. I take the piss because I'm not, y'
know, confident like, but I wanna be, honest.

He nods and looks at her. She becomes uncomfortable and moves away a little.

Tch. What y' lookin' at me for?

Frank Because – I think you're marvellous. Do you know, I think you're the first breath of air that's been in this room for years.

Rita (*wandering around*) Tch. Now who's taking the piss?

Frank Don't you recognise a compliment?

Rita Go 'way . . .

Frank Where to?

Rita Don't be soft. Y' know what I mean.

Frank What I want to know is what is it that's suddenly led you to this?

Rita What? Comin' here?

Frank Yes.

Rita It's not sudden.

Frank Ah.

Rita I've been realisin' for ages that I was, y' know, slightly out of step. I'm twenty-six. I should have had a baby by now; everyone expects it. I'm sure me husband thinks I'm sterile. He was moanin' all the time, y' know, 'Come off the pill, let's have a baby.' I told him I'd come off it, just to shut him up. But I'm still on it. (*She moves round to* **Frank**.) See, I don't wanna baby yet. See, I wanna discover meself first. Do you understand that?

Frank Yes.

Rita Yeh. They wouldn't round our way. They'd think I was mental. I've tried to explain it to me husband but between you an' me I think he's thick. No, he's not thick, he's blind, he doesn't want to see. You know if I'm readin', or watchin' somethin' different on the telly he gets dead narked. I used to just tell him to piss off but then I realised that it was no good doin' that, that I had to explain to him. I tried to

explain that I wanted a better way of livin' me life. An' he
listened to me. But he didn't understand because when I'd
finished he said he agreed with me and that we should start
savin' the money to move off our estate an' get a house out in
Formby. Even if it was a new house I wanted I wouldn't go
an' live in Formby. I hate that hole, don't you?

Frank Yes.

Rita Where do you live?

Frank Formby.

Rita (*sitting*)   Oh.

Frank (*getting up and going to the small table*)   Another drink?

She shakes her head.

You don't mind if I do? (*He pours himself a drink.*)

Rita No. It's your brain cells y' killin'.

Frank (*smiling*)   All dead long ago I'm afraid. (*He drinks.*)

Rita *gets up and goes to* **Frank**'s *chair. She plays with the swivel and
then leans on it.*

Rita When d' y' actually, y' know, start teaching me?

Frank (*looking at her*)   What can I teach you?

Rita Everything.

Frank *leans on the filing cabinet, drinks, shakes his head and looks at
her.*

Frank I'll make a bargain with you. Yes? I'll tell you
everything I know – but if I do that you must promise never
to come back here . . . You see I never – I didn't actually
want to take this course in the first place. I allowed myself to
be talked into it. I knew it was wrong. Seeing you only
confirms my suspicion. My dear, it's not your fault, just the
luck of the draw that you got me; but get me you did. And the
thing is, between you, me and the walls, I'm actually an
appalling teacher. (*After a pause.*) Most of the time, you see, it
doesn't actually matter – appalling teaching is quite in order
for most of my appalling students. And the others manage to

get by despite me. But you're different. You want a lot, and I can't give it. (*He moves towards her*.) Everything I know – and you must listen to this – is that I know absolutely nothing. I don't like the hours, you know. (*He goes to the swivel chair and sits*.) Strange hours for this Open University thing. They expect us to teach when the pubs are open. I can be a good teacher when I'm in the pub, you know. Four pints of weak Guinness and I can be as witty as Wilde. I'm sorry – there are other tutors – I'll arrange it for you . . . post it on . . . (*He looks at her*.)

Rita *slowly turns and goes towards the door. She goes out and quietly closes the door behind her. Suddenly the door bursts open and* **Rita** *flies in.*

Rita (*going up to him*)   Wait a minute, listen to me. Listen: I'm on this course, you are my teacher – an' you're gonna bleedin' well teach me.

Frank   There are other tutors – I've told you . . .

Rita   You're my tutor. I don't want another tutor.

Frank   For God's sake, woman – I've told you . . .

Rita   You're my tutor.

Frank   But I've told you – I don't want to do it. Why come to me?

Rita (*looking at him*)   Because you're a crazy mad piss artist who wants to throw his students through the window, an' I like you. (*After a pause*.) Don't you recognise a compliment?

Frank   Do you think I could have a cigarette?

Rita (*offering the packet of cigarettes*)   I'll bring me scissors next week and give y' a haircut.

Frank   You're not coming here next week.

Rita (*lighting his cigarette*)   I am. And you're gettin' y' hair cut.

Frank   I am not getting my hair cut.

Rita (*getting her bag*)   I suppose y' wanna walk round like that, do y'? (*She goes towards the door.*)

Frank   Like what?

Rita (*getting her coat*)   Like a geriatric hippie.

Blackout.

Rita *exits*.

Scene Two

Frank *is standing in the centre of the room. He glances at his watch, moves to the window, looks out, glances at his watch again and then moves across to the books. He glances at his watch and then his attention is caught by the door handle being turned. He looks at the door but no one enters although the handle keeps being turned. Eventually he goes to the door and pulls it open.*

Rita *is standing in the doorway, holding a small can of oil.*

Frank   Oh.

Rita   Hello. I was just oilin' it for y'. (*She comes into the room.*) I knew you wouldn't get round to it. Y' can have that.

She gives the oil can to **Frank**.

Frank   Erm – thanks. (*He puts the can on the filing cabinet and then goes and sits in the swivel chair.*)

Slightly amused, he watches her as she wanders round the room.

Rita (*turning to him*)   What y' lookin' at?

Frank   Don't you ever just walk into a room and sit down?

Rita   Not when I've got the chair with its back to the door.

Frank (*getting up*)   Well – if it'd make you happier you take my chair.

Rita   No. You're the teacher, you sit there.

Frank   But it doesn't matter where I sit. If you'd be happier with that chair then you sit there.

Rita Tch. Is that what y' call democracy at work? I don't wanna sit down anyway. I like walkin' around this room. (*After a pause.*) How d' y' make a room like this?

Frank I didn't make it. I just moved in. The rest sort of happened.

Rita (*looking round*) Yeh. That's cos you've got taste. I'm gonna have a room like this one day. There's nothing phoney about it. Everything's in its right place. (*After a pause.*) It's a mess. But it's a perfect mess. (*She wanders round.*) It's like wherever you've put something down it's grown to fit there.

Frank (*sitting down*) You mean that over the years it's acquired a certain patina.

Rita Do I?

Frank I think so.

Rita Yeh. 'It's acquired a certain patina.' It's like somethin' from a romantic film, isn't it? 'Over the years your face has acquired a certain patina.'

Frank *smiles*.

Rita (*sniffing*) You've not been drinking, have y'?

Frank No.

Rita Is that because of me, because of what I said last week?

Frank (*laughing*) My God. You think you've reformed me?

Rita (*going to the window*) I don't wanna reform y'. Y' can do what y' like. (*Quickly.*) I love that lawn down there. When it's summer do they sit on it?

Frank (*going to the window*) Who?

Rita (*going back to the desk*) The ones who come here all the time. The proper students.

Frank Yes. First glimmer of sun and they're all out there.

Rita Readin' an' studyin'?

Frank   Reading and studying? What do you think they
are, human? Proper students don't read and study.

Rita   Y' what?

Frank   A joke, a joke. Yes. They read and study,
sometimes.

Pause. **Rita** *dumps her bag on the chair and then goes and hangs up her
coat on the door.*

Rita   It looks the way I always imagined a public school to
look, y' know a boardin' school. When I was a kid I always
wanted to go to a boardin' school.

Frank   God forbid it; why?

Rita (*going to her chair at the desk*)   I always thought they
sounded great, schools like that, y' know with a tuck-shop
an' a matron an' prep. An' a pair of kids called Jones minor
an' Jones major. I told me mother once. (*She opens her bag and
takes out the copy of* Howards End, *ring-bound file, note-pad, ruler
and pencil-case, placing them methodically on the desk in front of her.*)
She said I was off me cake.

Frank (*with an exaggerated look at her*)   What in the name of
God is being off one's cake?

Rita   Soft. Y' know, mental.

Frank   Aha. I must remember that. The next student to
ask me if Isabel Archer was guilty of protestant masochism
shall be told that one is obviously very off one's cake!

Rita   Don't be soft. You can't say that.

Frank   Why ever not?

Rita   You can't. If you do it, it's slummin' it. Comin' from
you it'd sound dead affected, wouldn't it?

Frank   Dead affected?

Rita   Yeh. You say that to your proper students they'll
think you're off your – y' know . . .

Frank   Cake, yes. Erm – Rita, why didn't you ever become
what you call a proper student?

Rita   What? After goin' to the school I went to?

Frank   Was it bad?

Rita *starts sharpening the pencils one by one into perfect spikes, leaving the shavings on the desk.*

Rita   Nah, just normal, y' know; borin', ripped-up books, broken glass everywhere, knives an' fights. An' that was just in the staffroom. Nah, they tried their best I suppose, always tellin' us we stood more of a chance if we studied. But studyin' was just for the wimps, wasn't it? See, if I'd started takin' school seriously I would have had to become different from me mates, an' that's not allowed.

Frank   By whom?

Rita   By your mates, by your family, by everyone. So y' never admit that school could be anythin' other than useless.

Frank *passes her the ashtray but she ignores it and continues sharpening the pencils on to the table.*

Rita   Like what you've got to be into is music an' clothes an' lookin' for a feller, y' know the real qualities of life. Not that I went along with it so reluctantly. I mean, there was always somethin' in me head, tappin' away, tellin' me I might have got it all wrong. But I'd just play another record or buy another dress an' stop worryin'. There's always somethin' to make you forget about it. So y' do, y' keep goin', tellin' yourself life's great. There's always another club to go to, a new feller to be chasin', a laugh an' a joke with the girls. Till, one day, y' own up to yourself an' y' say, is this it? Is this the absolute maximum I can expect from this livin' lark? An' that's the big moment that one, that's the point when y' have to decide whether it's gonna be another change of dress or a change in yourself. An' it's really temptin' to go out an' get another dress y' know, it is. Cos it's easy, it doesn't cost anythin', it doesn't upset anyone around y'. Like cos they don't want y' to change.

Frank   But you – erm – you managed to resist another new dress?

Rita   Can't y' tell? Look at the state of this; I haven't had a new dress in twelve months. An' I'm not gonna get one either, not till – till I pass me first exam. Then I'll get a proper dress, the sort of dress you'd only see on an educated woman, on the sort of woman who knows the difference between Jane Austen an' Tracy Austin. (*She finishes sharpening the last pencil, and arranges it in line with the others. She gathers the pencil shavings into her hand and chucks them in the waste-bin.*) Let's start.

Frank   Now the piece you wrote for me on – what was it called. . . ?

Rita (*getting out her cigarettes and lighter*)   *Rubyfruit Jungle*.

Frank   Yes, it was – erm . . .

Rita   Crap?

Frank   No. Erm – the thing is, it was an appreciation, a descriptive piece. What you have to learn is criticism.

Rita   What's the difference? (*She lights a cigarette.*)

Frank   Well. You must try to remember that criticism is purely objective. It should be approached almost as a science. It must be supported by reference to established literary critique. Criticism is never subjective and should not be confused with partisan interpretation. In criticism sentiment has no place. (*He picks up the copy of* Howards End.) Tell me, what did you think of *Howards End*?

Rita   It was crap.

Frank   What?

Rita   I thought it was crap!

Frank   Crap? And who are you citing in support of your thesis, F.R. Leavis?

Rita   No. Me!

Frank   What have I just said? 'Me' is subjective.

Rita   Well it's what I think.

Frank   You think *Howards End* is crap? Well would you kindly tell me why you think it's quote, 'crap', unquote.

Rita   Yeh, I will tell y'. It's crap because the feller who wrote it was a louse. Because halfway through that book I couldn't go on readin' it because he, Mr Bleedin' E.M. Forster says, quote 'We are not concerned with the poor' unquote. That's why it's crap. An' that's why I didn't go on readin' it, that's why.

Frank (*astounded*)   Because he said we are not concerned with the poor?

Rita   Yeh, that's it!

Frank   But he wasn't writing about the poor.

Rita   When he wrote that book the conditions of the poor in this country were appalling. An' he's sayin' he couldn't care less. Mr E.M. Bleedin' Foster.

Frank   Forster.

Rita   I don't care what his name was, he was sittin' up there in his ivory tower an' sayin' he couldn't care less.

Frank *laughs*.

Rita   Don't laugh at me.

Frank (*getting up*)   But you cannot interpret E.M. Forster from a Marxist viewpoint.

Rita   Why?

Frank   Look before discussing this I said no subjectivity, no sentimentality.

Rita   I wasn't bein' sentimental.

Frank   Of course you were. You stopped reading the book because you wanted Forster to concern himself with the poor. Literature can ignore the poor.

Rita   Well, it's immoral.

Frank (*wandering around*)   Amoral. But you wanted to know. You see what sort of mark you'd get if you approached Forster in this way during an examination?

Rita   What sort?

Frank   Well, you might manage one or two per cent if the examiner was sympathetic to the one dubious quality your criticism displays.

Rita   What's that?

Frank   Brevity.

Rita   All right. But I hated that book. Can't we do somethin' else? Can't we do somethin' I like?

Frank   But the sort of stuff you like is not necessarily the sort of thing that will form the basis of your examination next Christmas. Now if you're going to pass any sort of exam you have to begin to discipline that mind of yours.

Rita   Are you married?

Frank (*moving back to the swivel chair*)   It's – ogh . . .

Rita   Are y'? What's y' wife like?

Frank   Is my wife at all relevant?

Rita   What? You should know, you married her.

Frank   Well, she's not relevant. I haven't seen her for a long time. We split up. All right?

Rita   I'm sorry.

Frank   Why are you sorry?

Rita   I'm sorry for askin'. For being nosey.

Frank (*sitting in his swivel chair*)   The thing about *Howards End* is that . . .

Rita   Why did y' split up?

Frank (*taking off his glasses and looking at her*)   Perhaps you'd like to take notes! When you have to answer a question on

Forster you can treat the examiner to an essay called Frank's marriage!

Rita   Oh go 'way. I'm only interested.

Frank (*leaning towards her; conspiratorially*)   We split up, Rita, because of poetry.

Rita   Y' what?

Frank   One day my wife pointed out to me that for fifteen years my output as a poet had dealt exclusively with the period in which we – discovered each other.

Rita   Are you a poet?

Frank   Was. And so, to give me something new to write about she left. A very noble woman my wife. She left me for the good of literature.

Rita   An' what happened?

Frank   She was right. Her leaving was an enormous benefit to literature.

Rita   What, y' wrote a load of good stuff?

Frank   No. I stopped writing altogether.

Rita (*slightly puzzled*)   Are you takin' the piss?

Frank *gives a short laugh and leans back in his chair*.

Frank   No.

Rita   People don't split up because of things like that. Because of literature.

Frank   Maybe you're right. But that's how I remember it.

Rita   Were you a famous poet?

Frank   No. I sold a few books, all out of print now.

Rita   Can I read some of your stuff?

Frank   You wouldn't like it.

Rita   How d' y' know?

Frank   It's the sort of poetry you can't understand – unless you happen to have a detailed knowledge of the literary references.

Rita   Oh. (*After a pause.*) Do you live on y' own then?

Frank   Rita! Tch.

Rita   I was only askin'.

Frank   I live with a girl. Ex student. She's very caring, very tolerant, admires me tremendously and spends a great deal of time putting her head in the oven.

Rita   Does she try an' do herself in?

Frank   Mm? No, she just likes to watch the ratatouille cook.

Rita   The what?

Frank   Ratatouille. Though Julia has renamed it the 'stopouts dish'. It can simmer in an oven for days. In our house it often has no choice.

Rita   D' you stop out for days?

Frank   Occasionally. And that is the end of . . .

Rita   Why do y'?

Frank   And that is the end of that.

Rita   If y' were mine an' y' stopped out for days y' wouldn't get back in.

Frank   Ah, but Rita, if I was yours would I stop out for days?

Rita   Don't y' like Julia?

Frank   I like her enormously; it's myself I'm not too fond of.

Rita   Tch. Y' great . . .

Frank   A vote of confidence; thank you. But, I'm afraid, Rita, that you'll find there's less of me than meets the eye.

Rita See – look – y' can say dead clever things like that, can't y'? I wish I could talk like that. It's brilliant.

Frank Staggering. Now look, *Howards* . . . (*He swivels the chair round so that he faces away from* **Rita**.)

Rita Oh ey . . . leave that. I just like talkin' to y'. It's great. That's what they do wrong in schools y' know – (*She gets up and warms her legs by the fire.*) they get y' talkin' an' that, an' y' all havin' a great time talkin' about somethin' an' the next thing they wanna do is turn it into a lesson. We was out with the teacher once, y' know outside school, an' I'm right at the back with these other kids an' I saw this fantastic bird, all coloured it was, like dead out of place round our way. I was just gonna shout an' tell Miss but this kid next to me said, 'Keep your mouth shut or she'll make us write an essay on it.'

Frank (*sighing*)   Yes, that's what we do, Rita; we call it education.

Rita Tch. Y'd think there was somethin' wrong with education to hear you talk.

Frank Perhaps there is.

Rita So why are y' givin' me an education?

Frank Because it's what you want, isn't it? What I'd actually like to do is take you by the hand and run out of this room forever.

Rita (*going back to her chair*)   Tch – be serious . . .

Frank I am. Right now there's a thousand things I'd rather do than teach; most of them with you, young lady . . .

Rita (*smiling gently*)   Tch. Oh sod off . . . You just like saying things like that. (*She sits down.*)

Frank Do I?

Rita Yeh. Y' know y' do.

Frank   Rita – why didn't you walk in here twenty years ago?

Rita   Cos I don't think they would have accepted me at the age of six.

Frank   You know what I mean.

Rita   I know. But it's not twenty years ago, Frank. It's now. You're there an' I'm here.

Frank   Yes. And you're here for an education. (*He waves his finger*.) You must keep reminding me of that. Come on, Forster!

Rita   Tch. Forget him.

Frank   Listen to me; you said that I was going to teach you. You want to learn. Well that, I'm afraid, means a lot of work. You've barely had a basic schooling, you've never passed an examination in your life. Possessing a hungry mind is not, in itself, a guarantee of success.

Rita   All right. But I just don't like *Howards* bleedin' *End*.

Frank   Then go back to what you do like and stop wasting my time. You go out and buy yourself a new dress and I'll go to the pub.

Rita   (*after a pause*)   Is that you putting your foot down?

Frank   It is actually.

Rita   Oh. Aren't you impressive when y' angry?

Frank   Forster!

Rita   All right, all right, Forster. Does Forster's repeated use of the phrase 'only connect' suggest that he was really a frustrated electrician?

Frank   Rita.

Rita   In considering Forster it helps if we examine the thirteen amp plug . . .

Blackout.

Rita *goes out*.

Scene Three

Frank *working at his desk.*

Rita *flounces into the room and goes to the desk.*

Rita   God, I've had enough of this. It's borin', that's what it is, bloody borin'. This Forster, honest to God he doesn't half get on my tits.

She dumps her bag on the chair and makes towards the hook by the door, taking off her coat as she goes. She hangs the coat on the hook.

Frank   Good. You must show me the evidence.

Rita   Y' dirty sod.

Frank (*wagging his finger at her*)   True, true . . . it's cutting down on the booze that's done it. Now. (*He waves a sheet of paper at her.*) What's this?

Rita (*sitting by the desk*)   It's a bleedin' piece of paper, isn't it?

Frank   It's your essay. Is it a joke? Is it?

Rita   No. It's not a joke.

Frank   Rita, how the hell can you write an essay on E.M. Forster with almost total reference to Harold Robbins.

Rita   Well? You said bring in other authors.

Frank   Tch.

Rita   Don't go on at me. You said; y' said, 'Reference to other authors will impress the examiners.'

Frank   I said refer to other works but I don't think the examiner, God bless him, will have read (*He consults the paper.*) *A Stone for Danny Fisher.*

Rita   Well, that's his hard luck, isn't it?

Frank   It'll be your hard luck when he fails your paper.

Rita   Oh that's prime, isn't it? That's justice for y'. I get failed just cos I'm more well read than the friggin' examiner!

Frank   Devouring pulp fiction is not being well read.

Rita   I thought reading was supposed to be good for one. (*She gets out her cigarettes.*)

Frank   It is, but you've got to be selective. In your favour you do mention *Sons and Lovers* somewhere in here. When did you read that?

Rita   This week. I read that an' the Harold Robbins an' this dead fantastic book, what was it called? Erm – ogh what was it? It sounded like somethin' dead perverted, it was by that English feller . . .

Frank   Which English feller?

Rita   You know, the one who was like Noël Coward – erm. Oh, I know – Somerset Maughan?

Frank   A perverted book by Somerset Maugham?

Rita   No, it wasn't perverted it was great – the title sounds perverted . . .

He starts to laugh.

Rita   Don't laugh.

Frank   Do you mean *Of Human Bondage*?

Rita   Yeh – that's it. Well it does sound perverted doesn't it?

Frank   Well! (*After a pause.*) You read three novels this week?

Rita (*taking a cigarette from the pack*)   Yeh. It was dead quiet in the shop.

Frank   And if I asked you to make a comparison between those books, what would you say?

Rita   Well, they were all good in their own way.

Frank   But surely you can see the difference between the Harold Robbins and the other two?

Rita   Apart from that one bein' American like?

Frank   Yes.

Rita   Yeh. I mean the other two were sort of posher. But they're all books, aren't they?

Frank   Yes. Yes. But you seem to be under the impression that all books are literature.

Rita   Aren't they?

Frank   No.

Rita   Well – well how d' y' tell?

Frank   I – erm – erm – one's always known really.

Rita   But how d' y' work it out if y' don't know? See that's what I've got to learn, isn't it? I'm dead ignorant y' know.

Frank   No. You're not ignorant. It's merely a question of becoming more discerning in your choice of reading material.

Rita   I've got no taste. Is that what you're saying?

Frank   No.

Rita   It is. Don't worry. I won't get upset. I'm here to learn. My mind's full of junk, isn't it? It needs a good clearin' out. Right, that's it, I'll never read a Robbins novel again.

Frank   Read it, by all means read it. But don't mention it in an exam.

Rita   Aha. You mean, it's all right to go out an' have a bit of slap an' tickle with the lads as long as you don't go home an' tell your mum?

Frank   Erm – well, yes, that's probably what I do mean.

Blackout.

Rita *exits.*

Scene Four

Frank *is standing by the window.*

Rita *enters and shuts the door behind her, standing just inside the room.*

Frank *goes to his briefcase on the window-desk and starts looking for* **Rita**'s Peer Gynt *essay.*

Rita   I can't do it. Honest, I just can't understand what he's on about. (*She goes to her chair at the desk, dumps her bag and then goes and hangs up her coat.*) He's got me licked, I don't know what he's on about, 'Only connect, only connect', it's just bleedin' borin'. It's no good, I just can't understand.

Frank   You will. You will.

Rita   It's all right for you sayin' that. You know what it's about. (*She goes to her chair by the desk.*) But I just can't figure it.

Frank   Do you think we could forget about Forster for a moment?

Rita   With pleasure.

Frank *takes the* Peer Gynt *essay and stands over her for a moment. Then he perches on the corner of the desk.*

Frank   I want to talk about this that you sent me. (*He holds up a sheet of A4 paper.*)

Rita   That? Oh.

Frank   Yes. In response to the question, 'Suggest how you would resolve the staging difficulties inherent in a production of Ibsen's *Peer Gynt*,' you have written, quote, 'Do it on the radio', unquote.

Rita   Precisely.

Frank   Well?

Rita   Well what?

Frank   Well I know it's probably quite naïve of me but I did think you might let me have a considered essay.

Rita *sits down by the desk and unpacks the student's pad, pencil case, ruler, copy of* Peer Gynt *and eight reference books from her bag.*

Rita That's all I could do in the time. We were dead busy in the shop this week.

Frank You write your essays at work?

Rita Yeh.

Frank Why?

Rita Denny gets dead narked if I work at home. He doesn't like me doin' this. I can't be bothered arguin' with him.

Frank But you can't go on producing work as thin as this.

Rita Is it wrong?

Frank No, it's not wrong, it's just . . .

Rita See, I know it's short. But I thought it was the right answer.

Frank It's the basis for an argument, Rita, but one line is hardly an essay.

Rita I know, but I didn't have much time this week, so I sort of, y' know, encapsulated all me ideas in one line.

Frank But it's not enough.

Rita Why not?

Frank It just isn't.

Rita But that's bleedin' stupid, cos you say — you say, don't y' — that one line of exquisite poetry says more than a thousand pages of second-rate prose.

Frank But you're not writing poetry. What I'm trying to make you see is that whoever was marking this would want more than, 'Do it on the radio'. (*He gets up and moves around to the other side of* **Rita**'s *chair.*) There is a way of answering examination questions that is expected. It's a sort of accepted ritual, it's a game, with rules. And you must observe those rules. (*He leans with one hand on the back of* **Rita**'s *chair.*) When I was at university there was a student taking his final theology exam. He walked into the examination hall, took out his pen and wrote 'God knows all the answers', then he handed in his paper and left.

Rita (*impressed*)   Did he?

Frank   When his paper was returned to him, his professor had written on it, 'And God gives out the marks'.

Rita   Did he fail?

Frank (*breaking away slightly*)   Of course he failed. You see, a clever answer is not necessarily the correct answer.

Rita (*getting out her cigarettes*)   I wasn't tryin' to be clever; I didn't have much time an' I . . .

Frank   All right, but look, you've got some time now. (*He leans on her chair, bending over her.*) Just give it a quarter of an hour or so adding some considered argument to this: 'In attempting to resolve the staging difficulties in *Peer Gynt* I would present it on the radio because . . .' and outline your reasons supporting them, as much as possible, with quotes from accepted authorities. All right?'

Rita   Yeh. All right.

She picks up the essay, pen, copy of Peer Gynt, *eight reference books, sticks the cigarette in her mouth, and starts to move towards the window desk.*

Frank   Now, are you sure you understand?

Rita *stops and speaks over her shoulder with the cigarette still in her mouth.*

Rita   Yeh. What d' y' think I am, thick?

She takes her usual chair and puts it in front of the window desk. She sits down and puts her belongings on the desk, moving **Frank**'s *briefcase out of the way.*

Frank *moves the swivel chair to the end of his desk and settles down to marking essays.*

Rita *leans back in the chair and tries to blow smoke-rings.*

Rita   Y' know Peer Gynt? He was searchin' for the meaning of life wasn't he?

Frank   Erm – put at its briefest, yes.

Rita   Yeh. (*She pauses.*) I was doin' this woman's hair on Wednesday . . .

Frank   Tch . . .

Rita (*facing* **Frank**)   I'm gonna do this, don't worry. I'll do it. But I just wanna' tell y'; I was doin' her hair an' I was dead bored with what the others in the shop were talkin' about. So I just said to this woman, I said, 'Do you know about *Peer Gynt*?' She thought it was a new perm lotion. So I told her all about it, y' know the play. An' y' know somethin', she was dead interested, she was y' know.

Frank   Was she?

Rita   Yeh. She said, 'I wish I could go off searchin' for the meanin' of life.' There's loads of them round by us who feel like that. Cos by us there is no meanin' to life. (*She thinks.*) Frank, y' know culture, y' know the word culture? Well it doesn't just mean goin' to the opera an' that, does it?

Frank   No.

Rita   It means a way of livin', doesn't it? Well we've got no culture.

Frank   Of course you have.

Rita   What? Do you mean like that working-class culture thing?

Frank   Mm.

Rita   Yeh. I've read about that. I've never seen it though.

Frank   Well, look around you.

Rita   I do. But I don't see any, y' know, culture. I just see everyone pissed, or on the Valium, tryin' to get from one day to the next. Y' daren't say that round our way like, cos they're proud. They'll tell y' they've got culture as they sit there drinkin' their keg beer out of plastic glasses.

Frank Yes, but there's nothing wrong with that, if they're content with it.

During the following **Frank**'s *attention is caught gradually and he stops marking and starts listening.*

Rita But they're not. Cos there's no meanin'. They tell y' stories about the past, y' know, the war, or when they were fightin' for food an' clothin' an' houses. Their eyes light up as they tell y', because there was some meanin' to it. But the thing is that now, I mean now that most of them have got some sort of house an' there's food an' money around, they know they're better off but, honest, they know they've got nothin' as well. There's like this sort of disease, but no one mentions it; everyone behaves as though it's normal, y' know inevitable that there's vandalism an' violence an' houses burnt out an' wrecked by the people they were built for. There's somethin' wrong. An' like the worst thing is that y' know the people who are supposed to like represent the people on our estate, y' know the *Daily Mirror* an' the *Sun*, an' ITV an' the Unions, what are they tellin' people to do? They just tell them to go out an' get more money, don't they? But they don't want more money; it's like me, isn't it? Y' know, buyin' new dresses all the time, isn't it? The Unions tell them to go out an' get more money an' ITV an' the papers tell them what to spend it on so the disease is always covered up.

Frank *swivels round in his chair to face* **Rita**

Frank (*after a pause*) Why didn't you take a course in politics?

Rita Politics? Go 'way, I hate politics. I'm just tellin' y' about round our way. I wanna be on this course findin' out. You know what I learn from you, about art an' literature, it feeds me, inside. I can get through the rest of the week if I know I've got comin' here to look forward to. Denny tried to stop me comin' tonight. He tried to get me to go out to the pub with him an' his mates. He hates me comin' here. It's like drug addicts, isn't it? They hate it when one of them tries to break away. It makes me stronger comin' here. That's what Denny's frightened of.

Frank 'Only connect.'

Rita Oh, not friggin' Forster again.

Frank 'Only connect.' You see what you've been doing?

Rita Just tellin' y' about home.

Frank Yes, and connecting, your dresses/ITV and the *Daily Mirror*. Addicts/you and your husband.

Rita Ogh!

Frank You see?

Rita An' – an' in that book – no one does connect.

Frank Irony.

Rita Is that it? Is that all it means?

Frank Yes.

Rita Why didn't y' just tell me, right from the start?

Frank I could have told you; but you'll have a much better understanding of something if you discover it in your own terms.

Rita (*sincerely*) Aren't you clever?

Frank Brilliant. Now. *Peer Gynt*.

Rita All right, all right, hold on. (*She opens a couple of books and starts writing.*)

Frank *continues his marking and does not notice as* **Rita** *finishes writing. She picks up her chair, essay, pen and books, and moves across in front of his desk. She replaces the chair by the desk and stands watching him.*

Frank (*looking up*) What?

Rita I've done it.

Frank You've done it?

She hands him the essay.

Frank (*reading aloud*) 'In attempting to resolve the staging difficulties in a production of Ibsen's *Peer Gynt* I would present it on the radio because as Ibsen himself says, he wrote the play as a play for voices, never intending it to go on in a theatre. If they had the radio in his day that's where he would have done it.'

He looks up as she beams him a satisfied smile.

Blackout.

Scene Five

Frank *is sitting in the swivel chair and* **Rita** *stands by the filing cabinet.*

Frank   What's wrong? (*After a pause.*) You know this is getting to be a bit wearisome. When you come to this room you'll do anything except start work immediately. Couldn't you just come in prepared to start work? Where's your essay?

Rita (*staring out of the window*)   I haven't got it.

Frank   You haven't got it?

Rita   I said I haven't got it.

Frank   You've lost it?

Rita   It's burnt.

Frank   Burnt?

Rita   So are all the Chekhov books you lent me. Denny found out I was on the pill again; it was my fault, I left me prescription out. He burnt all me books.

Frank   Oh Christ!

Rita   I'm sorry. I'll buy y' some more.

Frank   I wasn't referring to the books. Sod the books.

Rita   Why can't he just let me get on with me learnin'? You'd think I was havin' a bloody affair the way he behaves.

Frank   And aren't you?

Rita *wanders. She fiddles with the library steps, smoothing the top step.*

Rita (*looking at him*)   No. What time have I got for an affair? I'm busy enough findin' meself, let alone findin' someone else. I don't want anyone else. I've begun to find me – an' it's great y' know, it is, Frank. It might sound selfish but all I want for the time bein' is what I'm findin' inside me. I certainly don't wanna be rushin' off with some feller, cos the first thing I'll have to do is forget about meself for the sake of him.

Frank   Perhaps, perhaps your husband thinks you're having an affair with me.

Rita   Oh go 'way. You're me teacher. I've told him.

Frank   You've told him about me? What?

Rita (*sitting down*)   I've – tch – I've tried to explain to him how you give me room to breathe. Y' just, like feed me without expectin' anythin' in return.

Frank   What did he say?

Rita   He didn't. I was out for a while. When I come back he'd burnt me books an' papers, most of them. I said to him, 'Y' soft get, even if I was havin' an affair there's no point burnin' me books. I'm not havin' it off with Anton Chekhov.' He said, 'I wouldn't put it past you to shack up with a foreigner.'

Frank (*after a pause*)   What are you going to do?

Rita   I'll order some new copies for y' an' do the essay again.

Frank   I mean about your husband.

Rita (*standing up*)   I've told him, I said, 'There's no point cryin' over spilt milk, most of the books are gone, but if you touch my *Peer Gynt* I'll kill y'.'

Frank   Tch. Be serious.

Rita   I was!

Frank   Do you love him?

Rita (*after a pause*)   I see him lookin' at me sometimes, an' I know what he's thinkin', I do y' know, he's wonderin' where the girl he married has gone to. He even brings me presents sometimes, hopin' that the presents'll make her come back. But she can't, because she's gone, an' I've taken her place.

Frank   Do you want to abandon this course?

Rita   No. No!

Frank   When art and literature begin to take the place of life itself, perhaps it's time to . . .

Rita (*emphatically*)   But it's not takin' the place of life, it's providin' me with life itself. He wants to take life away from me; he wants me to stop rockin' the coffin, that's all. Comin' here, doin' this, it's given me more life than I've had in years, an' he should be able to see that. Well, if he doesn't want me when I'm alive I'm certainly not just gonna lie down an' die for him. I told him I'd only have a baby when I had a choice. But he doesn't understand. He thinks we've got choice because we can go into a pub that sells eight different kinds of lager. He thinks we've got choice already: choice between Everton an' Liverpool, choosin' which washin' powder, choosin' between one lousy school an' the next, between lousy jobs or the dole, choosin' between Stork an' butter . . .

Frank   Yes. Well, perhaps your husband . . .

Rita   No. I don't wanna talk about him. (*She comes to the front of the desk*.) Why was Chekhov a comic genius?

Frank   Rita. Don't you think that for tonight we could give the class a miss?

Rita   No. I wanna know. I've got to do this. He can burn me books an' me papers but if it's all in me head he can't touch it. It's like that with you, isn't it? You've got it all inside.

Frank   Let's leave it for tonight. Let's go to the pub and drink pots of Guinness and talk.

Rita I've got to do this, Frank. I've got to. I want to talk about Chekhov.

Frank We really should talk about you and Denny, my dear.

Rita I don't want to.

Frank (*after a pause*)   All right. Chekhov. 'C' for Chekhov.

He gets up and moves towards the bookcase, taking **Rita***'s chair with him. He stands on the chair and begins rummaging on the top shelf, dropping some of the books on the floor.* **Rita** *turns to sit down and notices her chair has gone. She sees* **Frank** *and watches him as he finds a bottle of whisky hidden behind some books. He gets down and takes the whisky to the small table.*

Frank We'll talk about Chekhov and pretend this is the pub.

Rita Why d' y' keep it stashed behind there?

Frank (*pouring the drinks*)   A little arrangement I have with my immediate employers. It's called discretion. They didn't tell me to stop drinking, they told me to stop displaying the signs.

Rita (*climbing on to the chair to replace the books*)   Do you actually like drinking?

Frank Oh yes. I love it. Absolutely no guilt at all about it.

Rita Know when you were a poet, Frank, did y' drink then?

Frank Some. Not as much as now. (*He takes a drink.*) You see, the great thing about the booze is that it makes one believe that under all the talk one is actually saying something.

Rita Why did you stop being a poet?

Frank (*wagging his finger at her*)   That is a pub question.

Rita Well, I thought we were pretendin' this was the pub. (*She gets down from the chair.*)

Frank In which we would discuss Chekhov.

Rita   Well he's second on the bill. You're on first. Go on, why did y' stop?

Frank   I didn't stop, so much as realise I never was. I'd simply got it wrong, Rita. (*After a pause.*) Instead of creating poetry I spent – oh – years and years trying to create literature. You see?

Rita   Well I thought that's what poets did.

Frank   What? (*He gives* **Rita** *her drink.*)

Rita   Y' know, make literature. (*She perches on the small table.*)

Frank (*shaking his head*)   Poets shouldn't believe in literature.

Rita (*puzzled*)   I don't understand that.

Frank   You will. You will.

Rita   Sometimes I wonder if I'll ever understand any of it. It's like startin' all over again, y' know with a different language. Know I read that Chekhov play an' I thought it was dead sad, it was tragic; people committin' suicide an' that Constantin kid's tryin' to produce his masterpiece an' they're all laughin' at him? It's tragic. Then I read the blurb on it an' everyone's goin' on about Chekhov bein' a comic genius.

Frank   Well, it's not comedy like – erm – well it's not stand-up comedy. Have you ever seen Chekhov in the theatre?

Rita   No. Does he go?

Frank   Have you ever been to the theatre?

Rita   No.

Frank   You should go.

Rita (*standing up*)   Hey! Why don't we go tonight?

Frank   Me? Go to the theatre? God no, I hate the theatre.

Rita   Why the hell are y' sendin' me?

Frank   Because you want to know.

Rita (*packing her things into her bag*)   Well, you come with me.

Frank   And how would I explain that to Julia?

Rita   Just tell her y' comin' to the theatre with me.

Frank   'Julia, I shall not be in for dinner as I am going to the theatre with ravishing Rita.'

Rita   Oh sod off.

Frank   I'm being quite serious.

Rita   Would she really be jealous?

Frank   If she knew I was at the theatre with an irresistible thing like you? Rita, it would be deaf and dumb breakfasts for a week.

Rita   Why?

Frank   Why not?

Rita   I dunno – I just thought . . .

Frank (*pouring himself another drink*)   Rita, ludicrous as it may seem to you, even a woman who possesses an M.A. is not above common jealousy.

Rita   Well, what's she got to be jealous of me for? I'm not gonna try an' rape y' in the middle of *The Seagull*.

Frank   What an awful pity. You could have made theatre exciting for me again.

Rita   Come on, Frank. Come with me. Y' never tell the truth you, do y'?

Frank   What d' y' mean?

Rita   Y' don't; y' like evade it with jokes an' that, don't y'? Come on, come to the theatre with me. We'll have a laugh . . .

Frank   Will we?

Rita   Yeh. C'mon, we'll ring Julia. (*She goes to the telephone and picks up the receiver.*)

Frank   What?

Rita   C'mon, what's your number?

Frank (*taking the receiver from her and replacing it*)   We will not ring Julia. Anyway Julia's out tonight.

Rita   So what will you do, spend the night in the pub?

Frank   Yes.

Rita   Come with me, Frank, y'll have a better time than y' will in the pub.

Frank   Will I?

Rita   Course y' will.

She goes and gets both coats from the hook by the door, comes back and throws her coat over the back of the chair.

Frank (*putting down his mug on the bookcase*)   What is it you want to see?

Rita *helps* **Frank** *into his coat.*

Rita   *The Importance of Bein' Thingy* . . .

Frank   But *The Importance* isn't playing at the moment . . .

Rita   It is – I passed the church hall on the bus an' there was a poster . . .

Frank *breaks loose, turns to her and throws off his coat.*

Frank (*aghast*)   An amateur production?

Rita   What?

Frank   Are you suggesting I miss a night at the pub to watch *The Importance* played by amateurs in a church hall?

Rita *picks his coat up and puts it round his shoulders.*

Rita   Yeh. It doesn't matter who's doin' it, does it? It's the same play, isn't it?

Frank   Possibly, Rita . . . (*He switches off the desk lamp.*)

Rita (*putting on her coat and picking up her bag*)   Well come on – hurry up – I'm dead excited. I've never seen a live play before.

Frank *goes round switching off the electric fire and desk lamp and then picks up his briefcase.*

Frank   And there's no guarantee you'll see a 'live' play tonight.

Rita   Why? Just cos they're amateurs? Y've gorra give them a chance. They have to learn somewhere. An' they might be good.

Frank (*doubtfully*)   Yes . . .

Rita   Oh y' an awful snob, aren't y'?

Frank (*smiling acknowledgement*)   All right – come on.

They go towards the door.

Rita   Have you seen it before?

Frank   Of course.

Rita   Well, don't go tellin' me what happens will y'? Don't go spoilin' it for me.

Frank *switches off the light switch. Blackout.*

Frank *and* **Rita** *exit.*

Scene Six

Frank *enters carrying a briefcase and a pile of essays. He goes to the filing cabinet, takes his lecture notes from the briefcase and puts them in a drawer. He takes the sandwiches and apple from his briefcase and puts them on his desk and then goes to the window desk and dumps the essays and briefcase. He switches on the radio and then sits in the swivel chair. He opens the packet of sandwiches, takes a bite and then picks up a book and starts reading.*

Rita *bursts through the door out of breath.*

Frank   What are you doing here? (*He looks at his watch.*) It's Thursday, you . . .

Rita (*moving over to the desk; quickly*) I know I shouldn't be here, it's me dinner hour, but listen, I've gorra tell someone, have y' got a few minutes, can y' spare. . . ?

Frank (*alarmed*) My God, what is it?

Rita I had to come an' tell y', Frank, last night, I went to the theatre! A proper one, a professional theatre.

Frank *gets up and switches off the radio and then returns to the swivel chair.*

Frank (*sighing*) For God's sake, you had me worried, I thought it was something serious.

Rita No, listen, it was. I went out an' got me ticket, it was Shakespeare, I thought it was gonna be dead borin' . . .

Frank Then why did you go in the first place?

Rita I wanted to find out. But listen, it wasn't borin', it was bleedin' great, honest, ogh, it done me in, it was fantastic. I'm gonna do an essay on it.

Frank (*smiling*) Come on, which one was it?

Rita *moves upper right centre.*

Rita
'. . . Out, out, brief candle!
Life's but a walking shadow, a poor player
That struts and frets his hour upon the stage
And then is heard no more. It is a tale
Told by an idiot, full of sound and fury
Signifying nothing.'

Frank (*deliberately*) Ah, *Romeo and Juliet.*

Rita (*moving towards* **Frank**) Tch. Frank! Be serious. I learnt that today from the book. (*She produces a copy of* Macbeth.) Look, I went out an' bought the book. Isn't it great? What I couldn't get over is how excitin' it was.

Frank *puts his feet up on the desk.*

Rita Wasn't his wife a cow, eh? An' that fantastic bit where he meets Macduff an' he thinks he's all invincible. I was on the edge of me seat at that bit. I wanted to shout out an' tell Macbeth, warn him.

Frank   You didn't, did you?

Rita   Nah. Y' can't do that in a theatre, can y'? It was dead good. It was like a thriller.

Frank   Yes. You'll have to go and see more.

Rita   I'm goin' to. *Macbeth*'s a tragedy, isn't it?

Frank *nods.*

Rita   Right.

Rita *smiles at* **Frank** *and he smiles back at her.*

Rita   Well I just – I just had to tell someone who'd understand.

Frank   I'm honoured that you chose me.

Rita (*moving towards the door*)   Well, I better get back. I've left a customer with a perm lotion. If I don't get a move on there'll be another tragedy.

Frank   No. There won't be a tragedy.

Rita   There will, y' know. I know this woman; she's dead fussy. If her perm doesn't come out right there'll be blood an' guts everywhere.

Frank   Which might be quite tragic – (*He throws her the apple from his desk which she catches.*) but it won't be a tragedy.

Rita   What?

Frank   Well – erm – look; the tragedy of the drama has nothing to do with the sort of tragic event you're talking about. Macbeth is flawed by his ambition – yes?

Rita (*going and sitting in the chair by the desk*)   Yeh. Go on. (*She starts to eat the apple.*)

Frank   Erm – it's that flaw which forces him to take the inevitable steps towards his own doom. You see?

Rita *offers him the can of soft drink. He takes it and looks at it.*

Frank (*putting the can down on the desk*)   No thanks. Whereas, Rita, a woman's hair being reduced to an inch of stubble, or – or the sort of thing you read in the paper that's reported as being tragic, 'Man Killed By Falling Tree', is not a tragedy.

Rita   It is for the poor sod under the tree.

Frank   Yes, it's tragic, absolutely tragic. But it's not a tragedy in the way that *Macbeth* is a tragedy. Tragedy in dramatic terms is inevitable, pre-ordained. Look, now, even without ever having heard the story of *Macbeth* you wanted to shout out, to warn him and prevent him going on, didn't you? But you wouldn't have been able to stop him would you?

Rita   No.

Frank   Why?

Rita   They would have thrown me out the theatre.

Frank   But what I mean is that your warning would have been ignored. He's warned in the play. But he can't go back. He still treads the path to doom. But the poor old fellow under the tree hasn't arrived there by following any inevitable steps has he?

Rita   No.

Frank   There's no particular flaw in his character that has dictated his end. If he'd been warned of the consequences of standing beneath that particular tree he wouldn't have done it, would he? Understand?

Rita   So – so Macbeth brings it on himself?

Frank   Yes. You see he goes blindly on and on and with every step he's spinning one more piece of thread which will eventually make up the network of his own tragedy. Do you see?

Rita   I think so. I'm not used to thinkin' like this.

Frank   It's quite easy, Rita.

Rita   It is for you. I just thought it was a dead excitin' story. But the way you tell it you make me see all sorts of things in it. (*After a pause.*) It's fun, tragedy, isn't it? (*She goes over to the window.*) All them out there, they know all about that sort of thing, don't they?

Frank   Look how about a proper lunch?

Rita   Lunch? (*She leaps up, grabs the copy of* Macbeth, *the can of drink and the apple and goes to the door.*) Christ — me customer. She only wanted a demi-wave — she'll come out looking like a friggin' muppet. (*She comes back to the table.*) 'Ey Frank, listen — I was thinkin' of goin' to the art gallery tomorrow. It's me half-day off. D' y' wanna come with me?

Frank (*smiling*)   All right.

Rita *goes to the door.*

Frank (*looking at her*)   And — look, what are you doing on Saturday?

Rita   I work.

Frank   Well, when you finish work?

Rita   Dunno.

Frank   I want you to come over to the house.

Rita   Why?

Frank   Julia's organised a few people to come round for dinner.

Rita   An' y' want me to come? Why?

Frank   Why do you think?

Rita   I dunno.

Frank   Because you might enjoy it.

Rita   Oh.

Frank   Will you come?

Rita   If y' want.

Frank   What do you want?

Rita   All right. I'll come.

Frank   Will you bring Denny?

Rita   I don't know if he'll come.

Frank   Well ask him.

Rita (*puzzled*)   All right.

Frank   What's wrong?

Rita   What shall I wear?

Blackout.

Rita *goes out.*

Scene Seven

Frank *is sitting in the armchair listening to the radio.*

Rita *enters, goes straight to the desk and slings her bag on the back of her chair.*

She sits in the chair and unpacks the note-pad and pencil-case from her bag. She opens the pad and takes out the pencil-sharpener and pencils and arranges them as before. **Frank** *gets up, switches off the radio, goes to the swivel chair and sits.*

Frank   Now I don't mind; two empty seats at the dinner table means more of the vino for me. But Julia — Julia is the stage-manager type. If we're having eight people to dinner she expects to see eight. She likes order — probably why she took me on — it gives her a lot of practice —

Rita *starts sharpening her pencils.*

Frank   — and having to cope with six instead of eight was extremely hard on Julia. I'm not saying that I needed any sort of apology; you don't turn up that's up to you, but . . .

Rita   I did apologise.

Frank 'Sorry couldn't come', scribbled on the back of your essay and thrust through the letter box? Rita, that's hardly an apology.

Rita What does the word 'sorry' mean if it's not an apology? When I told Denny we were goin' to yours he went mad. We had a big fight about it.

Frank I'm sorry. I didn't realise. But look couldn't you have explained. Couldn't you have said that was the reason?

Rita No. Cos that wasn't the reason. I told Denny if he wasn't gonna go I'd go on me own. An' I tried to. All day Saturday, all day in the shop I was thinkin' what to wear. They all looked bleedin' awful. An' all the time I'm trying to think of things I can say, what I can talk about. An' I can't remember anythin'. It's all jumbled up in me head. I can't remember if it's Wilde who's witty an' Shaw who was Shavian or who the hell wrote *Howards End*.

Frank Ogh God!

Rita Then I got the wrong bus to your house. It took me ages to find it. Then I walked up your drive, an' I saw y' all through the window, y' were sippin' drinks an' talkin' an' laughin'. An' I couldn't come in.

Frank Of course you could.

Rita I couldn't. I'd bought the wrong sort of wine. When I was in the off licence I knew I was buyin' the wrong stuff. But I didn't know which was the right wine.

Frank Rita for Christ's sake; I wanted *you* to come along. You weren't expected to dress up or buy wine.

Rita (*holding all the pencils and pens in her hands and playing with them*) If you go out to dinner don't you dress up? Don't you take wine?

Frank Yes, but . . .

Rita Well?

Frank Well what?

Rita   Well you wouldn't take sweet sparkling wine, would y'?

Frank   Does it matter what I do? It wouldn't have mattered if you'd walked in with a bottle of Spanish plonk.

Rita   It was Spanish.

Frank   Why couldn't you relax? (*He gets up and goes behind* **Rita**'s *chair, then leans on the back of it.*) It wasn't a fancy dress party. You could have come as yourself. Don't you realise how people would have seen you if you'd just – just breezed in? Mm? They would have seen someone who's funny, delightful, charming . . .

Rita (*angrily*)   But I don't wanna be charming and delightful; funny. What's funny? I don't wanna be funny. I wanna talk seriously with the rest of you, I don't wanna spend the night takin' the piss, comin' on with the funnies because that's the only way I can get into the conversation. I didn't want to come to your house just to play the court jester.

Frank   You weren't being asked to play that role. I just – just wanted you to be yourself.

Rita   But I don't want to be myself. Me? What's me? Some stupid woman who gives us all a laugh because she thinks she can learn, because she thinks that one day she'll be like the rest of them, talking seriously, confidently, with knowledge, livin' a civilised life. Well, she can't be like that really but bring her in because she's good for a laugh!

Frank   If you believe that that's why you were invited, to be laughed at, then you can get out, now.

He goes to his desk and grabs the pile of essays, taking them to the window desk. He stands with his back to **Rita** *and starts pushing the essays into his briefcase.*

Frank   You were invited because I wished to have your company and if you can't believe that then I suggest you stop visiting me and start visiting an analyst who can cope with paranoia.

Rita I'm all right with you, here in this room; but when I saw those people you were with I couldn't come in. I would have seized up. Because I'm a freak. I can't talk to the people I live with any more. An' I can't talk to the likes of them on Saturday, or them out there, because I can't learn the language. I'm a half-caste. I went back to the pub where Denny was, an' me mother, an' our Sandra, an' her mates. I'd decided I wasn't comin' here again.

Frank *turns to face her.*

Rita I went into the pub an' they were singin', all of them singin' some song they'd learnt from the juke-box. An' I stood in that pub an' thought, just what the frig am I trying to do? Why don't I just pack it in an' stay with them, an' join in the singin'?

Frank And why don't you?

Rita (*angrily*) You think I can, don't you? Just because you pass a pub doorway an' hear the singin' you think we're all OK, that we're all survivin, with the spirit intact. Well I did join in with the singin', I didn't ask any questions, I just went along with it. But when I looked round me mother had stopped singin', an' she was cryin', but no one could get it out of her why she was cryin'. Everyone just said she was pissed an' we should get her home. So we did, an' on the way I asked her why. I said, 'Why are y' cryin', Mother?' She said, 'Because – because we could sing better songs than those.' Ten minutes later, Denny had her laughing and singing again, pretending she hadn't said it. But she had. And that's why I came back. And that's why I'm staying.

Blackout.

Rita *goes out.*

Scene Eight

Frank *is seated in the swivel chair at the desk reading* **Rita's** Macbeth *essay.*

Rita *enters slowly, carrying a suitcase.*

Frank (*without looking up*) One second.

She puts down the suitcase and wanders slowly with her back to **Frank**.

He closes the essay he has been reading, sighs and removes his glasses.

Frank Your essay. (*He sees the suitcase.*) What's that?

Rita It's me case.

Frank Where are you going?

Rita Me mother's.

Frank What's wrong? (*After a pause.*) Rita!

Rita I got home from work, he'd packed me case. He said either I stop comin' here an' come off the pill or I could get out altogether.

Frank Tch.

Rita It was an ultimatum. I explained to him. I didn't get narked or anythin'. I just explained to him how I had to do this. He said it's warped me. He said I'd betrayed him. I suppose I have.

Frank Why have you?

Rita I have. I know he's right. But I couldn't betray meself. (*After a pause.*) He says there's a time for education. An' it's not when y' twenty-six an' married.

Frank *gets up and goes towards* **Rita** *who still faces away from him.*

Frank (*after a pause*) Where are you going to stay?

Rita I phoned me mother; she said I could go there for a week. Then I'll get a flat. (*She starts to cry.*) I'm sorry, it's just . . .

Frank *takes hold of her and tries to guide her to the chair.*

Frank Look, come on, sit down.

Rita (*breaking away from him*)   It's all right – I'll be OK. Just give me a minute. (*She dries her eyes.*) What was me *Macbeth* essay like?

Frank   Oh sod *Macbeth*.

Rita   Why?

Frank   Rita!

Rita   No, come on, come on, I want y' to tell me what y' thought about it.

Frank   In the circumstances . . .

Rita (*going and hanging her bag on the back of the swivel chair*)   It doesn't matter, it doesn't; in the circumstances I need to go on, to talk about it an' do it. What was it like. I told y' it was no good. Is it really useless?

Frank *sits in the chair.*

Frank (*sighing*)   I – I really don't know what to say.

Rita   Well try an' think of somethin'. Go on, I don't mind if y' tell me it was rubbish. I don't want pity, Frank. Was it rubbish?

Frank   No, no. It's not rubbish. It's a totally honest, passionate account of your reaction to a play. It's an unashamedly emotional statement about a certain experience.

Rita   Sentimental?

Frank   No. It's too honest for that. It's almost – erm – moving. But in terms of what you're asking me to teach you of passing exams . . . Oh, God, you see, I don't . . .

Rita   Say it, go on, say it!

Frank   In those terms it's worthless. It shouldn't be, but it is; in its own terms it's – it's wonderful.

Rita (*confronting him across the desk*)   It's worthless! You said. An' if it's worthless you've got to tell me because I wanna write essays like those on there. (*She points to the essays on the desk.*) I wanna know, an' pass exams like they do.

Frank   But if you're going to write this sort of stuff you're going to have to change.

Rita   All right. Tell me how to do it.

Frank (*getting up*)   But I don't know if I want to tell you, Rita, I don't know that I want to teach you. (*He moves towards the desk.*) What you already have is valuable.

Rita   Valuable? What's valuable? The only thing I value is here, comin' here once a week.

Frank   But, don't you see, if you're going to write this sort of thing – (*He indicates the pile of essays.*) to pass examinations, you're going to have to suppress, perhaps even abandon your uniqueness. I'm going to have to change you.

Rita   But don't you realise, I want to change! Listen, is this your way of tellin' me that I can't do it? That I'm no good?

Frank   It's not that at . . .

Rita   If that's what you're tryin' to tell me I'll go now . . .

Frank *turns away from her.*

Frank (*moving away from the desk*)   No no no. Of course you're good enough.

Rita   See I know it's difficult for y' with someone like me. But you've just gorra keep tellin' me an' then I'll start to take it in; y' see, with me you've got to be dead firm. You won't hurt me feelings y' know. If I do somethin' that's crap, I don't want pity, you just tell me, that's crap. (*She picks up the essay.*) Here, it's crap. (*She rips it up.*) Right. So we dump that in the bin, (*She does so.*) an' we start again.

Act Two

Scene One

Frank *is sitting at his desk typing poetry. He pauses, stubs out a cigarette, takes a sip from the mug at his side, looks at his watch and then continues typing.*

Rita *bursts through the door. She is dressed in new, secondhand clothes.*

Rita   Frank! (*She twirls on the spot to show off her new clothes.*)

Frank (*smiling*)   And what is this vision, returning from the city? (*He gets up and moves towards* **Rita**.) Welcome back.

Rita   Frank, it was fantastic.

She takes off her shawl and gives it to **Frank** *who hangs it on the hook by the door.* **Rita** *goes to the desk.*

Rita (*putting down her bag on the desk*)   Honest, it was – ogh!

Frank   What are you talking about, London or summer school?

Rita   Both. A crowd of us stuck together all week. We had a great time: dead late every night, we stayed up talkin', we went all round London, got drunk, went to the theatres, bought all sorts of secondhand gear in the markets . . . Ogh, it was . . .

Frank   So you won't have had time to do any actual work there?

Rita   Work? We never stopped. Lashin' us with it they were; another essay, lash, do it again, lash.

Frank *moves towards the desk.*

Rita   Another lecture, smack. It was dead good though. (*She goes and perches on the bookcase.*)

Frank *sits in the swivel chair, facing her.*

Rita   Y' know at first I was dead scared. I didn't know anyone. I was gonna come home. But the first afternoon I was standin' in this library, y' know lookin' at the books, pretendin' I was dead clever. Anyway, this tutor come up to me, he looked at the book in me hand an' he said, 'Ah, are you fond of Ferlinghetti?' It was right on the tip of me tongue to say, 'Only when it's served with Parmesan cheese,' but, Frank, I didn't. I held it back an' I heard meself sayin', 'Actually, I'm not too familiar with the American poets.' Frank, you woulda been dead proud of me. He started talkin' to me about the American poets – we sat around for ages – an' he wasn't even one of my official tutors, y' know. We had to go to this big hall for a lecture, there must have been two thousand of us in there. After he'd finished his lecture this professor asked if anyone had a question, an', Frank, I stood up! (*She stands.*) Honest to God, I stood up, an' everyone's lookin' at me. I don't know what possessed me, I was gonna sit down again, but two thousand people had seen me stand up, so I did it, I asked him the question.

There is a pause and **Frank** *waits.*

Frank   Well?

Rita   Well what?

Frank   What was the question?

Rita   Oh, I dunno, I forget now, cos after that I was askin' questions all week, y' couldn't keep me down. I think that first question was about Chekhov; cos y' know I'm dead familiar with Chekhov now.

He smiles. **Rita** *moves to the chair by the desk and sits.* **Frank** *swivels round to face her.*

Rita   Hey, what was France like? Go on, tell us all about it.

Frank   There isn't a lot to tell.

Rita   Ah go on, tell me about it; I've never been abroad. Tell me what it was like.

Frank   Well – it was rather hot . . . (*He offers her a Gauloise.*)

Rita   No, ta, I've packed it in. Did y' drink?

Frank   Ah – a little. (*He puts the cigarettes on the table.*)

Rita   Tch. Did y' write?

Frank   A little.

Rita   Will y' show it to me?

Frank   Perhaps . . . One day, perhaps.

Rita   So y' wrote a bit an' y' drank a bit? Is that all?

Frank (*in a matter of fact tone*)   Julia left me.

Rita   What?

Frank   Yes. But not because of the obvious, oh no – it had nothing whatsoever to do with the ratatouille. It was actually caused by something called *oeufs en cocotte*.

Rita   What?

Frank   Eggs, my dear, eggs. Nature in her wisdom cursed me with a dislike for the egg be it cocotte, Florentine, Benedict or plain hard-boiled. Julia insisted that nature was wrong. I defended nature and Julia left.

Rita   Because of eggs?

Frank   Well – let's say that it began with eggs. (*He packs away the typewriter.*) Anyway, that's most of what happened in France. Anyway, the holiday's over, you're back, even Julia's back.

Rita   Is she? Is it all right?

Frank (*putting the typewriter on the window desk and the sheets of poetry in the top left drawer*)   Perfect. I get the feeling we shall stay together forever; or until she discovers *oeufs à la crécy*.

Rita   *Oeufs à la crécy*? Does that mean eggs? Trish was goin' on about those; is that all it is, eggs?

Frank   Trish?

Rita   Trish, me flatmate, Trish. God is it that long since I've seen y', Frank? She moved into the flat with me just before I went to summer school.

Frank   Ah. Is she a good flatmate?

Rita   She's great. Y' know she's dead classy. Y' know like, she's got taste, y' know like you, Frank, she's just got it. Everything in the flat's dead unpretentious, just books an' plants everywhere. D' y' know somethin', Frank? I'm havin' the time of me life; I am y' know. I even feel – (*Moving to the window*.) I feel young, you know like them down there.

Frank   My dear, twenty-six is hardly old.

Rita   I know that; but I mean, I feel young like them . . . I can be young. (*She goes to her bag*.) Oh listen – (*She puts the bag on the desk and rummages in it, producing a box*.) I bought y' a present back from London – it isn't much but I thought . . . (*She gives him a small box*.) Here.

Frank *puts on his glasses, gets the scissors out of the pot on the desk, cuts the string and opens the box to reveal an expensive pen.*

Rita   See what it says – it's engraved.

Frank (*reading*)   'Must only be used for poetry. By strictest order – Rita' . . . (*He looks at her*.)

Rita   I thought it'd be like a gentle hint.

Frank   Gentle?

Rita   Every time y' try an' write a letter or a note with that pen, it won't work; you'll read the inscription an' it'll make you feel dead guilty – cos y' not writing poetry. (*She smiles at him*.)

Frank (*getting up and pecking her on the cheek*)   Thank you – Rita. (*He sits down again*.)

Rita   It's a pleasure. Come on. (*She claps her hands*.) What are we doin' this term? Let's do a dead good poet. Come on, let's go an' have the tutorial down there.

Frank (*appalled*)   Down where?

Rita (*getting her bag*)   Down there – on the grass – come on.

Frank   On the grass? Nobody sits out there at this time of year.

Rita   They do – (*Looking out of the window.*) there's some of them out there now.

Frank   Well they'll have wet bums.

Rita   What's a wet bum. You can sit on a bench. (*She tries to pull him to his feet.*) Come on.

Frank (*remaining sitting*)   Rita, I absolutely protest.

Rita   Why?

Frank   Like Dracula, I have an aversion to sunlight.

Rita   Tch. (*She sighs.*) All right. (*She goes to the window.*) Let's open a window.

Frank   If you must open a window then go on, open it. (*He swivels round to watch her.*)

Rita (*struggling to open the window*)   It won't bleedin' budge.

Frank   I'm not surprised, my dear. It hasn't been opened for generations.

Rita (*abandoning it*)   Tch. Y' need air in here, Frank. The room needs airing. (*She goes and opens the door.*)

Frank   This room does not need air, thank you very much.

Rita   Course it does. A room is like a plant.

Frank   A room is like a plant?

Rita   Yeh, it needs air. (*She goes to her chair by the desk and sits.*)

Frank   And water, too, presumably? (*He gets up and closes the door.*) If you're going to make an analogy why don't we take it the whole way? Let's get a watering-can and water the carpet; bring in two tons of soil and a bag of fertiliser. Maybe we could take cuttings and germinate other little rooms.

Rita   Go 'way, you're mental you are.

Frank   You said it, distinctly, you said, a room is like a plant.

Rita   Well!

There is a pause.

Frank   Well what?

Rita   Well any analogy will break down eventually.

Frank   Yes. And some will break down sooner than others. (*He smiles, goes to the bookcase and begins searching among the books.*) Look, come on . . . A great poet you wanted – well – we have one on the course . . .

Rita *sits on the desk watching* **Frank**.

Frank   I was going to introduce you to him earlier. (*As he rummages a book falls to one side revealing a bottle of whisky which has been hidden behind it.*) Now – where is he. . . ?

Rita *goes over and picks up the whisky bottle from the shelf.*

Rita   Are you still on this stuff?

Frank   Did I ever say I wasn't?

Rita (*putting the bottle down and moving away*)   No. But . . .

Frank   But what?

Rita   Why d' y' do it when y've got so much goin' for y', Frank?

Frank   It is indeed because I have 'so much goin' for me' that I do it. Life is such a rich and frantic whirl that I need the drink to help me step delicately through it.

Rita   It'll kill y', Frank.

Frank   Rita, I thought you weren't interested in reforming me.

Rita   I'm not. It's just . . .

Frank   What?

Rita   Just that I thought you'd started reforming yourself.

Frank   Under your influence?

She shrugs.

Frank *stops searching and turns to face her.*

Frank   Yes. But Rita – if I repent and reform, what do I do when your influence is no longer here? What do I do when, in appalling sobriety, I watch you walk away and disappear, my influence gone forever?

Rita   Who says I'm gonna disappear?

Frank   Oh you will, Rita. You've got to. (*He turns back to the shelves.*)

Rita   Why have I got to? This course could go on for years. An' when I've got through this one I might even get into the proper university here.

Frank   And we'll all live happily ever after? Your going is as inevitable as – as . . .

Rita   *Macbeth?*

Frank (*smiling*)   As tragedy, yes: but it will not be a tragedy, because I shall be glad to see you go.

Rita   Tch. Thank you very much. (*After a pause.*) Will y' really?

Frank   Be glad to see you go? Well I certainly don't want to see you stay in a room like this for the rest of your life. Now. (*He continues searching for the book.*)

Rita (*after a pause*)   You can be a real misery sometimes, can't y'? I was dead happy a minute ago an' then you start an' make me feel like I'm having a bad night in a mortuary.

Frank *finds the book he has been looking for and moves towards* **Rita** *with it.*

Frank   Well here's something to cheer you up – here's our 'dead good' poet – Blake.

Rita   Blake? William Blake?

Frank   The man himself. *You* will understand Blake; they over-complicate him, Rita, but you will understand – you'll love the man.

Rita   I know.

Frank   What? (*He opens the book.*) Look – look – read this
. . . (*He hands her the book and then goes and sits in the swivel chair.*)

Rita *looks at the poem on the page indicated and then looks at* **Frank**.

Rita (*reciting from memory*)
   'O Rose, thou art sick!
   The invisible worm
   That flies in the night,
   In the howling storm,

   Has found out thy bed
   Of crimson joy:
   And his dark secret love
   Does thy life destroy.'

Frank   You know it!

Rita (*laughing*)   Yeh. (*She tosses the book on the desk and perches on the bookcase.*) We did him at summer school.

Frank   Blake at summer school? You weren't supposed to do Blake at summer school, were you?

Rita   Nah. We had this lecturer though, he was a real Blake freak. He was on about it every day. Everythin' he said, honest, everything was related to Blake – he couldn't get his dinner in the refectory without relating it to Blake – Blake and Chips. He was good though. On the last day we brought him a present, an' on it we put that poem, y' know, 'The Sick Rose'. But we changed it about a bit; it was – erm

   'O Rose, thou aren't sick
   Just mangled and dead
   Since the rotten gardener
   Pruned off thy head.'

We thought he might be narked but he wasn't, he loved it. He said – what was it. . . ? He said, 'Parody is merely a compliment masquerading as humour.'

Frank (*getting up and replacing the book on the shelf*)   So . . .
you've already done Blake? You covered all the *Songs of
Innocence and Experience*?

Rita   Of course; you don't do Blake without doing
innocence and experience, do y'?

Frank   No. Of course. (*He goes and sits in the swivel chair.*)

Blackout.

Rita *picks up her bag and shawl and exits.*

Scene Two

Frank *is sitting at his desk marking an essay. Occasionally he makes
a tutting sound and scribbles something. There is a knock at the door.*

Frank   Come in.

Rita *enters, closes the door, goes to the desk and dumps her bag on it.
She takes her chair and places it next to* **Frank** *and sits down.*

Rita (*talking in a peculiar voice*)   Hello, Frank.

Frank (*without looking up*)   Hello. Rita, you're late.

Rita   I know, Frank. I'm terribly sorry. It was
unavoidable.

Frank (*looking up*)   Was it really? What's wrong with your
voice?

Rita   Nothing is wrong with it, Frank. I have merely
decided to talk properly. As Trish says there is not a lot of
point in discussing beautiful literature in an ugly voice.

Frank   You haven't got an ugly voice; at least you *didn't*
have. Talk properly.

Rita   I am talking properly. I have to practise constantly,
in everyday situations.

Frank   You mean you're going to talk like that for the rest
of this tutorial?

Rita   Trish says that no matter how difficult I may find it I must persevere.

Frank   Well will you kindly tell Trish that I am not giving a tutorial to a Dalek?

Rita   I am not a Dalek.

Frank (*appealingly*)   Rita, stop it!

Rita   But Frank, I have to persevere in order that I shall.

Frank   Rita! Just be yourself.

Rita (*reverting to her normal voice*)   I am being myself (*She gets up and moves the chair back to its usual place.*)

Frank   What's that?

Rita   What?

Frank   On your back.

Rita (*reaching up*)   Oh – it's grass.

Frank   Grass?

Rita   Yeh, I got here early today. I started talking to some students down on the lawn. (*She sits in her usual chair.*)

Frank   You were talking to students – down there?

Rita (*laughing*)   Don't sound so surprised. I can talk now y' know, Frank.

Frank   I'm not surprised. Well! You used to be quite wary of them didn't you?

Rita   God knows why. For students they don't half come out with some rubbish y' know.

Frank   You're telling me?

Rita   I only got talking to them in the first place because as I was walking past I heard one of them sayin' as a novel he preferred *Lady Chatterley* to *Sons and Lovers*. I thought, I can keep walkin' and ignore it, or I can put him straight. So I put him straight. I walked over an' said, 'Excuse me but I couldn't help overhearin' the rubbish you were spoutin' about Lawrence.' Shoulda seen the faces on them, Frank. I said tryin' to compare *Chatterley* with *Sons and Lovers* is like trying to compare sparkling wine with champagne. The next thing is there's this heated discussion, with me right in the middle of it.

Frank   I thought you said the student claimed to 'prefer' *Chatterley*, as a novel.

Rita   He did.

Frank   So he wasn't actually suggesting that it was superior.

Rita   Not at first – but then he did. He walked right into it.

Frank   And so you finished him off, did you Rita?

Rita   Frank, he was asking for it. He was an idiot. His argument just crumbled. It wasn't just me – everyone else agreed with me.

Frank *returns to reading the essay.*

Rita   There was this really mad one with them; I've only been talkin' to them for five minutes and he's inviting me to go abroad with them all. They're all goin' to the South of France in the Christmas holidays, slummin' it.

Frank   You can't go.

Rita   What?

Frank   You can't go – you've got your exams.

Rita   My exams are before Christmas.

Frank   Well – you've got your results to wait for . . .

Rita   Tch. I couldn't go anyway.

Frank   Why? (*He looks at her.*)

Rita   It's all right for them. They *can* just jump into a bleedin' van an' go away. But I can't.

He returns to the essay.

Rita Tiger they call him, he's the mad one. His real name's Tyson but they call him Tiger.

Frank (*looking up*) Is there any point me going on with this? (*He points to the essay.*)

Rita What?

Frank Is there much point in working towards an examination if you're going to fall in love and set off for the South of . . .

Rita (*shocked*) What! Fall in love? With who? My God, Frank, I've just been talkin' to some students. I've heard of match-making but this is ridiculous.

Frank All right, but please stop burbling on about Mr Tyson.

Rita I haven't been burbling on.

He returns to the essay.

Rita What's it like?

Frank Oh – it – erm – wouldn't look out of place with these. (*He places it on top of a pile of other essays on his desk.*)

Rita Honest?'

Frank Dead honest.

Blackout.

Frank *exits.*

Scene Three

Rita *is sitting in the armchair by the window, reading a heavy tome. There is the sound of muffled oaths from behind the door.*

Frank *enters carrying his briefcase. He is very drunk.*

Frank Sod them – no, fuck them! Fuck them, eh, Rita? (*He goes to the desk.*)

Rita Who?

Frank You'd tell them wouldn't you? You'd tell them where to get off. (*He gets a bottle of whisky from his briefcase.*)

Rita Tell who, Frank?

Frank Yes – students – students reported me! (*He goes to the bookcase and puts the whisky on the shelf.*) Me! Complained – you know something? They complained and it was the best lecture I've ever given.

Rita Were you pissed?

Frank Pissed? I was glorious! Fell off the rostrum twice. (*He comes round to the front of his desk.*)

Rita Will they sack you?

Frank (*lying flat on the floor*) The sack? God no; that would involve making a decision. Pissed is all right. To get the sack it'd have to be rape on a grand scale; and not just the students either.

Rita gets up and moves across to look at him.

Frank That would only amount to a slight misdemeanour. For dismissal it'd have to be nothing less than buggering the bursar . . . They suggested a sabbatical for a year – or ten . . . Europe – or America . . . I suggested that Australia might be more apt – the allusion was lost on them . . .

Rita Tch. Frank, you're mad.

Frank Completely off my cake. I know.

Rita Even if y' don't think about yourself, what about the students?

Frank *What* about the students?

Rita Well it's hardly fair on them if their lecturer's so pissed that he's falling off the rostrum. (*She goes to her chair by the desk and replaces the book in her bag.*)

Frank I might have fallen off, my dear, but I went down talking – and came up talking – never missed a syllable – what have they got to complain about?

Rita Maybe they did it for your own good.

Frank Or maybe they did it because they're a crowd of mealy-mouthed pricks who wouldn't know a poet if you beat them about the head with one. (*He half sits up.*) 'Assonance' – I said to them – 'Assonance means getting the rhyme wrong . . .' (*He collapses back on to the floor again.*) They looked at me as though I'd desecrated Wordsworth's tomb.

Rita Look Frank, we'll talk about the Blake essay next week, eh?

Frank Where are you going? We've got a tutorial. (*He gets up and staggers towards her.*)

Rita Frank, you're not in any fit state for a tutorial. I'll leave it with y' an' we can talk about it next week, eh?

Frank No – no – you must stay – erm . . . Watch this – sober? (*He takes a huge breath and pulls himself together.*) Sober! Come on . . .

He takes hold of **Rita** *and pushes her round the desk and sits her in the swivel chair.*

Frank You can't go. I want to talk to you about this. (*He gets her essay and shows it to her.*) Rita, what's this?

Rita Is there something wrong with it?

Frank It's just, look, this passage about 'The Blossom', you seem to assume that the poem is about sexuality.

Rita It is!

Frank Is it?

Rita Well it's certainly like a richer poem, isn't it? If it's interpreted in that way.

Frank Richer? Why richer? We discussed it. The poem is a simple, uncomplicated piece about blossom, as if seen from a child's point of view.

Rita (*shrugging*) In one sense. But it's like, like the poem about the rose, isn't it? It becomes a more rewarding poem when you see that it works on a number of levels.

Frank Rita, 'The Blossom' is a simple uncomplicated . . .

Rita   Yeh, that's what you say, Frank; but Trish and me and some others were talkin' the other night, about Blake, an' what came out of our discussion was that apart from the simple surface value of Blake's poetry there's always a like erm – erm –

Frank   Well? Go on . . .

Rita (*managing to*)   – a like vein. Of concealed meaning. I mean that if that poem's only about the blossom then it's not much of a poem is it?

Frank   So? You think it gains from being interpreted in this way?

Rita (*slightly defiantly*)   Is me essay wrong then, Frank?

Frank   It's not – not wrong. But I don't like it.

Rita   You're being subjective.

Frank (*half-laughing*)   Yes – yes I suppose I am. (*He goes slowly to the chair of the desk and sits down heavily.*)

Rita   If it was in an exam what sort of mark would it get?

Frank   A good one.

Rita   Well what the hell are you sayin' then?

Frank (*shrugging*)   What I'm saying is that it's up-to-the-minute, quite acceptable, trendy stuff about Blake; but there's nothing of you in there.

Rita   Or maybe Frank, y' mean there's nothing of your views in there.

Frank (*after a pause*)   Maybe that is what I mean?

Rita   But when I first came to you, Frank, you didn't give me any views. You let me find my own.

Frank (*gently*)   And your views I still value. But, Rita, these aren't your views.

Rita   But you told me not to have a view. You told me to be objective, to consult recognised authorities. Well that's what I've done; I've talked to other people, read other books an' after consultin' a wide variety of opinion I came up with those conclusions.

He looks at her.

Frank (*after a pause*)   Yes. All right.

Rita (*rattled*)   Look, Frank, I don't have to go along one hundred per cent with your views on Blake y' know. I can have a mind of my own can't I?

Frank   I sincerely hope so, my dear.

Rita   And what's that supposed to mean?

Frank   It means – it means be careful.

Rita *jumps up and moves in towards* **Frank**.

Rita (*angrily*)   What d' y' mean be careful? I can look after myself. Just cos I'm learnin', just cos I can do it now an' read what I wanna read an' understand without havin' to come runnin' to you every five minutes y' start tellin' me to be careful. (*She paces about.*)

Frank   Because – because *I* care for you – I want you to care for yourself.

Rita   Tch. (*She goes right up to* **Frank**. *After a pause.*) I – I care for you, Frank . . . But you've got to – to leave me alone a bit. I'm not an idiot now, Frank – I don't need you to hold me hand as much . . . I can – I can do things on me own more now . . . And I am careful. I know what I'm doin'. Just don't – don't keep treatin' me as though I'm the same as when I first walked in here. I understand now, Frank; I know the difference between – between – Somerset Maugham an' Harold Robbins. An' you're still treating me as though I'm hung up on *Rubyfruit Jungle* (*She goes to the swivel chair and sits.*) Just . . . You understand, don't you Frank?

Frank   Entirely, my dear.

Rita   I'm sorry.

Frank   Not at all. (*After a pause.*) I got round to reading it you know, *Rubyfruit Jungle*. It's excellent.

Rita (*laughing*)   Oh go 'way, Frank. Of its type it's quite interesting. But it's hardly excellence.

Blackout.

Rita *exits.*

Scene Four

Frank *is sitting in the swivel chair.*

Rita *enters and goes to the desk.*

Rita   Frank . . .

He looks at his watch.

Rita   I know I'm late . . . I'm sorry.

He gets up and moves away.

Rita   Am I too late? We were talkin'. I didn't notice the time.

Frank   Talking?

Rita   Yeh. If it'll go in my favour we were talking about Shakespeare.

Frank   Yes . . . I'm sure you were.

Rita   Am I too late then? All right. I'll be on time next week. I promise.

Frank   Rita. Don't go.

Rita   No – honestly, Frank – I know I've wasted your time. I'll see y' next week, eh?

Frank   Rita! Sit down!

Rita *goes to her usual chair and sits.*

Frank (*going to the side of her*)   When you were so late I phoned the shop.

Rita   Which shop?

Frank   The hairdresser's shop. Where you work. Or, I should say, worked.

Rita   I haven't worked there for a long time. I work in a bistro now.

Frank   You didn't tell me.

Rita   Didn't I? I thought I did. I was telling someone.

Frank   It wasn't me.

Rita   Oh. Sorry. (*After a pause.*) What's wrong?

Frank (*after a pause*)   It struck me that there was a time when you told me everything.

Rita   I thought I had told you.

Frank   No. Like a drink?

Rita   Who cares if I've left hairdressin' to work in a bistro?

Frank   I care. (*He goes to the bookshelves and takes a bottle from an eye-level shelf.*) You don't want a drink? Mind if I do?

Rita   But why do you care about details like that? It's just boring, insignificant detail.

Frank (*getting a mug from the small table*)   Oh. Is it?

Rita   That's why I couldn't stand being in a hairdresser's any longer; boring irrelevant detail all the time, on and on . . . Well I'm sorry but I've had enough of that. I don't wanna talk about irrelevant rubbish any more.

Frank   And what do you talk about in your bistro? Cheers.

Rita   Everything.

Frank   Everything?

Rita   Yeh.

Frank   Ah.

Rita   We talk about what's important, Frank, and we leave out the boring details for those who want them.

Frank   Is Mr Tyson one of your customers?

Rita A lot of students come in; he's one of them. You're not gonna give me another warning are y', Frank?

Frank Would it do any good?

Rita Look for your information I do find Tiger fascinatin', like I find a lot of the people I mix with fascinating; they're young, and they're passionate about things that matter. They're not trapped – they're too young for that. And I like to be with them.

Frank (*moving and keeping his back to her*) Perhaps – perhaps you don't want to waste your time coming here any more?

Rita Don't be stupid. I'm sorry I was late. (*After a pause she gets up.*) Look, Frank, I've got to go. I'm meeting Trish at seven. We're going to see a production of *The Seagull*.

Frank Yes. (*He turns to face her.*) Well. When Chekhov calls . . .

Rita Tch.

Frank You can hardly bear to spend a moment here can you?

Rita (*moving towards him a little*) That isn't true. It's just that I've got to go to the theatre.

Frank And last week you didn't turn up at all. Just a phone call to say you had to cancel.

Rita It's just that – that there's so many things happening now. It's harder.

Frank As I said, Rita, if you want to stop com –

Rita (*going right up to him*) For God's sake, I don't want to stop coming here. I've got to come here. What about my exam?

Frank Oh I wouldn't worry about that. You'd sail through it anyway. You really don't have to put in the odd appearance out of sentimentality; (*He moves round to the other side of the desk.*) I'd rather you spared me that.

Frank *goes to drink.*

Rita   If you could stop pouring that junk down your throat in the hope that it'll make you feel like a poet you might be able to talk about things that matter instead of where I do or don't work; an' then it might be worth comin' here.

Frank   Are you capable of recognising what does or does not matter, Rita?

Rita   I understand literary criticism, Frank. When I come here that's what we're supposed to be dealing with.

Frank   You want literary criticism?

He looks at her for a moment and then goes to the top drawer of his desk and takes out two slim volumes and some typewritten sheets of poetry and hands them to her.

Frank   I want an essay on that lot by next week.

Rita   What is it?

Frank   No sentimentality, no subjectivity. Just pure criticism. A critical assessment of a lesser-known English poet. Me.

Blackout.

Rita *exits.*

Scene Five

Frank *is sitting in a chair by the window desk with a mug in his hand and a bottle of whisky on the desk in front of him listening to the radio. There is a knock at the door.*

Frank   Come in.

Rita *enters and goes to the swivel chair behind* **Frank**'s *desk.*

Frank (*getting up and switching off the radio*)   What the – what the hell are you doing here? I'm not seeing you till next week.

Rita   Are you sober? Are you?

Frank   If you mean am I still this side of reasonable comprehension, then yes.

Rita (*going and standing next to him*)   Because I want you to hear this when you're sober. (*She produces his poems.*) These are brilliant. Frank, you've got to start writing again. (*She goes to the swivel chair and sits.*) This is brilliant. They're witty. They're profound. Full of style.

Frank (*going to the small table and putting down his mug*)   Ah . . . tell me again, and again.

Rita   They are, Frank. It isn't only me who thinks so. Me an' Trish sat up last night and read them. She agrees with me. Why did you stop writing? Why did you stop when you can produce work like this? We stayed up most of the night, just talking about it. At first we just saw it as contemporary poetry in its own right, you know, as somethin' particular to this century but look, Frank, what makes it more – more . . . What did Trish say – ? More resonant than – purely contemporary poetry is that you can see in it a direct line through to nineteenth-century traditions of – of like wit an' classical allusion.

Frank (*going to the chair of the desk and standing by the side of it*)   Er – that's erm   that's marvellous, Rita. How fortunate I didn't let you see it earlier. Just think if I'd let you see it when you first came here.

Rita   I know . . . I wouldn't have understood it, Frank.

Frank   You would have thrown it across the room and dismissed it as a heap of shit, wouldn't you?

Rita (*laughing*)   I know . . . But I couldn't have understood it then, Frank, because I wouldn't have been able to recognise and understand the allusions.

Frank   Oh I've done a fine job on you, haven't I?

Rita   It's true, Frank. I can see now.

Frank   You know, Rita, I think – I think that like you I shall change my name; from now on I shall insist upon being known as Mary, Mary Shelley – do you understand that allusion, Rita?

Rita   What?

Frank   She wrote a little Gothic number called *Frankenstein*.

Rita   So?

Frank   This − (*Picking up his poetry and moving round to* **Rita**.) this clever, pyrotechnical pile of self-conscious allusion is worthless, talentless shit and could be recognised as such by anyone with a shred of common sense. It's the sort of thing that gives publishing a bad name. Wit? You'll find more wit in the telephone book, and, probably, more insight. Its one advantage over the telephone directory is that it's easier to rip. (*He rips the poems up and throws the pieces on to the desk.*) It is pretentious, characterless and without style.

Rita   It's not.

Frank   Oh, I don't expect you to believe me, Rita; you recognise the hallmark of literature now, don't you? (*In a final gesture he throws a handful of the ripped pieces into the air and then goes to the chair and sits.*) Why don't you just go away? I don't think I can bear it any longer.

Rita   Can't bear what, Frank?

Frank   You, my dear − you . . .

Rita   I'll tell you what you can't bear, Mr Self-Pitying Piss Artist; what you can't bear is that I am educated now. What's up, Frank, don't y' like me now that the little girl's grown up, now that y' can no longer bounce me on daddy's knee an' watch me stare back in wide-eyed wonder at everything he has to say? I'm educated, I've got what you have an' y' don't like it because you'd rather see me as the peasant I once was; you're like the rest of them − you like to keep your natives thick, because that way they still look charming and delightful. I don't need you. (*She gets up and picking up her bag moves away from the desk in the direction of the door.*) I've got a room full of books. I know what clothes to wear, what wine to buy, what plays to see, what papers and books to read. I can do without you.

Frank Is that all you wanted? Have you come all this way for so very, very little?

Rita Oh it's little to you, isn't it? It's little to you who squanders every opportunity and mocks and takes it for granted.

Frank Found a culture have you, Rita? Found a better song to sing have you? No — you've found a different song, that's all — and on your lips it's shrill and hollow and tuneless. Oh, Rita, Rita . . .

Rita RITA? (*She laughs.*) Rita? Nobody calls me Rita but you. I dropped that pretentious crap as soon as I saw it for what it was. You stupid . . . Nobody calls me Rita.

Frank What is it now then? Virginia?

Rita *exits.*

Frank Or Charlotte? Or Jane? Or Emily?

Blackout.

Scene Six

Frank *talking into the telephone. He is leaning against the bookshelf.*

Frank Yes . . . I think she works there . . . Rita White . . . No, no. Sorry . . . erm. What is it? . . . Susan White? No? . . . Thank you . . . Thanks . . .

He dials another number.

Yes . . . Erm . . . Trish is it? . . . Erm, yes, I'm a friend of Rita's . . . Rita . . . I'm sorry Susan . . . yes . . . could you just say that — erm — I've . . . it's — erm — Frank here . . . her tutor . . . Yes . . . well could you tell her that I have — erm — I've entered her for her examination . . . Yes you see she doesn't know the details . . . time and where the exam is being held . . . Could you tell her to call in? . . . Please . . . Yes . . . Thank you.

The lights fade to blackout.

Scene Seven

Rita enters and shuts the door. She is wrapped in a large winter coat. She lights a cigarette and moves across to the filing cabinet and places a Christmas card with the others already there. She throws the envelope in the waste-bin and opens the door revealing Frank *with a couple of tea-chests either side of him. He is taken aback at seeing her and then he gathers himself and, picking up one of the chests, enters the room.* Rita *goes out to the corridor and brings in the other chest.*

Frank gets the chair from the end of his desk and places it by the bookcase. He stands on it and begins taking down the books from the shelves and putting them into the chests. Rita watches him but he continues as if she is not there.

Rita   Merry Christmas, Frank. Have they sacked y'?

Frank   Not quite.

Rita   Well, why y' – packing your books away?

Frank   Australia. (*After a pause.*) Some weeks ago – made rather a night of it.

Rita   Did y' bugger the bursar?

Frank   Metaphorically. And as it was metaphorical the sentence was reduced from the sack to two years in Australia. Hardly a reduction in sentence really – but . . .

Rita   What y' gonna do?

Frank   *Bon voyage.*

Rita   She's not goin' with y'?

Frank *shakes his head.* **Rita** *begins helping him take down the books from the shelves and putting them in the chests.*

Rita   What y' gonna do?

Frank   What do you think I'll do. Aussie? It's a paradise for the likes of me.

Rita   Tch. Come on, Frank . . .

Frank   It is. Didn't you know the Australians named their favourite drink after a literary figure? Forster's Lager they call it. Of course they get the spelling wrong – rather like you once did!

Rita Be serious.

Frank For God's sake, why did you come back here?

Rita I came to tell you you're a good teacher. (*After a pause.*) Thanks for enterin' me for the exam.

Frank That's all right. I know how much it had come to mean to you.

Rita *perches on the small table while* **Frank** *continues to take books from the upper shelves.*

Rita You didn't want me to take it, did y'? Eh? You woulda loved it if I'd written, 'Frank knows all the answers', across me paper, wouldn't y'? I nearly did an' all. When the invigilator said, 'Begin,' I turned over me paper with the rest of them, and while they were all scribbling away against the clock, I just sat there, lookin' at the first question. Y' know what it was, Frank? 'Suggest ways in which one might cope with some of the staging difficulties in a production of *Peer Gynt.*'

Frank *gets down, sits on the chair and continues to pack the books.*

Frank Well, you should have had no trouble with that.

Rita I did though. I just sat lookin' at the paper an' thinkin' about what you'd said. I tried to ignore it, to pretend that you were wrong. You think you gave me nothing; did nothing for me. You think I just ended up with a load of quotes an' empty phrases; an' I did. But that wasn't your doin'. I was so hungry. I wanted it all so much that I didn't want it to be questioned. I told y' I was stupid. It's like Trish, y' know me flatmate, I thought she was so cool an' together – I came home the other night an' she'd tried to top herself. Magic, isn't it? She spends half her life eatin' wholefoods an' health foods to make her live longer, an' the other half tryin' to kill herself. (*After a pause.*) I sat lookin' at the question, an' thinkin' about it all. Then I picked up me pen an' started.

Frank   And you wrote, 'Do it on the radio'?

Rita   I could have done. An' you'd have been proud of me if I'd done that an' rushed back to tell you – wouldn't y'? But I chose not to. I had a choice. I did the exam.

Frank   I know. A good pass as well.

Rita   Yeh. An' it might be worthless in the end. But I had a choice. I chose, me. Because of what you'd given me I had a choice. I wanted to come back an' tell y' that. That y' a good teacher.

Frank (*stopping working and looking at her*)   You know – erm – I hear very good things about Australia. Things are just beginning there. The thing is, why don't you – come as well? It'd be good for us to leave a place that's just finishing for one that's just beginning.

Rita   Isn't that called jumpin' a sinkin' ship?

Frank   So what? Do you really think there's any chance of keeping it afloat?

She looks at him and then at the shelves.

Rita (*seeing the empty whisky bottles*)   'Ey, Frank, if there was threepence back on each of those bottles you could buy Australia.

Frank (*smiling*)   You're being evasive.

Rita (*going and sitting on a tea-chest*)   I know. Tiger's asked me to go down to France with his mob.

Frank   Will you?

Rita   I dunno. He's a bit of a wanker really. But I've never been abroad. An' me mother's invited me to hers for Christmas.

Frank   What are you going to do?

Rita   I dunno. I might go to France. I might go to me mother's. I might even have a baby. I dunno. I'll make a decision, I'll choose. I dunno.

Frank *has found a package hidden behind some of the books. He takes it down.*

Frank   Whatever you do, you might as well take this . . .

Rita   What?

Frank *(handing it to her)*   It's erm – well, it's er – it's a dress really. I bought it some time ago – for erm – for an educated woman friend – of mine . . .

Rita *takes the dress from the bag.*

Frank   I erm – don't – know if it fits, I was rather pissed when I bought it . . .

Rita   An educated woman, Frank? An' is this what you call a scholarly neckline?

Frank   When choosing it I put rather more emphasis on the word woman than the word educated.

Rita   All I've ever done is take from you. I've never given anything.

Frank   That's not true you've . . .

Rita   It is true. I never thought there was anythin' I could give you. But there is. Come here, Frank . . .

Frank   What?

Rita   Come here . . . *(She pulls out a chair.)* Sit on that . . .

Frank *is bewildered.*

Rita   Sit . . .

Frank *sits and* **Rita**, *eventually finding a pair of scissors on the desk, waves them in the air.*

Rita   I'm gonna take ten years off you . . .

She goes across to him and begins to cut his hair.

Blackout.

Methuen Contemporary Dramatists
include

Peter Barnes (three volumes)
Sebastian Barry
Dermot Bolger
Edward Bond (six volumes)
Howard Brenton
  (two volumes)
Richard Cameron
Jim Cartwright
Caryl Churchill (two volumes)
Sarah Daniels (two volumes)
Nick Darke
David Edgar (three volumes)
Ben Elton
Dario Fo (two volumes)
Michael Frayn (three volumes)
John Godber (two volumes)
Paul Godfrey
John Guare
Peter Handke
Jonathan Harvey
Declan Hughes
Terry Johnson (two volumes)
Sarah Kane
Bernard-Marie Koltès
David Lan
Bryony Lavery
Deborah Levy
Doug Lucie

David Mamet (three volumes)
Martin McDonagh
Duncan McLean
Anthony Minghella
  (two volumes)
Tom Murphy (four volumes)
Phyllis Nagy
Anthony Nielsen
Philip Osment
Louise Page
Stewart Parker (two volumes)
Joe Penhall
Stephen Poliakoff
  (three volumes)
Christina Reid
Philip Ridley
Willy Russell
Ntozake Shange
Sam Shepard (two volumes)
Wole Soyinka (two volumes)
David Storey (three volumes)
Sue Townsend
Michel Vinaver (two volumes)
Arnold Wesker (two volumes)
Michael Wilcox
David Wood (two volumes)
Victoria Wood

Methuen World Classics
include

Jean Anouilh (two volumes)
John Arden (two volumes)
Arden & D'Arcy
Brendan Behan
Aphra Behn
Bertolt Brecht (seven volumes)
Büchner
Bulgakov
Calderón
Čapek
Anton Chekhov
Noël Coward (eight volumes)
Eduardo De Filippo
Max Frisch
John Galsworthy
Gogol
Gorky
Harley Granville Barker
 (two volumes)
Henrik Ibsen (six volumes)
Lorca (three volumes)

Marivaux
Mustapha Matura
David Mercer (two volumes)
Arthur Miller (five volumes)
Molière
Musset
Peter Nichols (two volumes)
Clifford Odets
Joe Orton
A. W. Pinero
Luigi Pirandello
Terence Rattigan
 (two volumes)
W. Somerset Maugham
 (two volumes)
August Strindberg
 (three volumes)
J. M. Synge
Ramón del Valle-Inclán
Frank Wedekind
Oscar Wilde

Methuen Modern Plays
include work by

Jean Anouilh
John Arden
Margaretta D'Arcy
Peter Barnes
Sebastian Barry
Brendan Behan
Dermot Bolger
Edward Bond
Bertolt Brecht
Anthony Burgess
Howard Brenton
Simon Burke
Jim Cartwright
Caryl Churchill
Noël Coward
Lucinda Coxon
Sarah Daniels
Nick Darke
Nick Dear
Shelagh Delaney
David Edgar
David Eldridge
Dario Fo
Michael Frayn
John Godber
Paul Godfrey
David Greig
John Guare
Peter Handke
David Harrower
Jonathan Harvey
Iain Heggie
Declan Hughes
Terry Johnson
Sarah Kane
Charlotte Keatley
Barrie Keeffe
Howard Korder

Robert Lepage
Stephen Lowe
Doug Lucie
Martin McDonagh
John McGrath
Terrence McNally
David Mamet
Patrick Marber
Arthur Miller
Mtwa, Ngema & Simon
Tom Murphy
Phyllis Nagy
Peter Nichols
Joseph O'Connor
Joe Orton
Louise Page
Joe Penhall
Luigi Pirandello
Stephen Poliakoff
Franca Rame
Mark Ravenhill
Philip Ridley
Reginald Rose
David Rudkin
Willy Russell
Jean-Paul Sartre
Sam Shepard
Wole Soyinka
Shelagh Stephenson
C. P. Taylor
Theatre de Complicite
Theatre Workshop
Sue Townsend
Judy Upton
Timberlake Wertenbaker
Roy Williams
Victoria Wood

For a Complete Catalogue of Methuen Drama titles
write to:

Methuen Drama
215 Vauxhall Bridge Road
London SW1V 1EJ

or you can visit our website at:

www.methuen.co.uk